The Most Dangerous Trade

How Short Sellers Uncover Fraud, Keep Markets Honest, and Make and Lose Billions

Richard Teitelbaum

WILEY

Published by John Wiley & Sons, Inc., Hoboken, New Jersey.

Published simultaneously in Canada.

For general information on our other products and services or for technical support, please contact our Customer Care Department within the United States at (800) 762-2974, outside the United States at (317) 572-3993 or fax (317) 572-4002.

Wiley publishes in a variety of print and electronic formats and by print-on-demand. Some material included with standard print versions of this book may not be included in e-books or in print-on-demand. If this book refers to media such as a CD or DVD that is not included in the version you purchased, you may download this material at http://booksupport.wiley.com. For more information about Wiley products, visit www.wiley.com.

Library of Congress Cataloging-in-Publication Data:

Teitelbaum, Richard, 1961–
  The most dangerous trade : how short sellers uncover fraud, keep markets honest, and make and lose billions / Richard Teitelbaum.
     pages cm
  Includes index.
  ISBN 978-1-118-50521-2 (cloth) – ISBN 978-1-118-77424-3 (epdf) – ISBN 978-1-118-61614-7 (epub)
  1. Short selling (Securities) 2. Fraud. 3. Investments. 4. Speculation. I. Title.
  HG6041.T43 2015
  332.64′5–dc23

                                                                      2015017857

Cover Design: Wiley
Cover Images: businessman walking ©iStock.com/4×6;
background ©iStock.com/delirium

Printed in the United States of America

10 9 8 7 6 5 4 3 2 1

Dedicated to former mayor of New York City, Michael Bloomberg, without whom this book would not have been possible.

Contents

Preface

A t its crux, short selling is about failure. Things break down. Whereas most of mankind basks in a natural optimism, there are those who navigate the darker side of events—the miscalculations, fraud, and follies that spur us onward toward disaster. Catastrophe's natural handmaidens are greed and, yes, plain evil.

The natural state of a collapsing universe is the breaking down of order. Short sellers understand this and seek to profit from it.

I knew these dynamics before starting this project in 2012. After all, I quoted the pessimist philosopher Arthur Schopenhauer in college and still enthuse over Samuel Beckett plays. In hindsight, I'm embarrassed to say, my effort was more about careerism than anything else. Colleagues and rivals were churning out acclaimed books in the wake of the 2008–2009 financial crisis. I was toiling for *Bloomberg News*, at a sparsely read monthly magazine under the yoke of a petulant editor. Yes, I was proud of a good portion of my work—racking up a record 23 cover stories. Some of it explored the underside of the financial crisis. But my peers were on *Charlie Rose* or, worse, had even penned movie deals.

John Wiley & Sons approached me, suggesting I write a book profiling short sellers—something I suspect they soon came to regret. Short sellers, a misfit breed of investor tilting against the relentless onslaught of hype emanating from Wall Street's powerful marketing machinary, make a colorful cast of characters—an assortment of loners, firebrands, cynics, liars, and losers. What could go wrong?

My paranoid suspicion—evidence for which is utterly circumstantial—is that the wheels began to fall off the project before it began, with an investigative story I wrote for the January 2012 issue of the magazine. In July 2008, U.S. Treasury Secretary Henry Paulson met at the offices of Eton Park Capital Management with a group of hedge fund managers and other Wall Street types, many of them alumni of Goldman Sachs, where he was CEO from 1999 to 2006. According to a source at the meeting, the secretary disclosed material nonpublic information—that the government was planning to put mortgage guarantors Fannie Mae and Freddie Mac into conservatorship—wiping out equity holders in those state-sponsored companies. Disclosing this was not illegal, as I reported, citing legal experts. Yet Paulson had recently said such a move was unlikely.

Nothing much came of that story until September 2012, when the *Wall Street Journal* reported that the U.S. Securities & Exchange Commission (SEC) had launched an investigation into the matter. I was on book leave, and *Bloomberg News* did not, according to standard practice, match the story. Nothing much seems to have come of the SEC investigation.

Except perhaps this: A month or so after the *Journal* story, while still on book leave, I was summoned to Bloomberg headquarters and informed that I was being demoted to essentially a data entry position. They somehow neglected to change my senior writer title. Of course plenty of people are demoted all the time. Later, Bloomberg LP revealed that then-mayor Michael Bloomberg had a business relationship with Paulson. Indeed, they are co-chairs of an environmental organization called the Risky Business Project, along with ex-hedge fund manager and Goldman Sachs alumnus Thomas Steyer.

But if this book was to chronicle breakdowns—financial, regulatory, ethical, structural—my star-crossed efforts to bring the project together seemed to eerily reflect that. Subjects declined to be interviewed. Others did so only off the record. I was given bogus information, including a false address by one subject, and others claimed to have no record of past returns. A retired woman short seller relayed to me that she had become so averse to the short-selling profession that she no longer dated men under six feet tall.

One source, after an Italian dinner in a rough part of town, asked to talk to me on "deep background" in a dark and deserted parking lot behind the restaurant, away from prying eyes and ears. I thought, briefly, I was about to get whacked.

Bad news mounted. The façade of my Greenwich Village apartment building required immediate replacement, costing $30 million in total. The jackhammers were merciless. On the eve of a key investment conference in Dallas, Superstorm Sandy swamped New York. My flight was canceled, scuttling interviews, and the resulting floodwaters knocked out electricity and forced battalions of mice into my co-op, necessitating bouts of successive efforts to eradicate them. Fortunately, we already had a good exterminator, because my crisscrossing of the country staying at cheap hotels had ushered in a virulent infestation of bed bugs. Interestingly, they seemed to prefer my voluminous cartons of interview notes and books to our beds.

The last of my roster of short sellers agreed, after initial refusals, to cooperate in the first half of 2013. I was on course to blow my deadline not by weeks but months. Like so much else, in this project, it was humbling, embarrassing—but nothing like what I was about to experience.

On July 5, the lion's share of reporting and writing was complete. My book leave had ended and the new job in data entry was going surprisingly well, in its own fashion.

The phone rang. It was from the hospital. My special-needs daughter Nina was in septic shock. "It's bad," the doctor intoned, when my wife passed the phone to him, panic in his voice. "It's really bad."

Toxins were filling her body. The window of opportunity to arrest it is vanishingly small—every hour from its inception increases the mortality rate by 20 percent, I've been told.

A series of operations on Nina proved successful—she would spend months in and out of intensive care. I returned to data entry at Bloomberg, but struggled to complete my remaining chapters with my daughter in the hospital. She is recovering.

Next came a series of unrelated deaths in a staccato procession: A brother-in-law (of a heart attack), my 90-year-old mother-in-law, and my first editor at *Fortune* magazine, John Curran, 59 (of amyotrophic lateral sclerosis). Sources and characters in my narrative were dying, too—*Barron's* Alan Abelson, 87, died of a heart attack, and Doug Millett, 49, formerly of Kynikos Associates and largely responsible for exposing the Enron fraud, succumbed to a cancer of the salivary glands. Already suspicious, I was fast becoming superstitious.

In November 2013, Bloomberg LP, in company argot, fired me—along with a raft of vastly more talented journalists. Another phenomenally expensive operation for Nina lay ahead, but of course I had no idea whether her medical care had influenced the decision (Nina's hospital tab for her first night was $330,637.54). Short sellers had taught me that paranoia is often well-founded. "What you see," one short seller told me, "is not what really is."

Fictions and delusions collapse as a consequence of their internal dynamics. Bad things happen. That's the most important thing that short sellers—damaged, battered, often nearly broke—can remind us. If they make a buck or two in the process, who am I to judge?

Chapter 1

Ackman: The Activist Grandstander

I t had taken William Ackman more than 18 months to get this far—with zero to show for it. Over that time, the founder of Pershing Square Capital Management, with more than $15 billion in assets under management, had been hammering away at Herbalife, what can only be called a marketing machine that used so-called independent distributors to peddle nutrition and weight-loss products through a vast pyramid scheme. There was an enormous amount of money at stake—Ackman, who goes by Bill, had at one point borrowed some 20 percent of Herbalife's stock, worth more than $1 billion, through his brokers and then sold it. His goal: Expose the company as a fraud and repay those borrowed shares for pennies on the dollar—or nothing at all.

That's how short-selling works—and Pershing Square had by now spent more than $50 million in research and fees alone on the effort.

Now, in July 2014, the six-foot-three-inch-tall Ackman was wrapping up an impassioned, polished presentation for the media and investors that laid out the details of how Herbalife entrapped its distributors through a system of so-called "nutrition clubs" that were meant to lure people into the base of the pyramid scheme and goose sales by foisting products on them. In the U.S., the lion's share of distributors were low-income people, typically Hispanic-Americans, but Herbalife was pushing its weight-loss products in countries from India to Zambia.

Ackman singled out the Herbalife CEO. "Michael Johnson will go down in history as the best CEO of a pyramid scheme in the world," he said, pointing out that the former Walt Disney and Univision Communications executive had extensive experience in marketing to Hispanic-Americans. He alluded to another famed notorious pyramid scheme, that of financier Bernard Madoff, who duped investors of some $20 billion. He compared Herbalife's marketing to that of the Nazis.

Then things got personal. His voice trembling with emotion, Ackman detailed his immigrant forbears' history in the United States, his great-grandfather apprenticing as an assistant tailor, the family's coat business, and his father's own formidable achievements as a mortgage broker. "I am a huge beneficiary of this country, okay?" he said, choking up with emotion. "Michael Johnson is a predator. Okay? This is a criminal enterprise. Okay? I hope you're listening, Michael. It's time to shut the company down!"

"This is an ingenious fraud," Ackman said and, wrapping himself in the Stars and Stripes, added that Pershing Square preferred to invest in companies that help America. "I said I'm going to take this to the end of the earth. We're going to do whatever makes sense."

Before taking a break, he fired off: "This company is a tragedy and it's also a travesty."

Whew! Pass the water.

Beyond the Ackman histrionics, his argument had merit.

The accusation was that Herbalife virtually forced its distributors to commit to buying more product than they could sell to earn a living wage, and Ackman, with the help of a contract research firm, had just furnished the evidence for his claim that Herbalife was a sophisticated pyramid scheme, illegal under U.S. Securities & Exchange Commission (SEC) and Federal Trade Commission rules.

The son of a successful commercial real estate broker, Ackman was born with a proverbial silver spoon in his mouth—and a highly polished one at that. He grew up in lush Chappaqua, New York—these days home to former President Bill Clinton and his wife, former Secretary of State Hillary—graduating from one of the nation's foremost public secondary educational institutions, Horace Greeley High School. Ackman picked up both a B.A., magna cum laude, and an M.B.A. from Harvard. Immediately after graduation in 1992, with no formal training, Ackman launched his own hedge fund, Gotham Partners, which he eventually shuttered in the face of investor withdrawals—but not before making a high-profile, unsuccessful bid to gain control of New York's Rockefeller Center. Even friends say the hyperambitious Ackman comes off as overconfident and a know-it-all—but one whose big bets and relentless drive have generated 20 percent–plus returns for investors in his current flagship fund, called Pershing Square Capital Management.

Ackman began his Herbalife campaign at a December 2012 event sponsored by the Sohn Conference Foundation—a charity that finances pediatric cancer research and care. Dubbing the presentation "Who Wants to Be a Millionaire?" after the television game show, he and colleagues spent an astonishing three-plus hours detailing a convincing case that Herbalife, which peddles nutrition bars, vitamins, and powdered smoothie mixes of soy, sugar, and protein, was a giant pyramid scheme with sales that year that would amount to $4.1 billion.

The business model required that independent Herbalife distributors pull in more and more distributors into their network to make real money, pushing those newbies in turn to recruit other hapless friends, acquaintances, and relatives to do the same. The takeaway: Products went in large part to distributors themselves instead of end customers, with the lion's share of the money paid to distributors for bringing in fresh candidates to the sales force, not selling the products.

That's basically the definition of a pyramid scheme—in which an ever-growing number of recruits is duped into paying off the previous set. "Basically, the large numbers are such that if you go back to that pyramid, you need a bigger and bigger base at the bottom to support it," Ackman explained. "Problem is, the money at the top is made from losses of the people at the bottom, and there are a very few people at the

top and a huge number at the bottom." The arrangement works until it
runs out of recruits.

By late 2012, Pershing Square was shorting Herbalife's stock,
borrowing millions of shares and then selling them, hoping that
exposing the alleged fraud would prompt regulators—the SEC, the
Federal Trade Commission, the Justice Department or perhaps states'
attorneys general—to step in and bring the stock crashing down,
profiting Pershing Square investors. In the perfect scenario, the price
would go to zero and the hedge fund wouldn't need to repurchase stock
at all.

Failing that, the accompanying publicity, much of it based on
third-party analysis by a boutique research firm called Indago Group,
might cause investors to dump shares, scare the company's auditors who
sign off on financial statements, or even rattle prospective Herbalife
distributors who might have otherwise been attracted to the business
scheme, effectively deflating what to Ackman was a blatant if fairly
sophisticated scam.

For Ackman this was not just another investment gambit—it was
a crusade.

Herbalife was also an extraordinarily risky bet, with Ackman
borrowing and selling about one fifth of Herbalife's total stock outstanding. The shares could be called back by their owners for any
reason—meaning Pershing Square was on the hook if those he had
effectively borrowed the shares from wanted them back. Yet, the shares
dropped 8 percent in the days leading up to the initial December 19,
2012, presentation as rumors of Ackman's upcoming speech began to
swirl. He didn't disappoint.

Ackman's first rousing speech, which he made without prepared notes, hammered away at Herbalife products' stratospheric
pricing—three times as much as competing goods. He pointed out the
lack of research and development (R&D) and marketing. And Ackman
railed against Herbalife's use of Nobel laureate advisory board member
Lou Ignarro—not for research, but for touting Herbalife's products
at conferences. Former Secretary of State Madeleine Albright was a
consultant too. Ackman showed a Herbalife video that the company
played for its distributors, with one of the higher paid ones driving a
Ferrari and living in a lavish Southern California mansion.

But it all came down to one simple accusation. "Participants in the Herbalife scheme, the distributors, obtain their monetary benefits primarily from recruitment rather than the sale of goods and services to distributors, not consumers," Ackman told attendees back in 2012. That was, almost verbatim, the Federal Trade Commission's definition of a pyramid scheme. In a perfect world, it would have been an open-and-shut case.

Initially Ackman's bet looked like a winner. The day of the presentation, Herbalife shares tumbled a further 12 percent, hitting $33.34, and they continued to fall thereafter. The day before Christmas 2012, Herbalife shares bottomed at $26.06. It looked as if in Herbalife, Ackman had picked an enormous loser, or in the case of Pershing Square investors, a gigantic winner to the tune of more than $1 billion.

Then, as is often the case in short-selling campaigns, the market began to turn. Somebody was buying, and Herbalife stock began to climb. As shares rose, a coterie of hedge fund managers and other investors jumped on the chance to initiate a short squeeze—buying Herbalife shares to drive up the price in hopes of forcing Ackman to cover, or buy back shares, at a big loss. A keenly watched metric in the short-selling game is called *days to cover*. That refers to the number of days, given average daily volume as a benchmark, it would take a short seller to cover a short position. And Herbalife's days to cover metric was off the charts.

So while Pershing Square's bet was huge, the size of his position left Ackman open to upward pressure on the share price if anyone wanted to buy shares and cause trouble by running up the price—a so-called "short squeeze" in Wall Street argot. And the prematurely silver-haired hedge fund manager—one acquaintance dubbed him the Yeti, after the abominable snowman—had plenty of enemies.

It's easy to see why. In an industry known for its titanic egos, even Ackman's stood out. According to those who have dealt with him, he constantly proffered unasked-for advice to friends and rivals and compared his record to that of Berkshire Hathaway CEO Warren Buffett. Ackman was also bluntly direct, passing on the name of his nutritionist to an acquaintance who had added a couple of pounds or setting up single colleagues on blind dates. A Pershing Square board member once inadvertently smeared a dab of cream cheese on his own jacket lapel during a morning meeting and failed to notice it. While someone else might have taken the board member aside or whispered to him, Ackman bellowed across the conference table: "You've got cheese on your jacket there!"

It did not escape notice that when Pershing Square floated shares of a closed-end fund it manages on the Amsterdam Stock Exchange, in October 2014, that he joked about the fact that they sold off, ending down 12 percent that day. "The stock is down, which is good," he quipped. "If it had gone up, we'd have sold too low." Holders included Qatar Holdings LLC, Blackstone Group, and Rothschild Bank AG.

Still, some look at Ackman's forthrightness and straight-shooting advice as just boldfaced honesty—commendable—while others do not. Even before the closed-end fund offering, Ackman managed Pershing Square like a disciplined governance-centric corporation with a board that includes former *New Republic* owner and editor-in-chief Martin Peretz; an ex-chief financial officer of McDonald's Corp., Matthew Paull; and Harvard Business School management professor Michael Porter, who is both a mentor and colleague. That compares to other funds, which can often seem like alpha male–dominated frat houses. Employees meet with the board without Ackman present so they can express their opinions about him forthrightly and deliver complaints about how the firm is run.

He maintains some high standards: Ackman, after consulting with the board, fired an employee for expensing a dinner that hadn't been on company time. (Of course, that was money out of his own pocket). More than anything else, though, what drove rivals of the 49-year-old hedge fund manager crazy was his knack for generating stellar returns, which, though volatile, were more than 20 percent annualized for his flagship fund—and with little leverage. That doesn't, ahem, include his closed Gotham Partners fund or his side pocket investments.

Full disclosure: Ackman, who is widely known for assiduously courting the media to an unusual, sometimes unseemly extent, declined to be interviewed for this book. It may have had to do with an unflattering article in the monthly *Vanity Fair* by the author William Cohan that appeared shortly before I made my request.

One investor harboring particular vitriol for Ackman at the time was Carl Icahn, chairman of Icahn Enterprises LP—the onetime 1980s corporate raider and greenmailer; that is, someone who would buy up shares in a company, threaten a takeover, and then sell them back to the target at above-market prices in exchange for simply going away. It was deemed a louche manner in which to earn a paycheck.

But Icahn had successfully refashioned himself into the more honorable profession of activist investor—shaking up corporate boards and enriching all shareholders, not just himself. And Icahn, a native of the rougher parts of the New York City borough of Queens, was pretty good at it—agitating for the sales, breakups, or restructurings of companies like Kerr-McGee, Time Warner, eBay, and Yahoo! Returns for his public investment firm were more than 20 percent annualized since 2000.

Ackman and Icahn shared a litigious history. Faced with investor withdrawals and illiquid holdings, Ackman in 2001 was winding down his first hedge fund, Gotham Partners, which itself had made some public short bets. He cold-called Icahn about buying the fund's 15 percent stake in Hallwood Realty Partners, a real estate investment trust.

The wily Icahn was amenable. Ackman had another, higher offer of $85 to $90 a unit on the table, yet he agreed instead to sell Gotham's Hallwood stake to Icahn for less, just $80 a unit plus what Icahn termed "schmuck insurance," incorporating a Yiddish term for a part of the male anatomy. Under the contract, according to Ackman, Icahn would pay 50 percent of his profits, above a 10 percent gain, if he sold or otherwise transferred the REIT units within three years. Ackman's view was that Icahn might bid for the whole company himself, because he was in fact unloading his shares on Icahn at what he deemed a fire-sale price, barely more than half their true value.

Well, Ackman was half right. Hallwood cashed out a year or so later for $136.70 per unit in cash, selling itself not to Icahn but to HRPT Properties Trust. Ackman called to congratulate Icahn and collect his "schmuck insurance." Icahn blew him off—refusing to pay—and the two investors ended up in court, where Ackman ultimately prevailed. The bitterness, however, had only festered over the years.

On January 25, 2013, in the kind of broadcasting melodrama that TV producers can usually only dream of, they both were call-in phone guests on CNBC's *Fast Money Half Time Report* TV program, hosted by Scott Wapner, by which time Herbalife shares were surging past $43.

Ackman would soon be losing money on his short sale. And the televised exchange quickly became personal.

"I've really sort of had it with this guy Ackman," groused Icahn, in his rough, outer borough accent. "He's like the crybaby in the school yard."

Icahn continued in a stream of consciousness-style rant of insults. "He's the quintessential example on Wall Street of if you want a friend, get a dog," he said. "Ackman is a liar."

Ackman returned the compliments—his diction crisp and Harvard perfect. "This is not an honest guy, and this is not a guy who keeps his word," he said, enunciating every syllable to perfection. "This is a guy who takes advantage of little people."

They spent a lot of time going over the Hallwood deal.

Icahn recalled having dinner with Ackman. "I couldn't figure out whether if he was the most sanctimonious guy in the world or the most arrogant," he said. "I was dizzy after having dinner with him."

The CNBC host struggled to bring the conversation back to Herbalife, but the two antagonists kept returning to the Hallwood deal a decade earlier. "I was concerned about dealing with Carl Icahn because Carl unfortunately does not have a good reputation," Ackman said. "Carl Icahn thought, 'this guy is roadkill on the hedge fund highway,'" referring to himself.

Icahn disputed the whole notion of the "schmuck" insurance. "I will swear to it on any bible you want," Icahn said. "I had a verbal agreement that he wasn't going to have any piece of the money on this."

Then Icahn launched into an attack on Ackman's strategies and tactics—lambasting them.

"Herbalife is a classic example of what he does," Icahn said. "He probably woke up in the morning and decided, 'What company can we do a bear raid on?'"

Icahn piled onto the dangerous nature of Pershing Square's Herbalife short and even suggested that the upstart hedge fund manager was intent on robbing retirees, that is, investors in the vitamin company, of their savings. Traders on the floor of the New York Stock Exchange stopped and stared at the televised duel, gaping at TV screens as the barrage of insults continued.

"I wouldn't have an investment with Ackman if you paid me to," Icahn declared. "Even if Ackman paid me." He even hinted at a possible buyout. "I will tell you, that I think HLF could be the mother of all short squeezes," he said.

Icahn declined to say whether he was buying Herbalife shares as part of a short squeeze strategy. He virtually invited investors to do so. "In a company like Herbalife, you can ask almost any pro, you don't go 20 percent short," Icahn said. "You go in and you get 20 percent, if there's ever a tender offer, which there well might be in Herbalife, what does he do? I'd like to get to ask, where does he get the stock? Let's say there's a tender offer for Herbalife and they call back the stock and if you know Wall Street, when there's a tender offer, everybody calls back the stock."

The consequences, with the stock trading at a bit over $40 a share, would undoubtedly be dire for Pershing Square. "That stock could rush to a $100, what the hell does Ackman do?" Icahn demanded.

Ackman was unflappable. "Number one, Carl's free to make a tender for the company," he responded succinctly. "Carl, you want to bid for the company? Go ahead and bid for the company."

Icahn sputtered with rage. "Hey, hey you don't have to tell me what I'm free to do," he responded. Ackman clearly had a way of getting under the septuagenarian's skin.

"Number two: We don't think there's going to be a tender for the company. We don't think this company is viable," Ackman said. "We don't think anybody's going to write a check for 4 or 5 billion dollars for a company that is fraudulent."

It was an astonishing airing of animosity and dirty linen—the kind of thing that generally isn't done on Wall Street, at least without the careful vetting of lawyers. After the on air-spat, Herbalife shares began to climb, actually piercing $80 by year-end 2013. Ackman's paper losses—mark-to-market, in industry speak—were likely expanding.

Icahn disclosed a 13 percent stake in Herbalife in February 2013 and soon took three Herbalife board seats. Third Point LLC's Daniel Loeb, a former friend of Ackman's who had been burned by investing in a Pershing Square side fund that made a disastrous, all-in bet on discount retailer Target Corp. using call options, also piled in to drive up the Herbalife share price. It was payback time.

In October 2013, Ackman, with Herbalife shares trading at $70, told investors in a letter that he had swapped 40 percent of his short position in Herbalife with what amounted to an equivalent exposure selling put options. Such options, give the seller to right to sell shares in the company at a set price, in this case likely roughly the price at the time the letter became public. If Herbalife tumbled Pershing Square would score, if not the firm would lose the premium it paid. "The restructuring of the position preserves our opportunity for profit—if the Company fails within a reasonable time frame we will make a similar profit as if we had maintained the entire initial short position—while mitigating the risk for further mark-to-market losses—because our exposure on the put options is limited to the total premium paid," the letter said, as reported in the *New York Post*. "In restructuring the position, we have also reduced the amount of capital consumed by the investment from 16 percent to 12 percent of our funds."

Ackman would make money if shares fell enough to hit the strike price and cover the cost of the options, usually a couple of bucks. It looked, almost, like he was heeding Icahn's advice.

In July 2014, Ackman was back on a publicity campaign to trumpet his latest research—and to rescue his souring bet. He was losing money on Herbalife, yet doggedly hell-bent on bringing the company down. "I will follow this trade to the end of the earth," he had said, taking care to say he would use his own money and not his investors', if that was the more prudent course of action. For the record, in another televised spectacle, Icahn and Ackman eventually made up, at least publicly, at the CNBC Institutional Investor Delivering Alpha Conference that same month. There was an awkward hug, which brought applause from the audience.

Ackman certainly primed the publicity pumps the day before his speech. "This will be the most important presentation I have made in my career," he boasted on CNBC as he made the rounds. "We are going to expose an incredible fraud tomorrow.... Come early. There is limited seating." Ackman promised new evidence, suggesting that a "death blow" to Herbalife was in the offing.

The plush, 487-seat wood-paneled auditorium at the AXA Equitable Center in Midtown Manhattan was full, as media, investors, and assorted hangers-on piled in. Next, a sultry-voiced female announcer introduced Ackman as if he were a talk-show host. "Ladies and gentlemen, please welcome founder and CEO of Pershing Square Capital Management, Mr. Bill Ackman," she enthused. The billionaire hedge fund manger bounded onstage decked out in a dapper dark blue suit and began his fire and brimstone sermon.

The new, groundbreaking information concerned so-called nutrition clubs, details of which were provided by Christine Richards, a former Dow Jones and *Bloomberg News* reporter who had penned *Confidence Game* (Bloomberg Press, 2010) an exhaustive book on an earlier Ackman short, insurer MBIA, which eventually netted him millions in profits after a three-year battle that included suits and investigations into Ackman and his fund by the New York State Attorney General at the time, Eliot Spitzer, the SEC, and the Justice Department. MBIA eventually lost its AAA S&P rating.

The upshot was this: Herbalife, he had discovered, was using a vast, secretive network of so-called "nutrition clubs"—informal meetings run by distributors—to offload company products on its distributors and lure in customers. They had to buy products, offer samples to potential buyers in shady, anonymous locations, and pay for this themselves. Desperate mothers, Richards reported, were feeding the nutrition mixes to their newborns, probably to help make ends meet.

Combined with Ackman's well-wrought pleas and references to his family history, it seemed a reasonably effective presentation. But the media and investors didn't buy it. Shares began to rise steadily during the presentation and finished the day up 25 percent at $67.77—its biggest one-day move ever.

The media was exuberant—perhaps deciding that Ackman's losing bet, which after all affected only millionaire investors, was far more interesting than any of the frankly damaging information the firm had revealed about Herbalife.

"The 'Death Blow to Herbalife' Promised by William Ackman Falls Short of Its Billing," the *New York Times* headline read.

"Herbalife Rallies in Face of New Attack by Ackman," said the *Wall Street Journal.*

While Ackman's short campaign against Herbalife remains a work in progress, it speaks emphatically to the dynamics of a financial system that seems to work relentlessly to punish those like Pershing Square that bet against stocks, rather than in favor of them. Ackman is no neophyte. In addition to MBIA, he has made successful wagers against the Federal Agricultural Mortgage Corp., or Farmer Mac, which makes loans to agricultural enterprises, as well as Realty Income, a real estate investment trust, and won big—at least as far as public documents can confirm.

Yet the vitriol heaped upon Ackman and his creed speaks volumes about the powerful forces that are aligned to defend even the most problematic companies—often helped as they are by a coterie of high-priced lawyers, like lobbyist Lanny Davis and Marty Lipton of Wachtell, Lipton, Rosen & Katz, and public relations powerhouses like Michael Sitrick's Sitrick and Company. It also shows a marked preference by many, though certainly not all, mainstream journalists to align themselves with established corporations rather than secretive Wall Street short sellers who can profit mightily when frauds are exposed. No matter that most so-called "dedicated" short sellers, those who, unlike Ackman, bet exclusively against stocks, seem inevitably to crash during extended bull markets.

James Chanos, for example, who went on to found the preeminent short-selling firm Kynikos Associates, was prominently mentioned in a 6,057-word cover story in the *Wall Street Journal* by reporter Dean Rothbart in 1985, as the decade's stock market bubble was rapidly inflating, quoting him extensively when examining the allegedly gamey tactics used to drive down share prices by short sellers. "They use facts when available, but some of them aren't above innuendo, fabrications, and deceit to batter down a stock," Rothbart wrote. Chanos was working at a Deutsche Bank subsidiary at the time—and was immediately informed his contract would not renewed.

In March 2006, correspondent Lesley Stahl of CBS News's *60 Minutes* aired a segment accusing a research firm, Gradient Analytics, of working with hedge fund firm SAC Capital Advisors to drive down the stock of Toronto-based drugmaker Biovail Corp. by publishing critical reports on the company. Two years later Biovail settled an SEC suit alleging accounting fraud for $10 million without admitting or denying the allegations.

More recently, and again in the midst of an expanding market bubble, *Bloomberg News*, in the September 2006 issue of its monthly magazine, *Bloomberg Markets*, published "Games Short Sellers Play." The article alleged that billions of dollars of phony sell orders were flooding the market and destroying promising young companies through the practice of n---d shorting—selling a stock without first locating an investor willing to lend it. It quoted a single short seller, Chanos himself, who dismissed the issue as a red herring—and relied on data that showed mostly that Wall Street settlement practices are sloppy, which they are.

But the story was notable in quoting an executive named Patrick Byrne, the CEO of a then-struggling e-commerce website called Overstock.com. The target of several short sellers, including David Rocker of Rocker Partners LP, it failed to note that Byrne's company had repeatedly missed its own earnings and revenue targets by wide margins over the years.

Nor did it mention that Byrne had told a skeptical accounting analyst that "you deserve to be whipped, f----d, and driven from the land." Or that Byrne had publicly declared on a conference call that an unnamed "Sith Lord" was orchestrating short-selling campaigns. Or that he had accused a female *Fortune* writer investigating Overstock.com of engaging in fellatio with various, unidentified Goldman Sachs traders.

Bloomberg TV used the story early the next year as the basis of a special report, hosted by Michael Schneider.

Other publications, especially those with limited expertise in covering Wall Street, were ready and happy to drive sales and circulation by blaming the shorts in a sort of bear-bashing cavalcade. Bryan Burroughs, co-author of the monumentally brilliant *Barbarians at the Gate: The Fall of RJR Nabisco* (Harper Collins, 1990), wrote a story for *Vanity Fair* in August 2008 laying blame for the collapse of investment bank Bear Stearns Cos. earlier that year at the feet of, predictably, unnamed short sellers. And Matt Taibbi—whose description of Goldman Sachs Group as a blood-sucking "vampire squid" would eventually go down in history—in October 2009 rehashed the same notion that it was n---d short-selling that had brought down both Bear and Lehman Brothers Holdings, failing to note their wildly extended balance sheets, with debt-to-equity ratios that topped 40 to one. Later, it turned out that Lehman had doctored its books each quarter.

The bad press may have prompted some monumentally dunderheaded regulatory moves. Amidst the collapse of Fannie Mae, Freddie Mac, Lehman, and American International Group, Wall Street executives, including Morgan Stanley's CEO John Mack, knowing they might be next in line to be brought down by panicked sellers, implored the SEC to ban the short selling of their company shares. In conjunction with the U.K. Financial Services Authority, SEC chairman Christopher Cox did that, albeit on a temporary basis, singling out 799 financial institutions—later expanded—for special protection from short sellers starting September 19, 2008, and ending October 2. Institutional investors were also required to disclose all new short positions.

In a study entitled *Shackling Short Sellers: The 2008 Shorting Ban*, released shortly after the restrictions were lifted, Ekkehart Boehmer of Mays Business School at the Texas A&M University, Charles M. Jones, of Columbia Business School, and Xiaoyan Zhang of the Johnson Graduate School of Management at Cornell University showed that while prices rose briefly, spreads widened and price impact increased, as did intraday volatility. Subsequent studies backed their conclusions.

Cox himself called it a mistake. "While the actual effects of this temporary action will not be fully understood for many more months, if not years, knowing what we know now, I believe on balance the commission would not do it again," he told Reuters. "The costs appear to outweigh the benefits."

Still, it remains a shame that so many juicy but dubious anecdotes have been written about short sellers, since the practice, regardless of whether one believes it healthy or harmful to the markets, has a fascinating history as it stands on its own merits—with good guys, bad guys, and mostly, and here's where it gets interesting, a whole range of characters in between. These are tales of fanatically committed people who perhaps because of the enormous pressures they endure year after year sometimes evolve into emotionally aggrieved and embittered individuals. Or maybe it's their distressed personalities that drive them into this punishing line of work to begin with. I don't know. Other times, they are just people with strong opinions and insights who stick to their beliefs.

While *The Most Dangerous Trade* is not a history of short selling, the background is fascinating—certainly worthy of a book in itself. The real stories of present-era short sellers, though, are gripping enough.

Note well: Some of the terminology is a bit scattershot or misleading. Short sellers, for example, despite common parlance, don't actually "borrow" shares. They contact a broker who says he or she has located an investor willing to lend shares, serving as a middleman for a steep price and taking an enormous cut—20 percent annualized or more of the amount borrowed in some cases. The shares are sold by the broker as well. The website of a now-defunct advocacy organization, the Washington, D. C.–based Coalition of Private Investment Companies, is still accessible and contains plenty of useful information on the subject.

Also, there are plenty of uses for short selling that have little if nothing to do with the focus of this book. Convertible arbitrage, for example, in its simplest form, involves buying a convertible bond and shorting the company's underlying stock—locking in the yield of the bond without the stock's risk—as a way to lock in gains with minimal volatility. That's no judgment on the company's management, viability, or even the priciness of its shares. One type of market-neutral investing balances out bullish bets on one industry stock, say General Motors Company, while shorting one of its rivals, such as Ford Motor Company, figuring the former is a better buy than the latter while netting out industry-specific risk. That's often called pairs trading and has been around for ages.

A strategy called capital structure arbitrage involves buying a particular class of bond or other corporate security because it looks relatively cheaper than, say, a shorter-term bond or preferred stock, which is shorted. And merger arbitrage often involves simply buying the stock of a takeover candidate while shorting that of the potential acquirer, which may be using its own shares as currency, benefiting when the spread between them disappears. The list goes on.

These are all legitimate strategies involving short selling that have little to do with most of the protagonists who are the focus of the book.

Full disclosure: I have, embarrassingly, failed to nail down, at least to any reasonable person's satisfaction, the precise origin of the term *short sale*. I can do what I usually do in such situations, however which is to repeat what I read or people tell me. Unfortunately, storied linguists like William Safire and Edwin Newman have passed on the subject.

The most obvious etymological derivation is that the term simply comes from the expression for selling someone short—that is, ascribing a value to a person or good that is below that of what is generally accepted, as in "Don't sell Snodgrass short." But that just hints at a resolution—although one that conveniently has been in English language usage for hundreds of years.

Another, somewhat more farfetched, explanation is that while a bullish or long investment has unlimited upside, the profit on a short sale is limited to the amount invested—a bigger or longer upside for the bull, in other words, and a more limited or shorter profit potential one for the bear. A stretch? I think so.

Likewise, it could just refer to the predilection of bulls to hold on to their investments for longer periods of time than shorts, who tend to book their profits, if they have them, quickly and quit while they were ahead. The *English Language & Usage Stack Exchange* cites a definition from *The Bryant and Stratton Business Arithmetic* of 1872. (I couldn't find one myself). It says simply that selling short is to imply selling before buying—that is, selling what one doesn't have leaving one short of the asset in question. Think along the lines of, "Joe, I'm short few dollars."

That works reasonably well for me and has the benefit of informing the early 20th-century proverb regarding short selling, whose attribution has, alas, also been lost to time: "He who sells what isn't his'n must pay the price or go to prison." In years past, not being able to furnish the shares owed to the party from which they have been borrowed was indeed a criminal offense. In some cases it still is.

(As an aside, the term "bear" probably derives from an ancient proverb that warns of selling a bear's skin before it's caught.)

The history of the short sale is so similarly aged as to have been lost to time—farmers, bankers, and merchants must have been doing it in one form or another for ages. But some of the choice examples are sufficient to suggest it is worthy of further investigation.

For example, the Dutch East India Company, the sprawling trading company with vast governmental and military powers that extended throughout the Far East, had an extensive shareholder base of wealthy and middle class investors in Holland. The stock price rose in a bubble-like fashion as talk of enormous wealth in far-off lands circulated. Some skeptical Dutch investors initiated short positions in 1609, most notable among them a merchant named Isaac LeMaire—who had a nose for sniffing out trouble and was not above spreading rumors. Shares tumbled and directors of the company complained to the Amsterdam stock exchange that they were the victims of a short-selling attack, which was bankrupting widows and orphans. The exchange responded that "the decline in the corporation's shares has been due to unsatisfactory business conditions," according to *The Art of Short Selling* by Kathryn Staley (John Wiley & Sons, 1997). Nevertheless, regulations against shorting were imposed the next year, and soon abandoned. There was no lesson learned: Tulipmania followed, beginning in 1634.

Britain effectively banned short selling in 1734 following the bursting of the similar great South Sea Bubble, in which shares of the South Seas Company tumbled from 1,200 to 86 pounds and short sellers were naturally blamed. The ban was widely ignored; although a new one focusing on banks was enacted following a major bank panic of 1866. That too was repealed in 1878, after a commission determined the collapse of the principal bank involved was a result of poor management and lending practices, not short sellers. It's always a question of shooting either the messenger or the short seller. While most people know John Maynard Keynes as the founder of Keynesian economic theory, he was also an active short seller, betting against the German mark during Weimar Republic years of hyperinflation in the 1920s only to be wiped out. "The market can remain irrational longer than you can remain solvent," he is said to have quipped. Keynes redeemed himself through his management of a Cambridge University endowment, the Chest fund, which returned more than 12 percent annually while he oversaw it from 1927 through 1945.

France experienced its own bubble decades before the French revolution. Much like the Dutch East India Company and the South Seas Company, the Mississippi Company, eventually called the Compagnie des Indes, generated enormous investor demand. A rakish Scotsman named John Law, one of the earliest proponents of paper, or fiat, currency persuaded the French government to issue bank notes backed by precious metals. As the power of Compagnie des Indes grew, it assumed greater power to collect taxes and print its own coinage. The French population was soon buying shares by the bushel full and prices soared, minting new millionaires daily. In 1720, as people tried to redeem the shares and the fiat currency Law had sold them, he devalued both. Compagnie des Indes shares collapsed to less than one twentieth of their peak value. Millionaires became paupers, short sellers were again blamed, and France entered a profound, extended depression that, according to some historians, was a fundamental cause of the French revolution. An anti-short selling rule was instituted in 1724.

Napoleon Bonaparte, incidentally, harbored a deep animosity toward short sellers because he believed they were interested in driving down the prices of government securities. That in turn would make it more difficult for him to finance La Grande Armée's campaign of conquest across Europe and was therefore treasonous. Once again, restrictions were enacted and later abandoned.

In America, the history of short-selling is more colorful still—dating back nearly to the days of Wall Street's famed buttonwood tree, under which the New York Stock Exchange's predecessor was founded. During the War of 1812 with Great Britain, for example, the New York legislative branch banned short selling as way to forestall panicked selling of bank shares. The prohibition was widely ignored, though it took until the late 1850s before the ban was formally repealed. As in other nations, it was a pattern that was to be repeated time and again over the decades.

Until the establishment of the SEC, in 1934, U.S. markets were, for all intents and purposes, unregulated—a Wild West free-for-all bereft of rules. That left the field open for blatant market manipulation—often by the renowned robber barons of the Gilded Age. This occurred in both inflating and driving down stock prices. In a so-called corner, one or two investors would buy up all available shares of a company, forcing the short seller to buy to cover at outrageous mark-ups. (A squeeze involves multiple participants.) There were a variety of shenanigans, including bribes and rumors, according to *All About Short Selling* by Tom Taulli (McGraw Hill, 2011).

Famed financiers Jay Gould and Jim Fisk teamed with Daniel Drew to flood the market in the late 1860s with new issues of Erie Railroad shares, driving its market capitalization to $57 million from $34 million, not to mention $20 million in convertible bonds that were sold abroad. They then yanked millions from banks, creating a panic that drove down share prices, and secretly covered their short positions on the railroad. The pair then turned against Drew, who had remained short, and engineered a massive short squeeze that cost him $1 million.

Corporate insiders also got in on the short-selling act. President John Gates of American Steel and Wire Company, a barbed-wire monopoly, shorted his own company's stock amidst a softening business and layoffs—cashing in as share prices fell. A storied gambler—known as Bet-A-Million Gates—he eventually sold the company to John Pierpont Morgan in 1901, and it became part of U.S. Steel Corp.

The greatest stock short seller of the 20th century was undoubtedly Jesse Lauriston Livermore, the "Boy Plunger." Born in 1877 into a farm family near Worcester, Massachusetts, he ran away from home at age 14 to take a job posting quotes at the Boston branch of the brokerage firm PaineWebber. He dabbled in dubious securities proffered by unsavory dealers known as bucket shops, yet somehow managed to profit.

In 1906, he is said to have shorted Union Pacific Corp, the San Francisco railroad giant, the day before the great earthquake. No one can explain why. The next year, he shorted the market during the panic of 1907, noting that speculators had overextended themselves and were subject to margin calls. Livermore only covered his short positions at the request of John Pierpont Morgan himself, realizing he wouldn't be able to collect his gains if the brokerage firms he traded with went belly up. His net worth: an estimate $3 million, or $75 million in 2014 dollars, an amount he subsequently lost on cotton speculation, filing for bankruptcy in 1915.

Livermore was down but not out. He borrowed money and eventually left the stock market to trade commodities and eventually recovered. He codified his trading strategies in a 1923 book, *Reminiscences of a Stock Operator* by Edwin Lefevre, and claimed all of his mistakes derived from not following them. Investors today still refer to it. He made money in the bull markets of the 1920s, and became close friends with Bernard Baruch, the financier and philanthropist who served as an advisor to Presidents Woodrow Wilson and Franklin D. Roosevelt. Baruch was also a noted short seller himself—booking gains on Brooklyn Rapid Transit and Amalgamated Copper, while failing to do so on Radio Corporation of America. By 1929, Livermore had noticed many of the same market characteristics that had preceded the panic of 1907—rising margin debt, pricey stocks, exuberance. He shorted stocks and made $100 million, or $1.37 billion in 2014 dollars.

What happened next is, from what I can gather, unknown. Livermore was a famed womanizer, with a yacht, houses around the world, and an armada of limousines. He was on his fifth marriage, but by 1934 he had managed to lose the $100 million. No one knows how, though trusts he had set up kept him from any real financial hardship.

He committed suicide with a revolver in the cloakroom of New York's Sherry-Netherland hotel on Fifth Avenue in 1940. His farewell note to his wife read: "Can't help it. Things have been bad with me. I am tired of fighting. Can't carry on any longer. This is the only way out. I am unworthy of your love. I am a failure. I am truly sorry but this is the only way out for me. Love Laurie."

There were other famed short sellers of the crash—"Sell 'em" Ben Smith and the president of Chase Bank, Albert Wiggen, who bet against his own bank using money he borrowed from it. Republican President Herbert Hoover believed that a cabal of Democratic short sellers were aligned against him, aiming to bring down the markets to support Franklin Delano Roosevelt—and railed against them. The Pecora Commission, headed by Ferdinand Pecora, counsel for the Senate Banking and Currency Committee, found that it was the government that was involved in double dealing and new disclosure rules were enacted.

The 1934 founding of the SEC under Roosevelt helped bring at least a semblance of order to the wild speculation, promotions, and manipulations of the stock market. Its first chairman: Joseph Kennedy, the former prohibition-era bootlegger and father of President John F. Kennedy. He too had been a successful short seller—and there was undoubtedly an element of Roosevelt hiring the fox to guard the henhouse. One often-cited but probably insignificant change: the *uptick rule*, which barred the shorting of a stock unless it had moved higher in its previous trade. That stayed on the books until 2007, leading some to conclude its repeal was a factor in the 2008–2009 collapse. I've seen no evidence to support that view.

The Investment Company Act of 1940 severely restricted diversified mutual funds from shorting. The 1949 launch by former *Fortune* magazine editor Alfred Winslow Jones of what is generally considered the first modern day *hedge fund*, which typically buys some stocks while shorting others, using leverage, was a game changer. "The Jones that Nobody Keeps Up With" was what Carol Loomis, a now retired *Fortune* writer, dubbed him in a deliciously revealing article. Slowly at first and then in increasing numbers, others emulated Jones and shorting became, if not pervasive, at least an established part of the sophisticated investors' arsenal.

Today there are more than 8,000 hedge funds, according to Hedge Fund Research, a Chicago form that tracks them. Most engage in some form of shorting.

Short selling was continually investigated as a source of market volatility—or at least downward movements in stocks, since nobody ever seems to protest when stocks rise sharply. The October 19, 1987, crash was fueled by a bubble of optimism, in part because of the spreading popularity of so-called portfolio insurance, which promised to short stock indexes in the event of a market sell-off, thereby locking in gains. Institutional investors threw caution to the wind. Following the crash, a House of Representatives Committee looked into the impact of short sellers on the meltdown. The ultimate conclusion was that their contribution was negligible. So-called circuit-breakers were instituted to halt trading when the market plunged precipitously—the triggers have been updated periodically.

In 1992, George Soros, with billions of dollars in his Quantum Fund, believed a sharp currency move was in the offing. The British pound was part of the so-called European Rate Mechanism—designed to keep European currency exchange rates in narrow ranges. Prime Minister Margaret Thatcher was bent on keeping the pound pegged to the German deutsche mark at a rate above 2.7 marks to the pound. Yet the U.K. inflation rate was three times that of Germany.

While the U.K. raised interest rates to entice investors to buy the pound, some investors, notably Soros, believed such a move was unsustainable. In what became known as the *Black Wednesday Currency Crisis*, the U.K. raised rates from 10 to 12 percent and then promised 15 percent to entice investors to buy pounds. The move failed. Soros shorted an estimated $10 billion in pounds in the market and ultimately forced the U.K. to withdraw from the ERM. The fund pocketed more than $1 billion from the trade—costing the U.K. government many times that. The move earned Soros the sobriquet "The Man Who Broke the Bank of England."

The move didn't earn Soros many friends. When Malaysia's currency collapsed in 1997 amidst the Asian contagion, the country's Prime Minister, Mahathir bin Mohamad, accused Soros—a Holocaust survivor with a history of championing human rights and open societies—of targeting the nation. "It is a Jew who triggered the currency plunge," he said.

The technology bubble of the 1990s eviscerated short sellers or even just value-conscious investors—despite Fed chairman Alan Greenspan's 1996 warning of irrational exuberance. Famed hedge fund manager Julian Robertson of Tiger Management mothballed his business as stocks like Microsoft, Intel, and Sun Microsystems soared, not to mention Internet companies with more dubious business models like theglobe.com, Pets.com and Etoys.com, which often did not generate earnings all. Being correct brought little satisfaction. Loews Corp, headed by famed value investor Larry Tisch, initiated a giant short bet against the S&P 500 beginning in 1996. He finally closed it out in March 2000, the very month the NASDAQ Composite Index reached its peak. The bet cost the storied conglomerate some $2 billion.

Following the terror attacks on the World Trade Center and Pentagon on September 11, 2001, which shut down the U.S. stock markets, Wall Street brokerage firms asked short sellers not to seek profit from the anticipated selloff in share prices when markets opened, which they did three days after the attack. It would be an interesting exercise to see who did or did not.

There were reports, including some in major media publications, that Al Qaeda-linked groups may have shorted stocks or used put options in advance of the attacks, with some less-established outlets asserting that they had specifically targeted the airlines involved and insurers that had underwritten catastrophic claims against the towers. Nothing I have read lends credence to this notion.

In 2004, the SEC approved a new rule, Regulation SHO, designed to reduce n---d short selling, that is, selling a stock without first having a broker locating a holder willing to lend it within a three-day window, or settlement period. The rule requires that the SEC publish a list of the stocks with the most violations of this settlement matter. Again, whether this rule has had any impact remains dubious.

There was a major irony in the temporary ban on shorting financial stocks on September 19, 2008. The move was taken at the behest of investment banks that had been making hundreds of millions of dollars from hedge funds lending them the stocks they were shorting, including their own. The banks argued it was short sellers, not genuine market fear of their outrageous leverage, driving down share prices.

The SEC also required institutional money managers to report new short positions—another way to quash short sales.

Short sellers will never be in the clear. The Financial Crisis Inquiry Report ascribed the 2008–2009 financial crisis to regulatory failures, poor corporate governance, and, of course, widespread excessive borrowing. Short-selling isn't mentioned even as a contributing factor to the crisis. Yet, it's a truism that such investors will be blamed in any market pull back.

On a clear chilly morning in December 2012, Dave Davidson, a continent away from Ackman, is in his smallish, bare one-room office in Greenbrae, California, tucked under the 101 Freeway that leads from San Francisco through undulating hills and mountains to points in northern Marin, Sonoma, and beyond. It's just a rented desk from a firm called Banyan Securities, where partner Claudio Chiuchiarelli seems to have a soft spot for taking in orphan contrarian market thinkers.

There is a view under that dark ribbon of asphalt and concrete across Larkspur Creek to Corte Madera. Davidson is an aging jock. He has given up rugby but still believes competiveness is the key to success on Wall Street. Davidson wears a fleece-lined vest, shorts, and sneakers as he focuses intently on his computer. His $66 million fund is losing money as the market climbs relentlessly in late 2012. How could it not? The Federal Reserve has interests at about 2.0 percent and is furiously buying up Treasuries and mortgage-backed securities as part of its quantitative easing program. This infuriates Davidson; it's an example of financial repression, in his view—deliberately keeping rates low as a means of forcing investors to buy stocks. "Where is the sanity?" reads the greeting on Davidson's Bloomberg terminal page. The future embodies devastating deflation and financial collapse.

Davidson graduated in 1977 from the University of Southern California in Los Angeles and worked as a medical technician before hitting Wall Street as the bull market shifted into high gear in 1984, taking on a string of sales positions—first in retail at PaineWebber and Donaldson, Lufkin & Jenrette Securities and then in institutional sales at Montgomery Securities and Volpe & Covington. He co-founded Pacific Growth Equities and then decided to manage money for himself and others through his own firm, SC Capital Management.

In 2000, he briefly hooked up with short seller Bill Fleckenstein of Fleckenstein Capital's R.T.M. Fund in 2000, playing the macro expert, he says, to his colleague's fundamentalist approach—as the technology bubble collapsed. The two split over a disagreement about R.T.M.'s management fees. Davidson started Shoreline Fund I with $10 million in assets under the SC Management brand in December 2004.

Davidson's process, which he refreshingly talks about at length and in depth, is elegantly simple—which may be precisely why he has trouble pulling in money from big name investors, who sometimes prefer reams of fundamental research from an analyst team. Davidson focuses on those stocks with the largest market capitalizations of $5 billion or more, and generally requires short candidates have 1 million shares a day in trading volume to ensure liquidity. It isn't brain surgery, but may require more of a stomach.

Davidson looks at former market leaders whose technical charts, 100-day moving averages, say, are falling amid strong daily volumes. Momentum is a positive force. "It's my belief that price and volume predict change," he says. He points out that he also takes heed of fundamentals like earnings and sales growth.

At his desk, he excitedly points to brightly lit red companies that fit the descriptions. He typically focuses on a list of 70 to 100 companies, in six to nine sectors. Today, it's Apple and Micron Technology, for example, that are sells for the moment. That can change, but Davidson believes it is a good indicator of future share prices. "My process is a predictive system," he says.

Broadly speaking, Shoreline I actually does what it is supposed to do—it is up when the S&P 500 is down, sometimes by a far greater amount than the inverse would suggest it should be. Since inception it has lost to the benchmark HFRI index of short-biased hedge funds in just 2 of 10 years. Overall, Shoreline I has returned 2.62 percent versus a loss of 20.6 percent for the short index. In 2008, the worst year of the financial crisis, Shoreline I gained 56.9 percent, double the 28.4 percent gain for the short index—versus a 37 percent plunge by the S&P 500.

Shoreline I also sometimes rises when the S&P 500 does, because of Davidson's willingness to cut and run. By remaining in liquid stocks, he can get out quick. "I can take my positions out to the trading desk and be out in 30 minutes," he says with an air of satisfaction. One of his adages undoubtedly helps. He says he won't fight the general market trend, major economic indicators, or Federal Reserve moves. Davidson covers his shorts and waits. "When things don't work, just take your exposure off," he says. "You wait until something turns your way. If I'm wrong, I just get out of the way."

Investors, though, aren't so patient—they seldom are with short selling strategies. Shoreline assets were down from $200 million, and that in itself is an added pressure for Davidson. "We had a 40 percent redemption in 2010," he says, as investors pulled out in the midst of a rollicking bull market. In 2012 he predicted another 20 percent redemption for the year.

And 2013 brought still worse news. A big Shoreline investor, a fund of funds, got tangled up in an unrelated management scandal and withdrew millions from the various funds it invested in. Much of that was pulled out in 2014 from Shoreline. And so despite such monster years as 2000, 2002, and 2008, when Shoreline posted returns of 46.5 percent, 37.2 percent, and 56.9 percent, respectively, Davidson is now down to just $2 million in assets in early 2015, essentially his own money.

Davidson, and other short sellers, for all their steely determination, will have their mettle tested daily. After all, they ply the stock market's most dangerous trade.

Chapter 2

Asensio: Exile on Third Avenue

The meeting turned nasty even before it began. Manuel Asensio walked off the elevator wearing a gray-striped Norman Hilton suit into the National Association of Securities Dealers (NASD) offices at One Liberty Plaza—a hulking black steel skyscraper in lower Manhattan. He was an hour late and offered no apologies.

As the dapper Asensio entered the lobby, a NASD case manager walked up to greet him, extending his hand as he did so. Asensio ignored it, and turned to his lawyer.

"I can't believe that this guy thinks I'm going to shake his hand," he told him. There were really no reasons for niceties from Asensio's perspective. The NASD had been routinely badgering him for thousands of pages of documents over the years, and he thought their goal was to drive him out of business.

The NASD had summoned Asensio in September 2004 to answer questions about his short-selling firm as well as six research reports published on the Asensio.com website. The research was part of a series describing alleged Medicare fraud at PolyMedica Corp, a NASDAQ-listed telemarketer of blood glucose test kits.

Then things got ugly. At the hearing, Asensio wouldn't respond when asked about ownership of his firm, Integral Securities. Because it wasn't an NASD member, he said he didn't have to answer. In his street-inflected Brooklyn accent, he called the proceedings "a fraudulent, corrupt, intentional attempt to discredit my firm, keep me from doing my work." Asensio declared that the American Stock Exchange, NASD, and New York Stock Exchange were all guilty of harassment.

Asensio accused the NASD officers of staring, "making faces," and "mocking" him. They were "hostile," "crooks," and "corrupt regulators." After two hours of interrogation by NASD officers, Asensio announced that he had "provided more than enough time." He got up and stalked out of the conference room.

The eruption cost him dearly. A NASD panel decided that Asensio had violated rule 8210, failing to respond in full to questions. Asensio says NASD officials offered him a deal: Pay $15,000 to settle and the matter would be effectively dropped. But that would not prevent the organization from coming after him in the future whenever he tried to uncover fraud. Asensio says he refused.

NASD's sentence: the organization's version of capital punishment—a lifetime bar from the securities industry.

"I call it 'the evil decision,'" says Asensio. "It's corruption, and that's what it should be called."

At the same time, today he says he is contrite. Asensio wishes passionately that he had handled the situation more delicately. "It was a colossal error in judgment," he says. "I was there after two years of persecution. At that point, I went ballistic."

Provocateur, Internet personality, and invective-throwing activist, Asensio has for years been among the most contentious players in a contentious industry—a paradigm of high-decibel short-selling. With his streetwise demeanor, Asensio has personally harangued the CEOs of companies he targets, yelling at one of them in court: "You are the devil incarnate." He keeps a Cuban passport, rides a vintage BMW R65 motorcycle, and once declared to the *Wall Street Journal*: "God has given me this power—It's the power of good versus evil."

Since the bar, however, Asensio's short-selling has been drastically sidelined and his strident advocacy muzzled. Funds, endowments, and family offices have shuttered accounts. Others have yanked money from his firm, which at its peak had more than $500 million in assets.

During what Asensio describes as his heyday, he was dubbed the "Demolition Man," and could send a stock plummeting with a single research report. Even since the bar, it still remains foolhardy to ignore his calls, such as one in December 2010 when he pegged Netflix, trading at $150, as overpriced. Though the stock barely moved at the time, one year later it was trading at $29. In early 2015 Netflix traded above $650.

Asensio calls the investigation a retaliation designed to punish him for his advocacy efforts. The NASD, whose regulatory powers were incorporated into the Financial Industry Regulatory Authority in 2007, at the time described the probe as part of a routine sweep to gauge compliance with a new regulation separating research from investment banking adopted following the analyst scandals of the early 2000s.

Asensio says that is nonsense. None of the firms he ran—Asensio & Company, Integral, or the website Asensio.com—did any investment banking business, either underwriting securities or providing advisory services.

"They created a frivolous investigation," Asensio says. "These regulators are private organizations that have been given the same powers as a government entity without the checks and balances."

Asensio's modus operandi is to research and identify what he considers frauds and then expose them in the media, on his eponymous website, or in the courts, driving down their share price along the way. He has made millions doing so. He used to call the strategy "hostile adversarial." He now prefers the more academic-sounding term "informational arbitrage."

Asensio is the acknowledged pioneer. A working paper by the National Bureau of Economic Research from January 2014 looked at the performance of 17 firms that publish negative research reports from July 2006 to December 2011. It found that 60 days after the initial report, the stock of companies Asensio targets fell 58.9 percent, more than any other firm.

All told, he calculates a total of more than 50 full-fledged short campaigns, more than half of which have resulted in share declines of 75 percent or more. These have provoked more than a half-dozen lawsuits, usually in the wake of screaming publicity battles.

Regulators often fare no better—Asensio prompted an investigation into American Stock Exchange listing standards and accused the U.S. Securities and Exchange Commission (SEC) and its then-chairman, Mary Schapiro, of lying about financial dealings when she headed the NASD. He helped launch an advocacy group, Alliance for Economic Stability, that accuses her of a variety of ethics violations.

"He's highly intelligent, works like a dog, but has utterly no common sense," says Richard Getty, a lawyer who represented Asensio in one of the litany of suits he has endured over the years.

Asensio sometimes exults in his outsider status and makes no attempt to sugarcoat his approach. "Money managers and regulators despise us because we upset their system," he says, carefully enunciating each word for effect. "We bring chaos to the system. We bring volatility. We are hostile to the system."

In the case of PolyMedica, the Federal Bureau of Investigation (FBI) raided its offices beginning on August 16, 2001. The company settled the fraud charges—among other things, it had been improperly submitting reimbursement claims and had violated the False Claims Act by not obtaining signed doctors' orders or prescriptions for the products it sold—and paid a $35 million fine. That wasn't enough for Asensio, who had called for at least $400 million in fines and described the outcome as "entirely a function of a political process." PolyMedica was bought by Medco Health Solutions in August 2007. Express Scripts bought Medco in 2012, and PolyMedica eventually filed for chapter 11 bankruptcy after it was purchased in connection with a management-led buyout.

Many, though not all, short sellers shun publicity, operating beneath the radar. Not Asensio. "He is the intellectual godfather of the Internet-enabled investor," says one fellow short seller. "He pulls no punches. He says, 'This is the guy who is lying.'"

Before the NASD barred him, Asensio's nose for fraud had attracted an impressive client list, including John Paulson, founder of hedge fund

Paulson & Co., who made more than $7 billion in the sub-prime collapse of 2008 and other prominent managers.

Even today, fans include Leon Cooperman of hedge fund Omega Advisors. "When he gets into something he's really obsessive," says Cooperman, who has knows Asensio socially and does not invest with him. "If he was shorting something and I owned it, I'd really grill my analyst to make sure he knew what he was talking about." Asensio won't disclose current or former clients.

Asensio's trail of "hostile adversarial" campaigns goes back to 1996, when he issued a "strong sell" recommendation on NYSE-listed Diana Corp., a Milwaukee-based meat distributor that was, on the cusp of the Internet bubble, trumpeting a new phone switch design that it claimed had revolutionary features demanded by Internet service providers. Asensio canvassed equipment makers like Flextronics, who told him the switch design was unbuildable. Asensio issued a 16-page report, detailing its technological flaws. Shares eventually fell to 7 cents from $100 when he issued the report.

Other frauds, or "promotes" as shorts call them, followed: A chain of laundromats, a maker of dubious engine turbochargers, and myriad technology companies are among the companies Asensio helped expose. So too was a Bronx, New York, outfit making a device to measure jaundice in newborns based on 1950s-era gadgetry. The claims of promoters, it seems, was limited only by their greed.

"On a case-by-case basis, his record is almost perfect," says one rival short seller, who asked not to be identified. "That's incredible."

Ultimately, Asensio's line of work has made him accustomed to making enemies. Lawsuits and inquiries have dogged him throughout his career. Among the insults target companies and others have used to describe him: "liar," "thief," and "Ass-ensio."

On a broiling August afternoon, Asensio is slouched in a black office chair at his Manhattan office. With shaved head and dressed in cutoff shorts, laceless sneakers, and a rumpled polo shirt, he looks more like a beachcomber than a Wall Street shark. At five feet eleven inches and a lithe 165 pounds, Asensio sizes up visitors with deep-set brown eyes.

Mia, his daughter's longhaired Chihuahua, playfully yelps. "She likes you," he observes. "That's unusual."

The threadbare office speaks to Asensio's outsider status. On the walls, instead of slick corporate art, are social-realist posters. "Work Better. Live Better," they read.

There are also old stock and bond certificates from the land of his birth: Cuban Cane Products Co. and Blanco Territorial de Cuba.

Like a lot of immigrants, Asensio worships the American work ethic. On a visit to a local sandwich shop, he points to the lone counterwoman. "Do you see how she's running this place all by herself?" he marvels, and then lapses into Spanish as he chats her up about business. Later, walking through a park frequented by transients, he shows his disdain for what he perceives as slackers: "The sense of entitlement of these guys is amazing."

Friends shrug it off. "Manuel definitely views the world as black and white," says Allan Block, a friend and CEO of Block Communications Inc., a Toledo, Ohio Communications Company that owns the *Pittsburgh-Gazette*, which often publishes op-ed pieces by Asensio. "Well, the world is not black and white."

Though he doesn't like to talk about it, short selling has made Asensio wealthy; he keeps an apartment on Manhattan's eastside and a luxury apartment in Miami, and dines at the finest steakhouses. He collects the artwork of contemporary Cuban artists like Alexis Leyva Machado and when in South Florida zips around on a classic 1979 BMW R65 motorcycle. But to hear Asensio tell it, uncovering fraud is less a career than a cause—part of the eternal struggle between right and wrong.

"Morality is important to me," says Asensio. "Whether you're dealing with FINRA, a court, or a short sale."

As he grapples with his exile high above Third Avenue, it's a subject he returns to again and again. He shows a black loose-leaf binder with articles by sociologists on the subjects of why people do what they do. It includes a paper by Ziva Kunda, the late social psychologist known for her work in motivational reasoning, and another by Jonathan Haidt, a New York University Stern School of Business professor who specializes in the psychological bases for morality across different cultures.

Asensio says he understands "instinctive" decision making"—what psychologists describe as the tendency of people to stick by choices they make on impulse. By contrast, "deliberative" decision-making requires time, and results in a more nuanced, balanced outcome. "The person making the instinctual decision will always make up a reason not to change that decision," Asensio says. Ergo, FINRA is unlikely to ever reverse its ruling.

Psychology aside, Asensio had been a thorn in the side of FINRA and other regulators for years. The targets of his short campaigns were often listed on the NASDAQ Stock Market, which was for a long time part of FINRA's NASD predecessor. The association fined him for myriad infractions over the years.

Beginning in 2000, Asensio let loose a blistering series of letters to regulators of the American Stock Exchange (AMEX) criticizing the market's lax listing standards. At the time, AMEX was a NASD subsidiary. "We believe that the AMEX's leaders have intentionally protected certain stock scams," Asensio wrote in a November 2000 letter to Representative John Dingell, chairman of the House Committee on Commerce, who launched an investigation into AMEX practices.

The specifics of Asensio's answers to the NASD—the basis of its ruling to bar him—are opaque based on available documents. Transcripts of such hearings are not posted, and the whole process of adjudication by so-called self-regulatory organizations like FINRA is cloaked in secrecy.

Excerpts from NASD transcripts show that before the hearing that led to the ban, Asensio & Company changed its name to Integral Securities, that would not be a broker-dealer. "There was nothing underhanded or contrived about it," says Asensio. "It was for the purpose of eliminating NASD jurisdiction."

Regardless, he has suffered the blowback. Appeals have all proven fruitless. When Asensio applied to FINRA in 2009 to be reinstated, under the sponsorship of a new company, ISI Capital, he was rejected. FINRA created a new rule to prevent a disbarred member from ever rejoining. He calls it "the Anti-Asensio rule" (an SEC commission scuttled the proposal after Asensio opposed it). Asensio next appealed his bar to the SEC, of which Schapiro had been named chairman, which backed FINRA's bar (Schapiro recused herself). Then, in 2012, Asensio's appeal to the U.S. Court of Appeals for the 11th Circuit was also denied.

Asensio has spent millions on his efforts. The opportunity costs are far greater. The bar means he was preoccupied and in the penalty box during the credit-fueled stock market meltdown of 2007–2009, when hedge funds managers like Paulson and Jim Chanos of Kynikos Associates pocketed billions.

He blames the bar for trashing his peace of mind. Mostly, though, he acknowledges the stain on his credibility and his family honor. "It struck at my heritage," he says, drawing on a Montecristo cigar. "I have a lot of pride in my family name."

The bitter lesson learned by Asensio is that for regulators, cracking down on short sellers produces little, if any collateral damage. "It's an easy political win to go after these guys," says Daniel Celeghin, a partner at consultant Casey, Quirk & Associates in Darien, Connecticut. "There is always this shoot the messenger mentality."

The bar against Asensio is testimony to how arbitrarily and capriciously such sanctions are applied. "Discretion without oversight is the enemy of fairness," he says. With hearings closed to the public, there is zero transparency. Dynamics like that conspire to sink a defendant who is disliked, uncooperative, hostile, or simply combative. Asensio is all of the above. "These cases are decided on a case-by-case basis," says professor Jill Fish of the University of Pennsylvania School of Law. "When you're dealing with a regulator, that can be a strategy that backfires."

It certainly did for the pugnacious Asensio—who seems to have been battling one system or another from his earliest days.

His tale begins in Batista-era Havana, where Manuel Pedro Asensio-Garcia was born in 1954. Asensio's father, Manuel Sr., and his uncle Abilio worked in an export–import business. His mother, Caridad, was a social worker and a descendant of Vicente Garcia Gonzalez, a nationalist hero of the Cuban Ten Years' War who was later reportedly poisoned by the Spanish with ground glass in 1886. Asensio still carries a Cuban passport.

After Fidel Castro overthrew Batista in 1958, his father supported the revolution. Asensio's pragmatic mother was skeptical as first opponents of Castro and then former allies were rounded up and summarily executed. His parents bundled the 6-year-old Manuel onto a steamer to Venezuela with an aunt and uncle, who officially adopted him to make the flight easier.

Asensio recalls embarking passengers being relieved of their jewelry by Castro's paramilitaries at the dock. He said goodbye to his father. "That was the last time I cried as a child," says Asensio.

After a spell in Caracas, his aunt and uncle dispatched him by plane to New York.

His new home was with his mother's sister Josephine, a factory seam-stress, in the working-class Brooklyn neighborhood of Borough Park. His mother soon joined them, and the extended Asensio clan settled into the bustling Jewish and Italian area of brick row houses, where the elevated subway clattered away day and night. His father, jailed for a spell in Cuba on political charges, eventually joined them,

Despite the poverty, it was one of the happiest times of his life. "None of the difficulties touched us," Asensio says. "We went to school together. We went to church together." He played stickball on the streets, always outnumbered by the local Jews. To make money, Asensio worked as a "Shabbat Goy," earning money by lighting ovens and turning on lights for orthodox Jews, who are forbidden from doing so on the day of rest. Only recently has he discovered that the Garcia side of his family has extensive Jewish roots, of which he is proud.

Asensio attended first public school and then St. Francis de Chantal, a nearby Catholic elementary institution overseen by a faculty of dis-ciplinarian nuns. "If we are ignorant, she is the seat of wisdom," reads an inscription by Saint Jane Frances de Chantal on the façade of the four-story, mid-century building. "If we are weak, she is strong."

From there it was on to the Bishop Ford Bishop Diocesan High School, where Franciscan brothers were in charge. As a freshman, Asen-sio became a track star clocking a half mile sprint at under two minutes. As always, he and his cousin were the only Cubans.

Asensio hustled for pocket money, working at a Carvel's ice cream shop, delivering groceries, or hawking newspapers. In 1970, his father, then working hourly jobs, scored a solid administrative post at IBM Corp.'s new personal computer factory in Florida. They were off to Boca Raton, where Asensio graduated from the local high school and began taking classes at community colleges. He worked at every opportunity, saving what he could.

From there, Asensio headed north to Philadelphia, to attend the Wharton Evening School, the business school's continuing education program. Scoring straight As helped him swing a transfer to the Wharton School proper on a work-study scholarship, graduating in 1977 with the degree he thought would be a passport to a Wall Street career.

That didn't happen. He still remembers the withering comment of a Morgan Stanley junior partner eyeing his cheap suit during the interview. "There's only so many investment bankers in the world and I don't think you look ... the type," he recalls the partner saying. The remark still stings. "In 1977, there were no spics on Wall Street," he says.

Bitter but wiser, Asensio left for Caracas, a stable and vibrant city at the time, awash in oil money. He landed a job at age 22 at an Alcoa subsidiary, arranging a long-term consumer financing. "I was the one who could speak English," Asensio chuckles. He later landed a superior spot at Société Financière Union.

Two years later, though, oil prices began to plummet. Asensio saw political-economic storm clouds gathering, and took his Venezuelan wife-to-be to Boston and Harvard Business School.

There, Asensio stumbled upon the kind of trade that comes along once or twice in a lifetime. It was 1981, and Seagram Company Ltd. and DuPont Company were in a contest to acquire Conoco Inc., the oil giant. Seagram was offering $110 a share when DuPont appeared as a white knight. In a two-step transaction that was pioneered by First Boston mergers and acquisitions co-heads Bruce Wasserstein and Joseph Perella, DuPont quickly bought 51 percent of Conoco's stock and offered the equivalent of $67 a share in DuPont stock for the balance. Since DuPont already controlled a majority of shares, those holding the rest would have to accept the $67 offer—a "cram down" in Wall Street parlance.

Unaccountably, Seagram left its $110 share offer on the table, even though it was virtually certain that it would be forced to accept the $67 DuPont stock cram down. The confusion helped prop up Conoco stock, which, illogically, was trading at $90 or so.

Asensio was busy calling investor relations, brokers, and merger arbitrage desks for insight into the deal. He also managed to find some put options that would give him the right to sell shares of Conoco at $90. The cost: $1 a piece. So, once Seagram's offer lapsed, someone on the other side of the trade would be forced to pay Asensio $90 for a $67 stock, locking in a profit of $23, for a mere $1 outlay, or a 2,300 percent return.

Asensio researched everything himself in his student dormitory. "I was reading the proxies, the 10-Qs, talking to companies and arbitrageurs," he says. Asensio says he bought as many puts as he could, and made nearly a half million dollars on the trade.

It was his first short investment—and it made him rich. "It allowed me to not have to worry about getting a job during recruiting season," he says.

The Cuban immigrant who couldn't get hired as a Morgan Stanley associate found himself on top of the world—in the ivory tower of capitalism. And Asensio wasn't shy about letting his classmates—who included JPMorgan Chase CEO Jamie Dimon and General Electric CEO Jeffrey Immelt—know about his success. Some resented it.

Asensio's machismo irked some people. On one occasion, his section was studying a case history of a woman executive who overcame a thorny business problem. Asensio declared: "I've been very impressed by the little lady." The class hissed. "He got notoriety for his politically incorrect statements," chuckles Glenn Wattley, a fellow classmate.

After Harvard, Asensio headed back to Boca Raton to set up First Boca Raton Investment Corp. It was not a runaway success. He provided advice to venture stage companies, which had begun to sprout in the area, as had a whole crop of dubious companies across South Florida. "This was my introduction to penny stock fraud," he says.

First Boca steered clear of them but did help to raise money for a dicey company called Therapeutic Technologies, which made machines to exercise the muscles of paralyzed patients. The company stiffed First Boca Raton on its bill, so Asensio had a local sheriff's department to haul away Therapeutic's office equipment.

The episode was recounted as a "bright" in the *Wall Street Journal*. Asensio was mortified.

In 1987, Asensio sold First Boca Raton, heading north to New York and Bear Stearns, a firm known for taking bets on unconventional hires. "In my case, a bad idea," Asensio writes in his autobiographical book, *Sold Short* (John Wiley & Sons, 2001).

John Paulson, the hedge fund manager, was Asensio's boss in Bear Stearns' mergers and acquisitions department. Asensio was struck by Paulson's fastidiousness. "He was meticulous. He always held the pen upright and then drew circles around what he had written," says Asensio. "John Paulson was always philosophical and thoughtful." Paulson, who later briefly shared office space at Asensio & Company, through a spokesman declined to comment about his relationship with the short seller.

Asensio gravitated toward corporate iconoclasts, even the most unpopular ones. These included Charles Hurwitz, the CEO of Maxxam Inc., a Bear Stearns client reviled by environmentalists for his efforts to cut down groves of California redwood trees in the 1990s.

"I liked Charles," says Asensio. "He was able to get control of companies with assets and cash flows and shake them up in creative ways."

Asensio says he wasn't a fit at Bear Stearns and set off to do something "entrepreneurial." He set up shop at a small brokerage, Baird, Patrick & Co., splitting his commissions with the firm. Every six months or so he would move on to a different firm to get higher payouts from his investment banking deals—Steinberg & Lyman, Moseley Securities, Ladenburg Thalmann, Thomson Mckinnon Securities, and so on. His autobiography skips over these years.

Asensio & Company opened its doors in 1992. The goal was to build a traditional brokerage. With the firm's certification as a minority-owned business, it was able to snag the role of lead manager for a $200 million underwriting of New York State municipal bonds, the ultimate low-margin, boring transaction.

With a four-person staff, Asensio & Company soon issued its first equity research report—surprisingly, a buy recommendation on Coca-Cola. The stock had nearly doubled over the previous three years, and with its P/E teetering at 27.4 times trailing earnings, many value investors figured it was overpriced. Asensio, however, forecast 15 to 20 percent earnings growth over the next four years as Coke expanded into more emerging markets, and he put a buy on it. Coke stock doubled over the next two years.

Still, with dozens of brokerage firms covering big companies like Coca-Cola, Asensio needed a way to differentiate his firm. With markets surging, one way to do that would be to find candidates for short selling.

The vitamin industry seemed like fertile territory, since the regulatory tide seemed to be turning against it. By 1995, the Food and Drug Administration was pushing for warning labels on diet aids, even as several states had moved to ban ephedrine, often used as an appetite suppressant. Asensio thought this boded poorly for the industry and began to dig for specific short candidates.

Insider selling provided a warning flag at a company called General Nutrition Companies, a Pittsburgh-based vitamin store chain. The previous November, General Nutrition's CEO had sold 80 percent of his shares and two vice presidents had sold all of theirs. Those were not votes of confidence. The company, a Wall Street darling, had saturated the country with 2,400 stores, yet average store sales were just $450,000. The stock had doubled the previous year and traded at a price earnings multiple of 29. With a market capitalization of $1.8 billion, General Nutrition's tangible net worth was just $2 million. To top it off, the company had already issued an earnings warning for the fourth quarter of 1995.

As Asensio talked to people in the industry, he heard talk of a study underway looking into the efficacy of vitamins sponsored by the National Cancer Institute. He began cold-calling NCI employees, searching for anyone with knowledge of the study. Finally, an associate of the study's director answered the phone and Asensio began peppering him with questions.

The study was shaping up as bad news: It was looking into the long-term effects of beta carotene on smokers and nonsmokers and included a control group receiving placebos. The study was halted when it became evident that those receiving placebos were faring much better than those getting the vitamin. The question for Asensio—how to profit from it?

Any negative news for the vitamin industry was bound to be even worse for General Nutrition, with its poor fundamentals, Asensio reasoned. When the NCI announced a special press conference, Asensio knew it would be big and bad. The firm put together a draft research report outlining its case against General Nutrition's fundamentals, and left space for the NCI findings.

On January 18, 1996, the NCI released not one but two studies— one suggesting that the use of beta carotene provided no benefits for heart or cancer patients and the other showing it actually to be harmful. "U.S. government officials were telling consumers that beta carotene was just a fraud," Asensio recalls.

He quickly wrote the studies' results into the Asensio & Company research report and sent out his "strong sell" recommendation via PR Newswire. The result: Nothing. Bullish Wall Street firms used the opportunity to reiterate their "buy" recommendations, saying such studies are routine. The stock closed up 35 cents at $21.25.

Frustrated, Asensio issued a second report the next day. "Investors continue to listen to analysts who have no choice but to continue to recite the company's position," it read.

The office phone rang. Finally, a response. "It was the general counsel calling to threaten litigation right away," Asensio says. The call was a rude welcome to the world of short selling. Yet Asensio's view was eventually vindicated. In May, when the company reported second quarter same-store sales would fall as much as 6 percent, Alex. Brown, PaineWebber, and Smith Barney cut their ratings, and the stock fell to $14 from $18.50.

Like a lot of investors, especially short sellers, Asensio discloses few specifics about his tactics—partly to avoid being accused of solicitation of customers, partly for competitive reasons. "We are constantly under scrutiny," he says. Asensio declines to reveal the assets he manages, or the number or names of his investors. He won't say when he opened any particular short position or when he covered it.

These positions are large, Asensio says, and he moves in and out of them quickly, both to take advantage of changing information and market swings and to minimize the *borrow*, or interest on borrowed shares to short, which can amount to 40 percent annualized. The Asensio.com website shows the price of target companies at the time Asensio issued its first report, its subsequent low, and the percentage decline to that low. It doesn't show any subsequent rebounds and warns that the numbers should not be viewed as indicative of investor returns.

Among other things, Asensio says he runs special purpose vehicles for larger pools of capital. In some circumstances, there are "carve-outs" to these, or walled-off money, for which Asensio & Company will surrender its carried interest, the 20 percent of any profit he normally keeps, if the name of the targeted short company becomes public. Some clients don't want to be associated with short sales. The website also refers to a firm proprietary short-selling account whose returns, it says, are greater than the calculated returns on its website.

Deep dive research drives all of his short investments, especially those involving suspected fraud. "I like to drill down for months to make an investment without speculation," Asensio says. "You need to have all the information, whether it's relevant or not."

Asensio says he prefers shorting a fraudulent company to one that is merely overvalued, like General Nutrition. "An overvalued company is an opinion where someone has miscalculated future earnings; valuation is a judgment," he says. "With fraud, you can have more conviction."

That preference for fraud led Asensio to Hemispherx Biopharma, a Philadelphia drug development company that was to become one of his most bitter and longest running campaigns. The obvious tip-off for Asensio was the drug maker's underwriter, Stratton Oakmont, a Lake Success, New York brokerage notorious for its pump-and-dump stock schemes and the subject of *The Wolf of Wall Street*, the 2013 film directed by Martin Scorsese and starring Leonardo DiCaprio. Indeed, Stratton Oakmont was expelled from the securities industry by the NASD just a year after taking Hemispherx public in 1995. "You look at the people," Asensio says. "Tigers can't change their stripes."

The focus of Asensio's analysis was Hemispherx's drug Ampligen, which by 1998 had been nearly 30 years in development. The company's CEO, William Carter, helped discover it while a 20-something researcher at Johns Hopkins University. Ampligen is a real chemical compound, described by Hemispherx as an antiviral drug that can stimulate the immune system and keep cancer cells from reproducing, among a wide variety of other possible uses.

Yet the Food and Drug Administration (FDA) has never given marketing approval to Ampligen for any use whatsoever, although it has been studied as a treatment for AIDS, hepatitis B, chronic fatigue syndrome, and a host of other maladies. Amazingly, Hemispherx had never even filed a new drug application with the FDA for Ampligen. Wags called it a cure in search of a disease.

Asensio began digging into Ampligen's history—trawling through medical and legal records. What he turned up wasn't pretty.

In 1986, Carter and colleagues had conducted a study on 10 patients with AIDS or similar diagnoses and published the encouraging results in the Lancet, the prestigious British medical journal. Based largely on that study, DuPont invested $30 million into Hemsipherx's predecessor company, HEB Research, to gauge its efficacy in treating HIV. When DuPont tried and failed to reproduce Carter's results, it accused him of falsifying research and sued to recover its investment, eventually settling the case.

In 1987, Peter Frost, a Houston AIDS patient, sued Carter, saying he had bought $157 worth of Hemispherx stock from him for the inflated price of $1 million in exchange for Carter admitting him into an Ampligen HIV study. Carter, though admitting the stock sale from his own personal account, denied the quid pro quo, and Frost dropped his suit, only to die shortly thereafter.

After that, HEB's board fired Carter, who sued the company and won his job back.

What Asensio desperately needed to be sure was that Ampligen was not a viable drug. He talked about Ampligen with doctors and drug industry scientists. The key takeaway: Ampligen is composed of a double-stranded ribonucleic acid, or RNA, a type of molecule that has a tendency to be extremely toxic. Accordingly, it was quite unlikely to ever receive an approval from the FDA. The drug did serve one non-FDA approved purpose—it gave Carter an excuse to sell more stock.

On September 22, 1998, Asensio posted his first Hemispherx research report on the Internet. He wrote that Ampligen was of "no medical or economic value" and that Hemispherx "had made fraudulent misrepresentations about Ampligen's FDA filing status." He also said that the company was "promoting futile projects simply in order to enable insiders to sell their otherwise worthless stock to the public."

The shares fell to $4.51 from $8 over three days. Hemispherx shot back with a press release accusing Asensio of being part of a conspiracy to manipulate its stock price. But that was just the opening volley. The shares were soon seesawing amid back and forth press releases from Asensio and the company. The stock would climb, for example, on a Hemispherx release promising a new clinical study, racking up losses for Asensio. It would then trade down, often after an Asensio.com post.

Over the years, Asensio continued to relentlessly bird-dog Hemispherx, exposing bogus company claims, for example, that Ampligen had been endorsed by an organization supporting research into chronic fatigue syndrome and revealing that the FDA had censured Carter for making inappropriate claims about Ampligen's safety. Surprisingly, patient advocacy groups were wont to support Carter, desperate as their constituents were for cures.

Asensio confronted Carter personally at one conference, shouting at him, "You belong in jail." Hemispherx sued Asensio in Federal Court in Philadelphia for fraud, defamation, and violation of the Racketeer Influenced and Corrupt Organizations Act (RICO). Though the court dismissed the fraud and RICO counts, the defamation claim was moved to state court. The jury ruled in Asensio's favor, though Hemispherx's appeals continued until 2010. Ultimately, it's the market's verdict that counts: Hemispherx shares in March 2015 traded for 25 cents.

Asensio says he can't remember what led him to start looking at KFx Inc., a Denver energy company that claimed to have a process to turn low-quality coal into clean fuel. That is not as surprising as it might sound. Short sellers share tips about potential frauds and other opportunities among themselves. Among the short-selling firms Asensio has worked with are Kingsford Capital Management in Richmond, California and the now-defunct Rocker Partners. A clutch of research firms also specialize in shorts, including Muddy Waters LLC, Citron Research LLC, and Integrity Research Associates.

That ecosystem gives ammunition to anti-short advocates, including stock promoters, like Carter, who warn ominously of an amorphous cabal of short sellers manipulating the market. Investors often believe it.

By early 2005, high-profile hedge funds had bought into KFx, including such dizzyingly successful ones as Perry Corp; Kingdon Capital Management, LLC; and Ritchie Capital Management, LLC. Since KFx went public via a reverse merger with a penny-stock shell company in 1998, shares had grown at a rate of 25 percent annualized.

The KFx story was premised on the dynamics of the coal markets. Nearly 50 percent of the world's coal is of the sub-bituminous, brown, or lignite variety—low-quality stuff that is saturated with moisture, pollutes heavily, and at $6 a ton costs about one-tenth what high-quality coal does. The moisture makes it more costly to transport and decreases its efficiency.

KFx held a patented process, dubbed K-Fuel, to remove the moisture using heat and pressurization and was building a plant in Gillette, Wyoming to test it. Entrepreneurs had tried to clean up low-grade coal for decades—it can be done but at a cost that was and remains wildly uneconomical.

The problem has to do with the moisture. When it falls below a certain level, the coal begins to reabsorb it from the atmosphere, increasing the chances of spontaneous combustion. That's not good.

Drying the coal also produces clouds of dust—which is both an environmental problem and a safety hazard, since such dust contributes to spontaneous combustion. Amazingly, KFx would eventually spend an astounding $166.1 million on the new test plant, even though at least some of management must surely have suspected that the process wasn't economical. The first run was scheduled for late 2005.

Asensio was no coal expert. He found a Department of Energy white paper that detailed the problems of cleaning coal. He also tracked down an executive he calls his "Deep Throat" at an electric utility that used dried coal in its own operations and so was schooled about the difficulties involved. "We would talk day and night, weekends, about how much trouble they had," Asensio says. He declines to identify the executive.

Beginning October 1, 2004, Asensio went hostile, issuing reports that cast doubt on KFx's progress and credibility. The reports detailed failed efforts by KFx and predecessors to market their K-Fuel technology. Asensio questioned the stock deals of KFx executives and aired K-Fuel criticism by rival mining industry experts.

KFx nevertheless announced the start up of the Gillette K-Fuel plant on December 10, 2005.

At an upbeat conference call on January 12, 2006, KFx chairman Ted Venners described the initial run as a success. "The main purpose for having operated the plant at that point was to verify that the product was stable and that it was less dusty," he said. "We had no dust." The stock surged.

When the Gillette plant finally shipped coal in July 2006, Asensio was ready. He had surreptitious video crews on hand, ex-FBI agents, to tape the shipment, destined for a terminal owned by a large utility called First Energy Corp.

He also arranged for them to take a sample of the coal—about 10 cents worth by his estimate—and have it analyzed by a laboratory, SGS North America. This was the same coal KFx had claimed was clean, dust-free, and not susceptible to spontaneous combustion. SGS said otherwise. "The tests showed that it was not any of those things," Asensio says.

An e-mail from Asensio detailing the results was leaked to KFx management, which sued the SGS laboratory, seeking the return of the coal—and demanding that it name Asensio & Company as its client.

On September 18, Asensio posted the video on Asensio.com, with swelling background music, showing dark plumes of coal dust, visible for miles, as they billowed from the shipping containers. A haze hangs over the plant. The stock tumbled.

The suit by KFx was running into trouble. A lawyer for the company deposed a former Asensio & Company employee, inducing him to violate a nondisclosure agreement—a possible criminal offense. Asensio's lawyer threatened a suit against KFx.

By the end of September, the promotion was falling apart. KFx, which changed its name to Evergreen Energy, acknowledged dust and other problems in its coal shipments, and the hedge funds were selling. Short interest rose to 28 percent. By the end of the year, Perry, Kingdon, and Ritchie had all exited their Evergreen positions.

At that point, Evergreen shares had fallen 41 percent from their highs, to $8.25. Asensio privately reached a settlement with Evergreen in April 2007. The next month, he terminated his Evergreen Energy coverage with shares at $6.50. "I offer Evergreen my best wishes," Asensio said in a statement at the time.

Today, Asensio won't disclose the terms of the settlement. Evergreen CEO Mark Sexton was fired the next month, and the company filed for bankruptcy liquidation in January 2012, its K-Fuel dreams up in smoke.

PolyMedica's reputation was already in tatters by the time Asensio & Company issued its first research report on the Woburn, Massachusetts company in October 2001. A year earlier, *Barron's* had reported that the Federal Bureau of Investigation was investigating PolyMedica for possible Medicare fraud, and the stock lost half its value. Asensio says he may have helped instigate that investigation since he had been in touch with the local offices of both the bureau and the Justice Department concerning PolyMedica well before that. In July 2001 the NYSE abruptly rejected its listing application. And in August, the *Wall Street Journal* reported a grand jury subpoena had been issued in a criminal investigation of the company. The next week, 85 FBI agents raided eight of PolyMedica's Florida offices over a two-day period. The stock fell 45 percent to $9.20 on that news.

At its core, PolyMedica was a simple telemarketer, selling blood glucose test kits at prices well above the going rate. In the process, it was bilking Medicare—not just because of what it charged, but because it was shipping kits with no doctors' orders to people who hadn't ordered them, or in some cases to people who had died. When kits were returned, as many inevitably were, PolyMedica was not reimbursing Medicare for them.

In the weeks following the terror attacks of September 11, 2001, though, PolyMedica shares rallied 78 percent, to $16.50. The unpleasant truth: Investors were betting that the war on Al Qaeda would take precedence over the PolyMedica investigation.

Asensio sensed a short opportunity. His sources told him the FBI investigation had been only temporarily delayed—and it certainly galled him to watch investors profiting from 9/11 in such a fashion. PolyMedica's results were flagging too: Profits fell 36 percent to $4.7 million in the quarter ended September 30.

For Asensio, the challenge was determining how deep the fraud ran at PolyMedica. A Justice Department slap on the wrist, say a $50 million fine, would have little impact on Polynesia's share price. Still, such an investigation might require Asensio canvassing hundreds of sources. "They have tens of thousands of customers, so I knew verification was going to be difficult," he says.

In addition to doctors, Asensio talked to customers who had received kits they hadn't ordered and former PolyMedica employees who, disgusted by the blatant Medicare rip-off, described company policies in detail. Asensio swapped information with FBI agents, who were keen on nailing what they considered a particularly flagrant Medicare fraud.

The key was gauging firsthand the volume of returns the company was experiencing. Asensio drove to a PolyMedica warehouse in Port Lucie, Florida. Camera in hand, he snapped away as trucks full of returned glucose kits drove by and began unloading. Asensio chatted up warehouse workers on their cigarette breaks. A security guard confronted him and Asensio was briefly taken into custody, where a local police officer issued him a bench summons.

Asensio waited until PolyMedica's earnings release to issue his October 25, 2001, report. "Based purely on fundamentals and irrespective of the likelihood that a federal indictment will result from PLMD's alleged criminal misconduct, we believe PLMD shares are worth less than $1 per share," he wrote. Asensio & Company put a "strong sell" rating on the stock.

Almost immediately, events began turning against Asensio and his fellow shorts. The research report had no discernable effect on the company's stock, which, after a brief rally, closed out the year at $16.60. Then began a slow-motion version of a short seller's nightmare. Over the next 36 months, no matter what damaging revelations surfaced—subpoenas, missed earnings estimates, or more evidence of fraud—PolyMedica's shares continued to rise.

The company's CEO, Steven Lee, resigned without explanation. The stock hit $24.

A federal study found abuses in the test kit industry. The stock rose to $28.

The SEC questioned PolyMedica's accounting for marketing costs. The stock hit $44.

After a round of layoffs and the resignation of the president of the test kit subsidiary, Polymedica hit $53.

What investors had begun to suspect was this—that under President George W. Bush, an anti-regulation, free-market advocate whose brother Jeb was Florida's governor at the time, there was scant interest in prosecuting PolyMedica.

By now Asensio's views too had begun to change. His sources in the FBI had turned increasingly skeptical that the local U.S. Attorney, Marcos Daniel Jimenez, was interested in punishing a local business—especially in what by 2004 was an election year.

PolyMedica's acting CEO, Samuel Shanaman, behind the scenes had been working to assuage the U.S. Justice Department and had increasingly been dropping references in conference calls to the "useful" dialogue he was having with authorities. A source close to the company said PolyMedica's investors were won over by the new CEO's efforts.

For Asensio, that was bad news. "I just eventually knew they weren't going to be prosecuted," he says.

That didn't prevent him from posting increasingly incendiary reports. "There are members of the Bush Administration who have an interest in advocating leniency towards PolyMedica," he wrote in an October 20, 2004, report. Any settlement for less than $400 million would be unfair and "questionable." Asensio stopped reiterating his "strong sell" rating. At this point, he wrote, the outcome was "entirely a function of a political process."

On November 4, 2004, PolyMedica announced a tentative settlement, agreeing to pay just $35 million, less than Asensio had guessed earlier. The same day, Asensio let loose one final blistering report: "The DOJ simply failed to perform its duty."

PolyMedica shares closed at $35, or $70 on a split-adjusted basis, up more than 400 percent from where they stood when Asensio had first put a strong sell rating on them. On August 28, 2007, PolyMedica was acquired by Medco Health Solutions for $53 a share in cash, $106 split adjusted.

Asensio won't talk about how much money he lost during the PolyMedica short campaign. "I didn't trade that one very well," he says glumly. One friend chalks the disaster up to Asensio's misplaced moralistic streak—something that is dangerous in short selling.

The PolyMedica episode, combined with his FINRA battles, prompt Asensio to compare what he sees as moral dissipation in the United States with what he experienced in Cuba. "I'm not quite sure which is more evil," says Asensio, "The evil of a hidden corruption where everyone is looking the other way and is legal and systematic versus a corruption that everyone knows about and isn't hidden."

With its cast of villains, big money wagers, and rags-to-riches narrative, Asensio's life story may seem like a Hollywood drama. It almost came to that in 2010. Director Brad Furman approached him with the idea for a television series portraying his short-selling exploits for HBO, the Time Warner cable television channel.

Asensio was game. Furman worked at his threadbare office to get a feel for the business, chasing down leads about possible frauds and answering phones. Comedian John Leguizamo, who starred in such movies as *Dr. Doolittle*, *Moulin Rouge*, and the *Ice Age* series, agreed to play Asensio. A pilot was written, contracts prepared, and production set.

Then, by early 2012, Asensio was having second thoughts on the project and began pushing hard on one nonnegotiable demand. He wanted HBO senior management to intercede with SEC chairman Schapiro to have Asensio's bar from the brokerage industry lifted. The project was scrapped.

Once again, Asensio wasn't endearing himself to people. "It speaks to the bizarre, magical realist view he has towards the world," said Leguizamo in a brief telephone interview. "He wasted two years of my life. Manuel Asensio is a deeply disturbed individual."

Asensio confirms the chain of events—but puts a different spin on it. Without a reinstatement by FINRA, the series would hardly have benefited him. "They'd take the glory and they'd take the money." Asensio wants to get back to research and investing, taking large concentrated bets, both long and short. "I don't want to be sued again," he says, a touch of fatigue in his voice. "I haven't been sued in a long time and I want to keep it that way."

A happy ending, it goes without saying, would provide a better storyline. "I'm interested in clearing my name," he says. Asensio needs a victory and some kind of redemption. "We would not know about Plato if the Greeks had lost the battle of Marathon," he says. "Jesus Christ would be just another dead Jew if he wasn't resurrected."

Chapter 3

Chanos: Connoisseur of Chaos

U nder a blue sky in Connecticut on an April afternoon, James Chanos eases his lean six-foot-two-inch frame out of his chauffeured Volvo sedan and strides past the hedges of 56 Hillhouse Avenue at the Yale School of Management. He wears thick rimless glasses, a casual blazer, jeans, and a tan wool sweater—the template of a hip, approachable Ivy League professor. Via the maze-like staircases and corridors that wind through the stately 19th-century building, Chanos arrives at room A60, where dozens of students are soon crowding into the lecture hall, taking their seats for the eight-class course he teaches—*Financial Fraud throughout History: A Forensic Approach.*

Academia is an unusual sideline for a hedge fund manager with a net worth in the hundreds of millions of dollars—and one whose name on Wall Street is synonymous with short-selling. Even aside from teaching, Chanos keeps a schedule best described as full throttle. When not running his short-selling focused firm, Kynikos Associates, which manages some $3 billion in assets, he can be found testifying before Congress. Chanos is a regular at political fundraisers. He makes the rounds on CNBC and Bloomberg TV, where his erudite analyses of overvalued companies, regulations, and macroeconomics make him a coveted guest. One recent theme: China's real estate bubble—a phenomenon that has led him to short such stocks as Agricultural Bank of China and a bevy of other Chinese finance companies and real estate developers.

At Yale, today's lesson includes a quick overview of choice frauds in the 18th, 19th, and early 20th centuries. Chanos reminds the class that afterwards, he's holding court at Frank Pepe Pizza Napolitana (Pepe's), a New Haven parlor famed for its white clam pies—with one proviso. "If anybody asks me again when I'm going to cover my China short, I'm going to pour beer on their head," he quips.

The hall erupts in laughter.

Chanos's class is definitely not just fun and games. A team of students kicks it off with a detailed 20-minute presentation dissecting the accounting of Bristol-Myers Squibb, the drug giant. Going into 2000, according to the presentation, the company was allegedly engaged in a massive program of channel stuffing—shipping unwarranted amounts of drugs to wholesalers as a way to boost revenues and earnings to meet internal goals and, by extension, the over-optimistic targets of Wall Street analysts. Along the way, the company had allegedly created improper reserves that it tapped to pad its income.

Chanos interrupts the slide show—grilling the students. "When is the easiest time to set up special reserves?" he demands.

Nobody answers.

"Usually there is an event when they will set up reserves. What is it?" he repeats.

The classroom remains silent, either too shy or intimidated to venture an opinion.

"Acquisitions," he declares. "This is a key point to watch out for, both in your projects and going forward when analyzing businesses, is when companies use acquisitions to classically cloud what's going on in their core existing businesses by taking broader restructuring charges." Bristol-Myers had bought the DuPont Pharmaceutical Group for $7.8 billion in mid-2001, having previously sold off a pair of shampoo and medical devices businesses, muddying its financial comparisons in the process.

"Management has a lot of latitude," he warns. "It's always a good idea to scrutinize companies that grow by acquisitions a little more closely."

Chanos continues, weaving the science and art of fraud detection into the students' presentation. "Beware also the serial restructurer, where the company is constantly taking restructuring charges and getting used to the idea that this is something you should ignore. And as a partner of mine once said very aptly: Recurring restructuring charges are reserves for bad business decisions. You give companies credit for good business decisions.... Somehow, they want you to disregard any reserves for bad business decisions: small acquisitions that are written off, unsold business inventories, plants they built that they never should have. This gives them the latitude to report the numbers in the best possible light."

Another piece of advice: Don't think for a moment that having a respected money manager invested in a stock is the same as a clean bill of health. "Most every successful short we've been involved with has had a big-name backer," he says.

Bristol-Myers ultimately settled with first the U.S. Securities & Exchange Commission (SEC) for $150 million in 2004 without admitting or denying guilt and later with the Justice Department for $300 million more, under a deferred prosecution agreement—a slap on the wrist. There was also the matter of disgorgement, the surrendering of illegal profits: Those totaled precisely $1. Chanos, for one, did not find that surprising given that the CEO during the period when much of the channel stuffing occurred was Charles Heimbold Jr., a major donor to the Republican Party. "Republican prosecutors decided to go light on the company," Chanos opines. The New Jersey U.S. Attorney at the time: Chris Christie, current governor of New Jersey.

In late 2001, the Bush administration named Heimbold ambassador to Sweden. The patsies: the former president of Bristol-Myers worldwide pharmaceuticals group and its ex-CFO, who were eventually indicted for federal securities violations. "They only went after the people who were fired or left the company," Chanos pointed out. And Bristol-Myers eventually was forced to restate earnings for 2000 and 2001. Kynikos did not short Bristol-Myers.

Certainly, Chanos belies the old platitude that those who can't do, teach. At age 57, he's the longest running short-selling act of any significance. Chanos has been at it for more than 30 years, overseeing a pure short-selling fund, Ursus, since 1985 and a more recent vintage long-short fund called Kynikos Opportunity. In addition to his myriad public appearances, he founded the Washington, D.C.-based Coalition of Private Investment Companies, an advocacy group for short sellers and other hedge funds.

To his critics—including rivals—he sets a dazzling yet flawed example. Chanos admits to being an epic partier. He has also been known as a major-stakes gambler, often blackjack, frequenting the high-roller tables at Las Vegas casinos.

Ashley Dupré, an alleged escort, house sat Chanos's Easthampton estate in 2006. Her relationship with then-New York Governor Eliot Spitzer lead to his abrupt resignation in 2007. Chanos was divorced from his wife, Amy, in 2006.

Chanos says he won't discuss his personal life on the record. He does mention that bench presses 340 pounds at a Manhattan gym he owns.

Chanos defenders—and there are legions—say all this is totally irrelevant, both professionally and, for that matter, ethically, since we know very little about his private life. "It's absolutely nobody's business," said Doug Millett, a former research chief for Kynikos in an interview in March, 2013, who died later that year of cancer. Certainly he is man of striking contradictions. Chanos has four children. He is president of the board of trustees of The Browning School in New York and a trustee at The Nightingale-Bamford School and the New-York Historical Society. Chanos agreed to serve as Millett's godfather when the latter weighed converting to Greek Orthodox Christianity in 2013. "He said 'I'm happy to do this for you, but I'm not lifting you into the water,'" said Millett, who is widely regarded as having done the legwork which uncovered the accounting irregularities of Enron Corp.—Kynikos's most famous short.

And for the record, Chanos is wealthy. In addition to his sprawling estate on Further Lane in East Hampton he owns a triplex on Manhattan's Upper East Side. Chanos dispenses money freely to politicians, mostly Democrats.

The pressures of the business undoubtedly take their toll. "Short-selling is a physically brutal thing," says Jim Smith, a former short seller who has known Chanos since the 1980s. "It's high emotional contact.

It's brutal on the brain, the emotions, the lifestyle. The wear and tear couldn't be clearer."

What is undeniable is that Chanos has shaped the profession—providing the gravitas to counterbalance the promotional froth of financial markets as well as the incessant criticism of the practice. He has been both pointed and eloquent in his demands for fairness, transparency, and accountability on Wall Street and with Washington regulators. In addition to his now moribund advocacy group, Chanos serves on a New York Federal Reserve Bank advisory committee.

Less well noted is that in Kynikos Associates, he has forged a successful enterprise in an environment designed to undermine the skeptics of the investing world. Chanos has built a distinct corporate culture, compensation schedule and research capability that has proved its mettle over not years, but decades. Says Smith: "If you want an allocation to the short side, you want to be with Chanos."

James Steven Chanos's journey into the sharp elbowed world of short-selling began in Wauwatosa, Wisconsin, outside Milwaukee. The oldest of three sons, his father, a second-generation Greek immigrant, ran a chain of dry cleaners. "It made us comfortable," says Chanos. His father sold the dry cleaning business to work in the corporate world at BASF, the German chemical company, and the family soon moved to Birmingham, Michigan. His mother was an office manager at a steel company. Chanos eagerly devoured the investing books his father checked out for him at the local library.

Chanos also learned the value of manual labor, taking on jobs as a busboy and, later, at a dye manufacturing plant in Germany over the summer, living with a local family. That helped spark a lifelong fascination with European history. Aided by his towering physique, Chanos was a passable forward on his high school basketball team—an acquaintance describes his distinctive jump shot.

From there, it was off to Yale, where his initial direction was pre-med. He worked summers in the steel industry, finding temporary employment at Inland Steel's Babcock & Wilcox division. Even into the late 1980s, Chanos was a dues-paying member of the local Pipefitters and Boilermakers Union. Not a typical hedgie, in other words.

It may be that the rigor of his studies at Yale baked into Chanos a wariness of consensus. His interests turned from pre-med to economics and political science. One major influence was the investing books he read, which further stoked his interest in the markets. Another was Edward Tufte, a professor of political science, computer science, and statistics, who became renowned as trailblazer in the field of data visualization—looking for new ways to present information through graphics. "He might have noted my skepticism toward conventional wisdom and concern about the lack of evidence of quality and integrity in human affairs," says Tufte.

Then there was Richard Levin, Chanos's professor for intermediate microeconomics who went on to become the longest-serving president of Yale, from 1993 to 2013. "He did make an impression," Levin says. "Jim likes getting into a good intellectual dispute. He's like a good professor."

It was to Levin that Chanos first proposed teaching a course on financial fraud. Levin, reportedly asked: "You're not going to teach them how to *commit* fraud, are you?" Chanos is one of several Yale alumni, including Thomas Steyer of Farallon Capital Management and Dinakar Singh of TPG-Axon Capital Management, who have managed money for the school's $24 billion endowment. Yale chief investment officer David Swensen was a pioneer in hedge fund investing.

Keith Allain, today coach of the Yale national championship winning ice hockey team, recalls Chanos, his freshman year roommate, and his ability to pack in enormous amounts of studying and partying—excelling at both. "He had this incredible ability to burn his candle at both ends," Allain recalls. Chanos was famous for the postgame parties he organized for the Bulldog hockey team, in particular his carefully recorded party tapes.

After graduation, in 1980, Chanos turned to Wall Street, with the economy mired in recession at the tail-end of an extended bear market. His first job was as a junior-level corporate finance analyst at the Chicago office of what soon became known as PaineWebber, the big retail brokerage firm. With a paycheck of $12,000 a year, he was discouraged, given the grunt work of crafting deal book pitches for corporate clients, mostly fixed income. Chanos was far more interested in stocks, and chatted up Bob Holmes, a banker on the equities side of the business, with one point of interest being the phenomenally successful stock buybacks of Henry Singleton at Teledyne Technologies a conglomerate, which were making shareholders rich.

Chanos was drafted to write the pitch book for a McDonald's Corp bond offering. His analysis showed that rather than issuing debt at 12 percent, the fast food chain would be far better off buying back its shares, like Teledyne. "The earnings per share went up much higher on a buyback than a debt deal and they didn't need the cash at the time," he recalls.

He went to talk to his boss. "Have you ever looked at asking them about a buy back?" Chanos asked.

"Why would we do that?" his boss asked.

"Here are my numbers," Chanos responded, showing him his calculations.

"Don't ever show that to the client," his boss snapped. "We're here to do a bond deal."

Chanos recalls going into Holmes's office and asking him, "What value am I here?"

Holmes and a New York partner, Ralph Worthington, soon left PaineWebber to set up Gilford Securities. The boutique firm, with offices in New York and Chicago, was named after the seaside town of Guilford, Connecticut, but the lawyer misspelled it.

Chanos's luck was about to change. At Gilford, he was assigned to cover MGIC Investment Corp, a former Nifty-Fifty insurer that was soon subsumed into a fast-growing company called Baldwin-United, whose ticker symbol was BDW.

Baldwin was a well-known piano maker that in the spirit of the times had morphed into a fast-growing seller of annuities—in this case, essentially certificates of deposit wrapped in an insurance product. They were specifically called single premium deferred annuities or SPDAs, which for an initial premium of, say, $21,000 or so paid a market rate of 14.25 percent with the rate guaranteed not to fall below 7.5 percent for the first 10 years.

There were also minimal withdrawal and surrender penalties for purchasers. Other Baldwin-United business lines included property and casualty insurance, a saving and loan business, and trading stamps. Everything except the annuity business was declining when Chanos began looking into the business. He learned the intricacies of statutory accounting, the complex set of bookkeeping rules that govern insurers rather than standard generally accepted accounting principles, or GAAP.

The first problem with Baldwin-United was that although the life insurance business of which the SPDA operation was comprised accounted for 70.7 percent of revenues, tax law changes by the Internal Revenue Service were about to make the annuities much less attractive for investors—including fat penalties for early withdrawals and changes in their tax treatment. People knew this, and sales of SPDAs were plummeting.

The capital structure of the firm was wildly out of whack with the competition too. Firms like Aetna, General Re, and Travelers sported debt-to-equity ratios that ranged from one to ten or less. Baldwin-United's was more than five to one.

Soon Chanos received a late night phone call.

"Are you Jim Chanos?"

"Yes."

"Are you the one asking the questions about Baldwin-United?"

"Yes."

"Do you know about the files at the Arkansas State Insurance Department?"

"No."

"You should ask for them. They are public information."

Despite the more than three decades that have passed, Chanos still bubbles with excitement when he describes the twists and turns of uncovering his first fraud—jumping up like a schoolboy from his seat to sketch out the complicated scheme on a white board in his midtown Manhattan offices.

After laboriously piecing together details of Baldwin-United's $1.17 billion purchase of MGIC, Chanos zeroed in on the fact that the firm was using cash from its SPDAs to buy money-losing MGIC real estate and equity in other Baldwin-United subsidiaries, a gambit to fund the annuities. More than half the premiums invested in 1981, according to Chanos's research report, "represented net transactions in Baldwin's affiliates."

The firm was using insurance money to in effect keep the SPDA balloon inflating, and nobody seemed inclined to pop the bubble. It also didn't help that Baldwin-United's chief financial and accounting officer was in the process of resigning—always a bad sign. "The handwriting is already on the wall. Regulators in both Arkansas and Wisconsin have informed us they intend to screen BDW's future internal financing plans very closely, and may require outside collateral (bank letters-of-credit, etc.)," he wrote.

The stock was trading at $24 a share when Gilford published the report on August 17, 1982. He forecast a near-term target price of $10 to $15. "At a recent price of $24 per share, the case for selling BDW shares is most compelling," his report concluded. Of course, the 1980s bull market was just beginning.

By early December, shares had risen to $44 even as the junior analyst—he was just 25—had begun to sharpen and focus his analysis. As the stock price rose, Chanos was derided by bullish analysts. In a new report, he now pointed out that net income figures were unreliable because of Baldwin-United's dubious tax accounting, cash flow was declining, and, again, that the insurance portfolios were stuffed with securities of affiliated companies or their holdings. He also showed that even using the company's own income statements it was losing money on an operating basis.

Gilford hired Ray Dirks, who had famously uncovered the Equity Funding scandal in the 1970s, to look into Baldwin-United. His verdict: Chanos's work was flawed. "The kid's all wet," Dirks told the New York office. "The company's fine." Baldwin-United shares eventually hit $56.

On Christmas Eve, Chanos received a stunning holiday gift—a phone call. "The Arkansas insurance regulators just seized the Baldwin-United insurance subsidiaries," a voice said. Baldwin-United the next year filed for bankruptcy, the largest in U.S. history up until that time. Shares ended up close to zero.

Hedge fund managers had been following the Baldwin-United case, and soon job offers piled in. Chanos remained loyal to Gilford. He followed up his Baldwin-United call with an impressive victory lap of other short calls, with sell recommendations on Coleco Industries, maker of the disastrous Adam Computer, and Waste Management, a trash-hauling roll-up.

Gilford, though, was changing its focus. Rather than churn out deeply researched reports on dubious companies, the firm wanted to get into the lucrative business of underwriting stocks. Chanos was assigned by Gilford to serve as the junior banker for the initial offering of a Huntington, Long Island company named CopyTele—which had no products and no sales but was being hyped as the next Xerox. The company claimed to be developing a high-resolution computer screen that Chanos describes as a "blank piece of plastic." One version was supposed to replace the top of copier machines, allowing for the printing of images from a computer and ushering in a new age of graphics reproduction.

Chanos remembers his dismay after realizing the product was baloney: "I told Bob Holmes 'There's nothing there! I can't do hard-hitting research and do IPOs.'"

The loyal Chanos nevertheless helped CopyTele go public, after which it became the subject of scathing articles in, among other places, *Fortune* magazine. Ironically, it also set off a battle between short sellers and those attempting to squeeze them—one of whom took out full page newspaper ads reading "Here's a Stock Thomas Edison Would Buy."

Chanos was mortified. "I'll always carry the millstone of being one of the junior underwriters on one of the great shorts of all time," he says. CopyTele still loses millions of dollars a year and continues to trade on the OTC bulletin board at a price of 8 cents a share as of March 2015.

CopyTele hastened Chanos's decision to leave Chicago for New York, where he landed an analyst position at Atlantic Capital, a broker-dealer subsidiary of Deutsche Bank that had been grandfathered to avoid Glass-Steagall rules separating commercial and investment banking. There his boss, Jim Levitas, encouraged him to pursue his skeptical research. Sometimes, as in the case of United-Baldwin, the job required ungodly amounts of fundamental research and sleuthing.

In other cases, it was breathtakingly simple. For example, one short selling idea that Chanos carried over from Gilford was Coleco. Its Adam home computer was supposed to be shipped in early 1983, but production problems kept delaying it, eventually threatening the critical Christmas season.

Meanwhile, the home computer craze was in full bloom, with the IBM PC Jr. and Commodore 64 flying off store shelves. An Adam prototype that appeared at a consumer electronics show in 1983 was rumored to be filled with the innards of an Apple II. When the Adam finally debuted that year it was skewered mercilessly in the media. "*Consumer Reports* just panned it," Chanos recalls. "They said do not buy this.

It's buggy and it crashes." How tough is it to write a sell recommendation based on a downbeat *Consumer Reports* article?

Plenty, as it turns out. True, Coleco's electronics business, including the disastrous Adam, collapsed with sales plunging from $404 million in 1984 to $100 million in 1985 and just $56 million in 1986.

Yet, as the Adam's bust was making headlines, Coleco was successfully ramping up the inexplicably popular Cabbage Patch Kids, "must have" dolls for the under-10 set that would prove a far bigger hit. Sales of the dolls soared from $67 million in 1983 to $540 million in 1984 and $600 million in 1985, when the fad eventually began to run its course. The stock price fell by nearly 50 percent from its November 1984 high of $19.125 to $10.125 in 1985. It then powered back before Coleco eventually was forced into chapter 11 bankruptcy in 1988. "We rode a bubble and then it collapsed, but then we stayed too long for another bubble on top of that," Chanos recalls.

Atlantic clients appreciated Chanos's bearish analysis—even if the upstart, who sported a thick mustache at the time, didn't always score. Many were already legends of the hedge fund industry—the volatile Michael Steinhardt; the former Hungarian refugee and macro investor George Soros, who himself would later make $1 billion shorting the British pound in 1992; and Julian Robertson, founder of Tiger Management LLC, which served as a storied training ground for dozens of hedge fund stars. Chanos at the age of 27 had carved out a comfortable niche for himself on Wall Street, with a deep-pocketed backer in Deutsche Bank and an impressive customer base who would channel commissions to the firm's trading desk.

Then in early September 1985 came a front-page story in the *Wall Street Journal* that would change everything. It was a 6,000-plus word front-page takedown of short sellers, featuring Chanos as one of the few willing to be quoted by name. Written by reporter Dean Rothbart, the article accused Chanos of being part of something he called "the network"—a group of secretive short sellers who shared ideas about which companies might be overpriced for whatever reason:

> To their critics, Wall Street's short sellers are worse than ambulance-chasing lawyers. Not only do they seek profit from others' misfortunes, but, the critics say, a new breed of activist short sellers tries to help the bad news happen.

Chanos didn't help his case when he joked about his profession. "People think I have two horns and spread syphilis," he said.

One corporate chairman of a New York Stock Exchange–listed company, who is not named in the article, described Chanos thus: "This guy has caused us such grief. We can't stand this guy." Rothbart went on to write, with no apparent chagrin, that the chairman's company was one of several that helped finance or aided a private investigation of Chanos as a way to shut him down. The story quoted a detective, describing what he found. "Chanos lives a nice, quiet yuppy existence," the gumshoe said.

Ironically, the article cited at least three maligned companies— insurer First Executive Corp, real estate syndicator Integrated Resources, and Coleco, that were targeted by Chanos or other short sellers. All three companies later filed for bankruptcy.

Deutsche Bank officials were not amused. They immediately told Chanos that his contract at Atlantic would not be renewed, but the bank would pay him through the end of the year. Surprisingly, Chanos bears Deutsche no animosity. "I understand from their perspective, they didn't really know what we did made a lot of money," he says. "I think from their perspective they said, 'Look we have corporate business, we want to stay on the right side of U.S. regulators—why do we need this?'"

Now he was jobless—the victim of a juicy newspaper hatchet job. Yet he still had a loyal client base that was in need of a service he was skilled at providing. Ross Hall, a Dallas-based fund of funds managed by Bill Brown and Glen Vinson, was looking for a manager to run a short portfolio for a wealthy family. Chanos's reputation from Baldwin-United drew Brown, but so did his gimlet-eye worldview. "He was a person you had to prove your position to," Brown says. "Everything was a hypothesis. You might call that skeptical."

Brown recalls Chanos taking a while to ponder the offer. "He's a cautious guy," says Brown. "He wanted to think about it. It took him a week or two."

Chanos definitely didn't want to get in over his head—and asked to bring in his boss Levitas as a partner. "I said, 'Look I don't anything about trading, I don't know anything about back office, I don't know anything about the guts of Wall Street,'" Chanos says. "'Could I bring Jim in as a partner?' And they agreed."

Kynikos, named after the ancient school of Greek skeptics who sought truth at the expense of status, popularity, or wealth, was born. The initial capital was certainly skimpy enough, just $16 million—$1 million from Chanos and Levitas and the rest from Ross Hall. The initial office was at 2 Rector Street, an elegant turn-of-the-century skyscraper that had seen better days, standing in the shadow of the towering World Trade Center and, appropriately, just around the corner from the graveyard at Trinity Church.

Today, Kynikos's ninth-floor offices are a bit more upscale, but not by much. The firm's name is spelled out with inexpensive-looking brass letters. The entrance through the cramped vestibule is a glass-paneled wood door that wouldn't look out of place in a suburban dentist's office, circa 1985. Perhaps the firm's lean years have left a mark.

The mood darkens further when a visitor scans the rows of dog-eared books lining Kynikos's spacious but threadbare conference room—which could have used a makeover a decade or so ago as well. The titles say it all: *On Risk and Disaster*, *The Dark Side of Valuation*, *Origins of the Crash*, *House of Cards*, and *How Markets Fail*.

Chanos today is wearing a gray suit, white shirt, and blue-patterned tie. He stretches out his lanky frame in a chair at the conference table as he describes Kynikos's early years and its evolving philosophy. Late 1985 was just about the midpoint of the 1980s bull market, and it might seem a poor time to kick off a fund dedicated to short selling. What Chanos learned early, however, was that there are different flavors of short selling opportunities—some not dependent at all on the direction of the overall market, although of course it's helpful to have wind at your back as a bear in a collapsing equity market.

There are four kinds of short sale opportunities, Chanos says. First are accounting frauds, like Baldwin-United, and later Enron and Tyco International. Someone cooks the books or omits material information. Then there are consumer fads—represented by the likes of Coleco's Cabbage Patch Kids. Consumers and investors get caught up in a new, trendy product with limited staying power or, better still, restaurants or food chains that flourish until people tire of, say, Krispy Kreme doughnuts. Third are broken industries, collapsing in the face of changing technologies or new competing business models that render them obsolete, regardless of turnaround efforts or how cheap their share prices.

Eastman Kodak is an example of this, as are a number of notable computer companies.

Chanos's favorite varietal is what he calls "booms that go bust." Think China today or the home mortgage originators in the run-up to the 2007–2009 housing meltdown and subsequent financial crisis. "Booms that go bust," emphasizes Chanos. "That's the big one. And that was our first big success at Kynikos in 1985 and 1986 in Texas." That was after he paid $1 to buy out Levitas, who didn't have the stomach for short selling.

Chanos had gotten a taste of excesses growing in the real estate market as far back as 1985 when he researched Integrated Resources, a real estate syndicator financed by Drexel Burnham Lambert underwritten junk bonds. But Jim Grant, a Chanos friend and editor of the perennially bearish *Grant's Interest Rate Observer*, put him in touch with Frederick "Shad" Rowe, a Dallas short seller and author of a particularly lucid and witty column for *Forbes* magazine.

The epicenter of the real estate bubble wasn't New York, Florida, or California, but Texas, coming as it did off the tail of the oil boom of the late 1970s and early 1980s. The Tax Reform Act of 1986 basically ended the tax shelter status of most real estate deals—spelling disaster for the syndicators—but it took awhile to sink in.

Chanos remembers calling Rowe.

"Jim Grant wants me to give you a call on Texas real estate."

"Chanos, you've got to come down here," exclaimed Rowe, a notably exuberant type. "This is insane."

Chanos jumped on a plane and was soon touring Texas exurbs—the kind of kick-the-tires investigation that can be just as important as pouring over a company's footnotes, balance sheets, and cash flow statements.

"It was on-the-ground research," Chanos says. "Shad drove me around for three days and we went around from building to building as they were already being called 'see-throughs.'"

Many of the shiny new buildings were open for business. There might be a dozen cars in the parking lot, and Chanos and Rowe would go into the building and see five or six new businesses—most of them appraisal companies, title insurers, syndicators, or other real estate-related companies. "So it was all this self-fulfilling boom," Chanos recalls.

The popular wisdom at the time was that Japanese investors, flush with U.S. dollars, would put them to work buying up the commercial real estate. It was just a matter of time. Hadn't they already purchased trophies like Rockefeller Center in New York and the Pebble Beach golf course in California?

The Texas banks had gotten very big, swollen with deposits. Credit was phenomenally easy. Meanwhile, in what would play out some years later, the saving and loans (S&Ls) had been deregulated under the Reagan administration and were moving beyond issuing simple home mortgages to investments in junk bonds, stocks, and commercial real estate. Some sported trading desks that resembled those at Wall Street trading firms like Salomon Brothers.

"It was our first sort of thematic short, but based on fundamentals in terms of looking at the companies that were either owners of the real estate or lenders to the real estate, and realizing that the cash flows from the buildings wasn't supporting the debt being incurred," says Chanos. "So you end up with a sort of Ponzi finance of borrowing money to service your interest. And inexorably, in those kinds of situations, the equity usually gets wiped out."

Up until now, though, Chanos had been an analyst, not a businessman. He had to learn the ropes not only of entrepreneurship, but the details and pitfalls of locating stock to borrow, covering positions, and pressing them or expanding his positions as stocks careened downward. He started out focused on Texas, shorting real estate developers like Southland Corp. and SouthMark Corp. in early 1986. From there, he expanded into banks like Texas Commerce Bankshares and MCorp, and finally into dozens of S&Ls. Then Kynikos expanded geographically into other parts of the country, including Arizona, that were experiencing similar, if less spectacular, real estate bubbles.

"Our timing was lucky," says Chanos. "It was Shad. That didn't have to do with me. A smart guy happened to bring me down there to look at this."

The upshot was that even though the Standard & Poor's (S&P) 500 was powering ahead through 1986 and into 1987, Chanos's fund, Ursus, posted dazzling returns in its infancy—33.4 percent in 1986 and

23.7 percent in 1987, when the fund also benefited from the October 19 stock market meltdown, when the Dow Jones Industrial Average tumbled a record 22.6 percent in a day.

Chanos was in Dallas the day after the crash riding an elevator to the lobby with Jim Smith, a broker who worked closely with Kynikos. "Whatever you do," Chanos told Smith following the Dow Industrials' 508 point plunge, "Don't let them see you smile."

Part of Kynikos's success may be due to the fact that the amount of money invested in short strategies probably shrank during this period, leaving the field open for Chanos. Still, the S&P 500 powered ahead in the years that followed—Kynikos and its Ursus fund still generated positive returns, based on the spreading real estate collapse and the S&L crisis. It posted gains of 13.5 percent in 1988, 30.6 percent in 1989, and a sizzling 68.6 percent in 1990, a year when the S&P 500 lost more than 3 percent.

After Ross Hall's exclusivity agreement lapsed in late 1987, big name investors came knocking—among them, many of the hedge fund managers who had read his research: Soros, Steinhardt, and Robertson, and some years later, the storied Ziff Brothers, whose combined wealth was recently pegged at $14.3 billion by *Forbes* magazine. Assets ballooned past $600 million.

In retrospect, though, Chanos was engaged in risky business. The fund was leveraged, using borrowed money to amplify returns; some positions approached 10 percent of assets—a serious situation if a target was acquired or subject to a *squeeze*, in which bulls collude to drive a stock up by snapping up shares and essentially forcing short sellers to cover their positions or face outrageous, theoretically unlimited losses. Kynikos was headed for a comeuppance.

Following the first U.S.–Iraqi Gulf War of 1990–1991, the American economy spring-boarded out of what turned out to be a mild recession, triggered as it was by a brief spike in oil prices, which soon declined after the United States–led coalition's unexpectedly quick victory. When the economy revved back to life, so too did the market for equities— with a vengeance.

The S&P 500 soared 30.2 percent in 1991, followed by gains of 7.5 percent and 10 percent the following two years. Kynikos suffered consecutive losses of 31.8 percent, 16.5 percent, and a stunning

44.5 percent in 1991, 1992, and 1993 respectively. The early part of the decade still brings to mind memories of searing pain for Chanos, who calls them "the dark ages."

What insights and anecdotes can he share on the subject?

"Nothing," Chanos chuckles. "As you will see from my numbers, it was a very difficult time. One thing we did wrong was we were leveraged from 1990 to 1994 and paid that price because the market just took off in 1991." The NASDAQ Composite was up nearly 80 percent that year. "From 1991 to 1993 there was just no place to hide.... Everything went up."

One particularly galling loss was against McDonnell-Douglas, the military airplane maker, which was experiencing cost overruns on its C-17 transport planes. Chanos bet against the company, only to lose money when it posted a remarkable turnaround. It turned out later that the Defense Department had improperly accelerated payments to the company.

The drawdown on Kynikos's assets, from a combination of market losses and withdrawals, was brutal. They dropped from $660 million at the end of 1990 to less than $175 million at the bottom of 1993. And the worst of it was that the terms under which Chanos was managing those millions prevented him from playing defense. "We had a mandate to be short," he says. When the stock screens on his computers turned green in the morning—signifying a run up in shares—he was not even supposed to cover his positions since he had been hired for the express purpose of shorting stocks, almost always as a hedge for bigger investors, who were invariably long to a far greater degree in their overall portfolios.

The year 1994 proved a watershed—giving the firm an opportunity to regroup. With the U.S. central bank raising the Federal Funds Target Rate six times, to 5.5 percent from 3 percent, the 10-year U.S. Treasury bond lost more than 8 percent in 1994 and stocks were basically flat, eking out just a 1.3 percent gain. Ursus returned 44.5 percent. "We had a monster year," Chanos recalls. It was certainly a much-needed respite. With losses mounting, he had been paying the Kynikos staff out of his own pocket. Ursus was structured as a traditional hedge fund, charging a 1 percent management fee and 20 percent of any profits. But that's clearly not a fee structure that can withstand an extended bull market. "We said, 'What did we do wrong here?'" Chanos remembers asking.

"We're surviving, but how are we going to prosper if the market just goes up forever again?"

In 1995, Chanos began an overhaul at Kynikos. First was to dispense with leverage. The firm would no longer borrow money to goose returns. Secondly, the company would diversify its portfolio. Instead of a maximum of 10 percent of assets in a position, Ursus would limit itself to just 5 percent. That meant expanding the number of holdings from 30–40 to 50–60.

Lastly, and most importantly, Kynikos changed its fee structure. Instead of the standard management fee and carried interest for its managed accounts, the lion's share of its business, Kynikos would earn 20 percent of the inverse of the S&P 500's gain for a year. By way of example, if the S&P 500 gained 30 percent and the Ursus fund lost 5 percent, it would be treated as a 25 percent gain, with the firm entitled to 20 percent of that amount.

The fee structure helps account for Kynikos's longevity, since it gives the firm the chance to earn performance fees in extended bull markets. Few, if any, other short sellers have adopted a similar fee structure, usually complaining about the complexity of accounting for the fee, which must be calculated on a monthly basis. Chanos himself is mystified why nobody has followed his lead. "I have no idea," he says, shaking his head.

Fees aren't the only thing setting Kynikos apart. Chanos runs the firm in a fashion at odds with other asset managers. He jumps up again to a white board to map out a diagram with stick figures, arrows, and light bulbs. As at most asset management firms, everything ultimately comes down to corporate culture. "That's a lot of who we are," Chanos says.

Most money management firms charge analysts with the role of generating investment ideas. Chanos calls that a bad proposition. "It has to do with culture, I think, and human motivational behavior," he says, lapsing into one of his frequent philosophical musings. Typically, analysts research industry, economic, or corporate developments and pitch a stock to a portfolio manager with the notion that buying or shorting a stock will generate a profit. "The whole initiative is for these people at the bottom, who are typically your younger and more inexperienced people, of coming up with ideas and giving the ideas, sending them up," he says. Chanos points to a light bulb he's drawn on the white board. "It's what I call intellectual ownership of an idea." The analyst who generates the idea gets credit or blame for it, and is very much incentivized to defend a position—even when new developments turn unfavorable or run counter to his thesis.

The analyst is on the hook. "Well from then on, if anything happens relating to that, everyone looks at you, right? You brought it in," Chanos says. "In that shop, you have intellectual ownership of the idea."

Then he points to the stick figures at the top of his whiteboard—representing him and his partners. "The problem is that the economic ownership of the idea resides up here," Chanos said. "In effect, if things go well, everybody does well. But if things don't go well, guess who gets looked at and blamed? You've put the onus of profit and loss and origination on the most junior members of the team. But if it all works out, a disproportionate share of the economic gain goes to the person at the top of the pyramid."

"If things are good—fine," he adds. "When things start going bad, that's a very unstable model." Analysts get blamed, responsibility denied and people fired.

This is why turnover is so high at hedge funds; it's also why they fold so quickly when trouble hits, Chanos says. Moreover, it encourages analysts to withhold important information that may run contrary to their original thesis. "It's creating a silo," he says. "You don't want to give bad news."

At Kynikos, the onus of developing investment ideas mostly rests with the partners, of which today there are six. The three big idea generators among the partners include Chanos himself, managing director Charles Hobbs, and research director chief David Glaymon. Other partners include Brian Nichols, who wears three hats as chief financial, compliance, and operating officer, head trader Bob Veninata, and head of stock loan Alan Best. A hedge fund with a partner totally devoted to locating and borrowing stock? "Absolutely," says Chanos. "It isn't at most firms, but it is at ours. Alan's been on the Street since 1966 or 1967, training most people in stock loan on the Street."

The partners may get their ideas just about anywhere—tips from other short sellers, economic reports, conferences, just an unreasonably sharp rise in a stock price, a newspaper article, or perhaps even a cocktail party conversation. They may spend a weekend reading through stacks of 10-K or other filings, do background research or ruminate. Then, if one of them thinks there's merit to an investment thesis, the partner assigns an analyst to do the grunt work—gather up sell-side research; interview customers, rivals, and suppliers; attend industry conferences; scout out company locations if necessary. The analyst will do web searches, map out spreadsheets to compare the stock with those of its peers, and learn the industry top to bottom.

An analyst has no idea where a profitable insight might surface, but he or she increases his or her chances by working overtime. All the information is channeled to the partner who makes the ultimate decision of how much capital, if any, to risk on a position.

The analyst's job is designed as a staff position, not generally a stepping stone to partner or a portfolio management slot—although David Glaymon is an exception. "We're up front with our analysts," says Chanos. "We do tell them that this is different than 99 percent of most money management firms or hedge funds, where the model is the guys at the top expect the guys at the bottom not only to work on the ideas but come up with the ideas."

There's an added benefit for analysts. "I will never yell at an analyst if a stock's not working out," says Chanos. "That's my job, that's my responsibility. I will get mad at an analyst if I don't get information. So it's a much truer staff model. And because all of the analysts are compensated not on their stocks but on the profitability of the firm, it generates lateral information flow. Someone sees something, hears something—they make sure the analyst covering it sees it and gets it to the partners."

While the partners have relatively conventional backgrounds—Deutsche Bank, Morgan Stanley, PaineWebber, and JPMorgan Chase—the analysts come from a variety of disciplines. "Hiring analysts, the thing we want to see most of is real intellectual curiosity," he says. "Assuming they have certain base quantitative skills, they know a little bit about corporate balance sheets and accounting and have done spreadsheets and things like that, but almost everybody we interview has that level of capability. We want to see some evidence, whether in written work or whatever, of the ability to ask questions and to follow inquiry if they don't know something or if something appears out of whack. Almost everything else we can teach."

Millett was a trader at the Chicago Board of Trade. Steve Schurr wrote for the *Financial Times*. Lily Jong curated the Ziff family art collection when the Kynikos offices were located at Ziff Brothers Investments. She spent her lunch hours asking about the short-selling business, Chanos recalls. "And she turned out to be one of my greatest analysts ever," he says. "She was an art history major from Columbia. But she was just always asking the right questions and just had that sixth sense."

Unusually, Chanos seems as eager to talk about his losing bets as his winners. That may be that he is simply bored repeating such famed successful shorts as Enron and Tyco International. It may be fear of lawsuits. Or it may be because he, like many of us, has learned more from his duds than his hits.

America Online is a case in point—especially as recounted by Katherine Burton in her book *Hedge Hunters* (Bloomberg Press, 2007). America Online, now known as AOL, posted sales of $1.1 billion in its fiscal year ended June 1996, nearly tripling from $394.3 million the year earlier. Research and development (R&D) costs and other expenses had risen in tandem, but AOL under CEO Steve Case had simply decided to lengthen the time over which it would expense those costs, giving the impression of far faster-growing earnings than a true assessment would suggest. (Around the same time, short seller David Rocker of Rocker Partners LP was questioning issues pertaining to the pricey CD ROMs AOL was mass mailing to prospective customers, which the company, in like fashion, booked as capital expenditures, even though logic would state they should have been treated as simple marketing costs, again allowing the company to post inflated earnings).

AOL continued to rise, gaining 20 points over a matter of months. Chanos got persistent phone calls from one particular investor, a well-known hedge fund manager, grilling him on the AOL position. Why was it losing money? Merrill Lynch loved it. The business was booming. Was Chanos sure he was correct?

The Kynikos short portfolio overall in 1997 was in positive territory and plenty of his other short positions were working out, including Boston Chicken, Oxford Health, and Sunbeam. The hedge fund manager persisted in badgering him about the AOL position, pointing to sell-side research.

The calls were frequent and annoying, and when the investor called on a Sunday night, the normally easygoing Chanos became irate. The *New York Times* had just written an upbeat AOL story, the client said. "I just wanted to talk to you about it," he pleaded. Chanos said if he received one more phone call, he would return his client's money.

Less than a week later the client called again. "I know what you said, but we have to talk about America Online," he said.

"No, we need to talk about getting you your money back," Chanos said, laughing. Being constantly interrogated about his investments was not part of the Kynikos job description. He declines to identify the investor on the record.

AOL was eventually forced to restate earnings because of its accounting fraud, but managed to buy Time Warner with over $100 billion of its own dubious stock in a deal announced in January 2000, just three months before the Internet-fueled market collapse. To critics, CEO Steve Case may go down in history as an ethically challenged executive—but he certainly made money for his AOL shareholders by finding in Time Warner a buyer for his inflated shares.

While AOL ultimately turned out to be a money loser for the firm, Chanos and his colleagues are proud to have nailed it, albeit years too early. AOL, later spun off from Time Warner, agreed to be bought by Verizon Communications in 2015.

Undoubtedly, Kynikos is most famous for its short on Enron. For those interested in the gripping details of the rise and collapse of the Houston energy trading giant, with its cast of thieves and larger than life miscreants, no better source exists than the rollicking tale as told by two *Fortune* writers, Bethany McLean and Peter Elkind: *The Smartest Guys in the Room* (Portfolio/Penguin, 2003). It should be required reading for every M.B.A. candidate and every stock market investor. There's also an Oscar-nominated documentary based on the book.

Though doubts about Enron's opaque accounting had surfaced in the media as far back as the 1990s, it was an article by Jonathan Weil in September 2000 that caught Chanos's eye. Or rather, the article was forwarded to Chanos because it appeared only in the Texas regional insert of the *Wall Street Journal*. Weil, who had a juris doctor degree from Southern Methodist University, certainly knew his way around a balance sheet. His article focused on the use of gain-on-sale accounting at three Houston-based companies—El Paso Energy, Dynegy, and Enron.

All three companies had transitioned from hard asset energy providers with pipelines and storage facilities, to financial firms—traders of energy-based contracts and derivatives as well as a variety of other instruments linked to commodities or interest rates. They were printing money amidst the deregulation of the U.S. energy markets at the time: A sharp spike in natural gas prices was goosing their reported earnings and share prices. The stock of Enron, the biggest such trader in America, had almost doubled year to date by the time Weil's story appeared and was trading at $84.875, or 60 times earnings.

The problem, Weil pointed out, was that all these companies used gain-on-sale accounting when calculating their earnings. Enron and the other companies were booking profits on electricity and other contracts that could run for 20 years or more—requiring them to estimate prices decades out. This was dicey. Further, all the companies declined to disclose their formulas or methodologies for producing those estimates. In other words, they had a license to report whatever earnings they felt like. "Our interest in Enron and other energy companies was piqued," Chanos told an SEC roundtable in May 2003. "In effect, 'earnings' could be created out of thin air if management was willing to push the envelope by using highly favorable assumptions." (After a series of other jobs, including one as Bloomberg News' star columnist, Weil joined Kynikos as a senior analyst in 2014).

It was time for serious financial digging—and that began with 1999 10-K filings, released in early 2000. Enron's return on capital was roughly 7 percent. That means that for every dollar invested, Enron was earning just seven cents. "Would you put your money in a hedge fund earning a 7 percent return?" Millett asked Fortune's McLean. Enron's traders, after all, as the book title proclaimed were, "the smartest guys in the room." Yet they couldn't keep pace with the long-term average of the S&P 500. The best estimate Kynikos could come up with was that Enron's cost of capital—that is, what it paid on a blended basis for its debt and equity—was 9 percent. So, even including the dubious gain-on-sale accounting, the firm was losing money in real terms.

Chanos also was wary of some vaguely defined "related party transactions" described in the 10-K and then in the quarterly filings, or 10-Qs. What were they? What was their purpose? "We could not decipher what impact they had on Enron's overall financial condition," Chanos told the roundtable. "Enron had organized these entities for the apparent purpose of trading with their parent company." They were run by Andrew

Fastow, Enron's CFO. It turned out that they had some wonderfully colorful names, to the delight of journalists, like Raptor, Talon, and Timberwolf. Although it was not clear at the time, they were designed to hide mark-to-market losses—and paid Fastow millions in the process.

It didn't take long for Kynikos to act. "We began shorting Enron common stock in November of 2000," Chanos said.

Most of everything else that Chanos and his colleagues found only added to their negative outlook—it was much like peeling an onion gone bad, whose every layer revealed more rot and questionable activities. Chanos likes to say that when he builds an argument for a short position, it's not a criminal case, from the Kynikos outlook, but a civil one. Chanos needed only a preponderance of evidence—he did not have to prove his case beyond a reasonable doubt. But the scary, if circumstantial, evidence on Enron piled up. Corporate insiders were selling shares—not a smoking gun because energy executives, obviously, need to finance homes and yachts. But it was nevertheless suspicious.

More damning: Enron executives had in late 2000 been talking at conferences about the great opportunities they foresaw in broadband, that is data communications capacity, which it was building out at a rapid pace—and claiming it already added $20 to $30 to the value of Enron stock, a figure it would later boost to $40. The company had acquired a small fiber optic network in the purchase of utility Portland General in 1996.

The Internet bubble had long since collapsed, however, and Kynikos was already investigating short positions on telecommunications companies based on the titanic oversupply of such Internet-dependent broadband capacity. Management was either lying or totally out of touch with the telecommunications market. (CEO Jeffrey Skilling was, perhaps, a technophobe and refused to use the Internet or e-mail).

In late January, the company declared at an analyst conference in Houston that its shares, which had begun the year trading at $85 share, should be trading at $126—a bizarre assertion to make from the very parties that stand to benefit from making such a claim.

In February, the *New York Times* ran a story concerning the California energy crisis—a shortage of electricity that many attributed to the deregulation of the electricity prices. The article pointed out that Enron had invoked a clause in its contract with consumers that allowed it to back out of its middleman position between the buyers and power providers, many of whom at that point were bankrupt. "Enron's credibility in the entire energy retail business began to crumble simply because the company refused to recognize sure losses in California," Chanos told a congressional committee in February 2002.

At the time, Chanos held an annual February "Bears in Hibernation" conference in Florida with a varied group of hedge funds managers. He laid out his suspicions about Enron. Apparently, many of the participants agreed because the short interest on Enron soon rose sharply.

In early March 2001, *Fortune* published a short article by McLean simply questioning Enron's high stock price, which had tumbled to $59. People were still calling it the "Goldman Sachs of energy trading," the piece pointed out, but its shares were trading at a multiple of 55 times trailing earnings, more than three times those of the storied investment bank.

Moreover, Enron simply wouldn't disclose how it made its money because, according to CEO Skilling, the company viewed that information as a competitive advantage—something it did not want to share with rivals. Chanos and Kynikos were big sources for the *Fortune* story, but remained anonymous at the time. Again, there was no major reaction to Enron's share price by investors, nor apparently by *Fortune* itself, which itself named Enron a "digitizing superstar" a few weeks later. (Chairman Ken Lay later reportedly had to be painstakingly airbrushed out of a group photo, which also included Time Warner's Levin, of "The Smartest People We Know," an article that was a November 2001 cover story). But investor uneasiness grew.

By the summer of 2001, natural gas and electricity prices began to tumble. As Chanos noted to the SEC and in subsequent congressional testimony, almost all trading firms claim to be sufficiently hedged in such situations to protect earnings. They seldom are. "Trading operations always seem to do better in bull markets and to struggle in bear markets," he said. Enron's stock was down to $44.

The company's 2001 second quarter 10-Q, released in August, also fueled rumors that Enron's falling shares could trigger a cash squeeze because some of the terms of the off-balance-sheet partnerships referenced the stock price. Most devastating however, was the unexpected resignation of CEO Skilling, the most vocal of those obsessed with the company's share price. He cited "personal reasons." Shares tumbled from $46 to $35 that month. "Because we viewed Skilling as the architect of the present Enron, his abrupt departure was the most ominous development yet," Chanos said. Kynikos increased its short position further, although it has not disclosed by how much.

And just in time too. On October 16, Enron reported an unexpected loss of $618 million. Shares inexplicably rose slightly. But the next day *Wall Street Journal* reporters Rebecca Smith and John Emshwiller, who had spent months developing sources and parsing through leaked and public documents, published the first of a devastating series, detailing the fraudulent accounting of the Raptor and other partnerships and the litany of Enron misstatements to both the SEC and the public.

Although plenty of other details would surface in the months and, indeed, years ahead, the series definitely pushed Enron over the precipice. The stock went into free-fall, hitting $13 by the end of the month. The company filed for bankruptcy on December 2. In May 2006, Skilling was convicted of multiple counts, including securities fraud, insider trading, conspiracy and making false statements to an auditor. He is serving time in Montgomery Federal Prison Camp in Alabama and is scheduled for release in 2019.

As for Ken Lay, he was also convicted of 10 counts of securities fraud or related charges—but died of a heart attack that year. A judge vacated the convictions.

Enron's auditor, Arthur Andersen, was found guilty of criminal charges involving its auditing of Enron. The verdict was later overturned, but the former "big five" accounting firm surrendered its licenses to practice. Its employee count is down from a high of 85,000 worldwide to just 200.

Chanos, a fan of ironic twists, relishes a delicious denouement. As Enron careened toward bankruptcy, a copycat company named Dynegy offered to buy it. Incredulous investors asked whether it had properly scrutinized Enron's financials. Dynegy responded that it had—and that it was reassured because both firms used identical accounting methodologies. Chanos promptly proceeded to short Dynegy, which flirted with bankruptcy in 2002. Chanos says Kynikos made as much money on Dynegy as it had on Enron. Dynegy eventually did file for bankruptcy in 2012 reemerging the same year.

Kynikos missed out on the proverbial inverse "10-bagger" with American International Group Inc., or AIG—a short position that Chanos hasn't talked about much. As the expert behind Baldwin-United, Chanos personally was the point man and took responsibility for the position. The famed insurance giant, founded in Shanghai's bund in 1919 by Cornelius Vander Starr, had over the decades expanded into a global behemoth with its fingers in virtually every corner of the insurance industry—property & casualty, life, reinsurance and even beyond, into fields like aircraft leasing.

Its CEO, the famously aggressive Maurice "Hank" Greenberg, pushed his people relentlessly hard, built obscure lines of business, and forged new ones. With dozens of interconnected subsidiaries—National Fire Insurance Company of Pittsburgh, SunAmerica, America General Life, Lexington Insurance, aircraft lessor International Lease Finance, even the ski resort of Stowe, Vermont—most analysts threw up their hands. It wasn't a company but a vast feudal financial empire—and because one of its holdings included a tiny S&L, it was overseen not by a major regulator but the tiny Office of Thrift Supervision. "Regulatory arbitrage," it was called.

Chanos thought he was up for the challenge and looked closely at the firm's financial services division, expending enormous energy and man hours trying to figure it out.

Chanos got close. One thing he knew was that AIG was big on what is known as finite reinsurance—that's when an insurer transfers the risk of a policy, typically over a certain amount it's on the hook for, to another insurer or third party as part of a deal. The counterparty then receives the ongoing premiums and pays the policy off if necessary. There's often a payment made to the company that assumes the policy, or vice versa.

In one such finite reinsurance deal, AIG under Greenberg sold the risk to Berkshire Hathaway's General Re subsidiary, which paid it a $500 million premium that AIG used to bulk up its loss reserves, bolstering earnings. (Several General Re executives, including its CEO, were convicted of what was deemed to be a fraudulent transaction. The case was overturned in 2011.) Under pressure from then–New York State Attorney General Eliot Spitzer, the AIG board forced Greenberg to resign in 2005.

Ultimately the firm, in Chanos's estimation, just stank. "There was a culture there of aggressiveness," he says. Chanos turned his attention to what was in effect finite earnings reinsurance to high-tech companies during the turn-of-the-century technology bubble. "They had a unit that sold reinsurance that was in effect coverage to high-tech companies who needed to meet earnings forecasts," he says.

Even today, Chanos admits it was an ingenious scam. AIG would cede, for example, $500 million of an insurance policy to a high-technology company. The tech company would collect the premiums and pay any claims. But most importantly, AIG paid the technology firm, say, a $25 million ceding commission. That would usually find its way into the technology company's earnings statement under "other income" but was not generally disclosed otherwise. Mirabile dictu: The tech company would hit its target earnings. The terms, however, were ultimately extremely advantageous to AIG.

"That was the first sign that there was a culture here of these guys selling a product that just doesn't pass the smell test. And by the way, [it] was probably wildly profitable for them," Chanos says. "And that's what got us going on AIG."

Chanos and his colleagues also made a valiant effort to untangle the AIG Financial Products unit that famously sold some $62 billion of credit default swaps—insurance protection—on toxic collateralized debt obligations, sales that ultimately blew up, leading to AIG's government takeover. But Kynikos gave up well before that. "It was a black box," he says, referring to AIG Financial Products. "And the financial disclosures weren't great."

"We were short it before the crisis because of accounting issues, and we knew something was wrong in financial services, but I could not prove it," he says. "I could not get a smoking gun and we ended up covering too early. Looking for certainty is a fool's errand. You're never going to get it. You can get some really great ideas that get you closer to 100 percent certainty, but you're never going to get to 100 percent certainty."

After the company disclosed that it received subpoenas from the SEC and then Attorney General Eliot Spitzer in February 2005, shares plunged more than 10 percent. The board fired Greenberg in March 2005, and the stock continued to decline, hitting $63 in March, but then more or less moved sideways for more than a year under Greenberg's replacement, Martin Sullivan.

Kynikos covered its short position in late 2006 and early 2007 as what he felt were more promising financial services stocks began to show signs of stress. Kynikos made a small profit on the position but nowhere near what he could have had he maintained or pressed his AIG position. As part of the $182.3 billion bailout, the government took over 79.9 percent of the stock in the September 2008 deal, reducing the value of the remaining position by nearly 80 percent in a single swoop. In this case, Chanos decided to move on too soon.

There were plenty of other opportunities—banks, loan originators, homebuilders, and Freddie Mac and Fannie Mae among them. Chanos spread his bets. Not surprisingly, the Ursus fund cleaned up in 2007 and 2008, generating returns of 26.4 percent and a sizzling 60.2 percent, respectively. Remember, those were years in which the S&P 500 returned just 5 percent and lost 37 percent, respectively, and Kynikos was getting paid on the difference. The long-short Kynikos Opportunity, with a more traditional fee structure, gained 13.4 percent and 15.9 percent, respectively, those years. For most shorts, it was like shooting fish in a barrel.

Chanos, like his rivals, was prevented from initiating new short positions on financial stocks due to a short-term September 19, 2008, ban by the SEC on such bets, made in collaboration with the U.K. Financial Services Authority. The U.S. ban ended on October 2, and a 2012 report by the New York Federal Reserve Bank confirmed what most everybody knew—that it was totally ineffective in stopping or even slowing the decline of financial stocks. The ban did have the effect of lowering liquidity and driving up trading costs, the report concluded.

The rebound from the financial crisis, beginning in March 2009, proved more challenging for Kynikos, and Ursus lost 30.5 percent that year, though the long-short Kynikos Opportunity fund gained 15.1 percent.

It certainly made sense to focus on accounting frauds rather than asset bubbles in a market quickly regaining its footing in the aftermath of the Great Recesssion. The Federal Reserve, after all, was buying back hundreds of billions of Treasury and mortgage bonds in its bid to keep interest rates low—the policy of quantitative easing that had some short sellers gnashing their teeth. Treasuries were yielding close to zero, virtually forcing investors into the stock market. Wagering against dubious accounting seemed a wise course in this era of financial repression.

Even with world stock markets battered, Kynikos came across a veritable gem of a fraud—one that ultimately led Chanos to a second greater short against one of the legends of the U.S. technology industry. The first dubious target was Autonomy Corp, an English software firm spun out from its parent, Cambridge Neurodynamics, a fingerprint recognition firm, in 1996. Autonomy listed its shares on NASDAQ two years later and made its founders rich, as shares soared more than tenfold in the technology bubble.

Autonomy by 2009 had a compelling business tale for investors, specializing in pulling vast amounts of data from myriad sources—databases, e-mails, text or audio files, websites—and then repurposing what it culled into usable and marketable information and services: market analytics, search engine optimization and even video surveillance. The space is called e-Discovery. Yet, underneath the brilliant code writing, Autonomy was, according to Kynikos, a classic serial acquirer of tech companies or "roll-up"—and was using accounting trickery to snooker investors.

Chanos has a special place in his heart for roll-ups—and it is neither warm nor cuddly. The purpose of such acquisitions is often, as he explained to his students in New Haven, to obscure poor underlying fundamentals in a core business. Often purchases are accompanied by restructuring charges and write-offs, which investors are encouraged to ignore. Serial acquirers encourage investors to look at earnings without any of the bad stuff.

And Autonomy, under its shiny-headed, smooth talking CEO, Michael Lynch, was an exemplar of the process. The firm acquired at least eight businesses from its inception until 2011—including its former parent. The idea was to take over the targets' customer bases and integrate their products into Autonomy's flagship product, the IDOL search engine. The evidence of misleading accounting in this case gave Chanos enormous confidence. "It was our biggest position in Europe in 2011," he says.

Chanos is also quick to point out that neither he nor his principal in London, Glaymon, were the first to take aim at Autonomy. "We weren't the only ones," he says. Paul Morland, an analyst at brokerage Peel Hunt, wrote six research reports beginning in 2008 that on several occasions brought up accounting maneuvers, all of which had the effect of over-stating performance, according to newspaper reports.

For this Morland was banned from Autonomy analyst calls, and employees were forbidden to speak to him. Two other brokerage analysts, were also deemed personae non gratae—Daud Khan of J.P.Morgan Cazenove and Roger Phillips at Merchant Equity Partners. So some in the City were wise to Autonomy, but the firm generated sufficient fees from its purchases to cause most to look the other way.

Similarly, industry technology analysts who questioned Autonomy's IDOL search engine were blacklisted, too. IDOL, Lynch claimed, had near-magical powers due to its harnessing of Bayesian analysis, a statistical approach pioneered by the 18th century English mathematician Thomas Bayes that updates statistical probabilities as new information is introduced.

While noting that customers were far less enthusiastic about IDOL than the company was, Kynikos got short Autonomy in early 2009, mostly focusing on a laundry list of accounting and disclosure issues. "There were lots of issues," says Chanos, pausing for effect. "I mean *lots* of them."

Autonomy claimed a 40 percent market share of the e-Discovery market—an industry space that included such heavyweights as Microsoft, EMC, and IBM. Likewise, claims of 20 percent revenue growth were far greater than those of rivals. In an opaque and early-stage industry, it was easy to make such assertions, but hard to believe or effectively disprove.

Autonomy's financial disclosure was abysmal, failing to provide standard metrics like maintenance revenue or details of its myriad acquisitions, which were typically of small private companies. And always in cash, since that meant the target would not engage in due diligence. Much of what it did disclose was made verbally in conference calls, not regulatory filing—license revenues, cash collections, subsidiary revenue contributions.

Nevertheless, what Autonomy did claim was indeed outstanding: margins of 44 percent in fiscal 2009. Those compare to just 36 percent for both Google and Oracle in the same period. By its own admission it was generating returns of just 14 percent on its net business assets. That's compared to about 48 percent for Google and 23 percent for Oracle.

One area of Kynikos's focus was deferred revenue growth—that is, the gain in sales and services that have been booked but not yet paid for because they have yet to be delivered. It's a key metric for software firms, especially when looked at as a percentage to realized revenues, because it signifies the company's growth trajectory—the higher the percentage, the better. Kynikos noted that whenever deferred revenue growth dipped below 70 percent of that of recognized revenue, Autonomy would make another purchase and the percentage would, not surprisingly, shoot up.

Most of Autonomy's purchases were of smaller private companies or divisions of companies like CA or Iron Mountain, without extensive published financial data to check on its claims. Chanos didn't trust the accounting of two private companies Autonomy acquired, Meridio and Zantaz, in 2007. He counted $111 million more in goodwill and intangibles than there should have been as a result of the purchases. This allowed Autonomy to keep costs of its income statements low, inflating earnings.

Kynikos got more clarity on this maneuver in early 2009, when Autonomy spent $775 million to buy Interwoven, a publicly-traded U.S. company, with detailed financials that he could verify. In this case goodwill and intangibles were overstated by a whopping $195 million. At this point it was clear that Autonomy would have to continue to buy bigger companies to boost its deferred revenue growth or find some other way to cover up the weakness of its underlying business.

Chanos initiated his short at 1,253 pence a share, but the share price quickly rose, hitting 1,500 in early 2010. In June 2011, Autonomy paid $350 million for Iron Mountain's digital archiving business, and shares hit 1,788 pence. Chanos's pain was severe.

But Lynch was about to make things much, much worse. "The only thing you can do in this kind of roll up is a) either sell yourself or b) change the strategy and hope the street doesn't notice," says Chanos. "That's what Tyco tried to do and of course blew up."

Enter Hewlett-Packard, the floundering American computer maker, under the stewardship of it new CEO, SAP veteran Leo Apotheker, intent on decisively shifting the storied computer maker away from hardware into software. Stunning the technology industry, in August 2011 he purchased Autonomy for a whopping $11.7 billion, a 64 percent premium over its market value at the time, in a deal that translated to 2,550 pence a share.

There was little Chanos could do except try and alert Hewlett-Packard's seemingly somnolent board of directors. "I even sent our write-ups to friends I had who I know had friends on the Hewlett board," Chanos says. Quoting some of his missives: "I don't get it, I don't understand it—what are you people looking at that I'm not? At the same time we're saying are you kidding me? This is a disaster. Why are you doing this? Have you looked at the numbers here?"

The deal closed anyway. "That was one of our biggest losers in our global portfolio in 2011," Chanos says, losing nearly 2 percentage points of performance. Thirteen months later, Hewlett-Packard took an $8.8 billion impairment charge to cover accounting irregularities it found at Autonomy and Apotheker was sent packing, replaced by former eBay chairman Meg Whitman. It issued a statement: "HP now believes Autonomy was substantially overvalued at the time of its acquisition due to the misstatement of Autonomy's financial performance, including its revenue, core growth rate, and gross margins, and the misrepresentation of its business mix."

Three investigations were launched, respectively, by the U.S. Justice Department, the SEC and the U.K.'s Serious Fraud Office. Lynch said in a website interview: "HP is looking for scapegoats and I'm afraid I'm not going to be one of those." Chanos indulged in a bit of schadenfreude, e-mailing memos to the street: "I said, 'By the way, you could have seen this beforehand.'"

The U.K. Serious Fraud Office dropped its investigation of Autonomy's alleged accounting fraud in January 2015, saying, "there is insufficient evidence for a realistic prospect of conviction." Hewlett-Packard continues to pursue its own case against Lynch.

Ironically, it was Autonomy that put Chanos on course to a major payday. "We were already at that point, in mid-2011, beginning to get concerned about Hewlett because of their inkjet business," Chanos says. Sales were declining and margins squeezed in the division. Kynikos had already been short printer maker Lexmark. More critically, Kynikos was worrying about a nascent global shift away from the personal computer (PC) altogether. "It was becoming apparent to me and some of the other people in the firm that the PC was on its way out, that in fact, the unending growth in PCs and notebooks was going to end because of the advent of mobile and smart phones and the cloud," he says. "We began doing a lot of work on the PC space directly."

The Autonomy purchase prompted an even more thorough, top to bottom reassessment of Hewlett-Packard. "Basically, I think, 'If they are dumb enough to buy Autonomy, what else have they been doing?'" says Chanos.

Indeed, Hewlett-Packard had been through three CEOs in five years. Its board of directors included executives who had presided over high-profile failures, including Ken Thompson of Wachovia and Patricia Russo of Alcatel-Lucent.

Most important, was the analysis of the company's acquisitions. It started with the 2002 purchase of Compaq Computer Corp for $24.2 billion, which required a $1.7 billion write down, after massive layoffs and declining earnings. That led to the board of directors' ouster of CEO Carly Fiorina, who was soon replaced by Mark Hurd. Under Hurd, Hewlett-Packard bought Electronic Data Systems for $13.9 billion in 2008, which required an $8 billion writedown. The company's $1.8 billion purchase of smartphone maker Palm Inc and its WebOS operating system in 2010 resulted in a $1.7 billion write down and impairment, with the operating system soon abandoned.

Hurd was widely acclaimed for his turnaround efforts—but he was forced to resign after being accused of inappropriate sexual advances by a woman he had hired. Apotheker was drafted to take his place, with only a cursory search by the board.

While others lauded the Hewlett-Packard turnaround, Chanos did not see it. "We looked at Hewlett and realized, my God, these people have been acquiring all their R&D through the years," Chanos says. "They spent almost nothing on R&D, 2 percent, unlike IBM and Samsung, who spend 6 percent. And the difference they make up by buying companies. Well, they have not bought good companies, and they have not integrated these companies."

Bulls pointed to Hewlett-Packard's low price to earnings (P-E) multiple of just 5.2 times forecast 2012 earnings, declaring it a bargain. Chanos instead called it "the ultimate value trap" and pointed out that focusing on P-E ratios ignored the company's deteriorating balance sheet, with debt to total capital increasing from just 6 percent to 40 percent since 2006 and tangible equity tumbling to a negative $6.3 billion. "Hewlett-Packard has essentially devolved into a tech roll-up whose constantly changing management team has wrecked the balance-sheet in pursuit of growth," was how one Kynikos research report summed it up.

Hewlett-Packard's shares fell from $29.51 at the time of the Autonomy acquisition to a low of less than $12 in late 2012. Kynikos covered some of its position at that point, but was still short shares as of April 2013, as he wrapped up his class at Yale. The firm was still short Hewlett-Packard in early 2015 even after the company's announcement of plans to split in two, with one business focused on corporations and the other on PCs and printers.

At 56 Hillhouse, afternoon light is filtering into the lecture hall. Chanos continues pacing back and forth, detailing frauds of an earlier era—he refers to John Kenneth Galbraith's concept of "the bezzle," the frauds that build up in flush economic times only to be discovered when markets collapse, much like Bernard Madoff's Ponzi-like enterprise, which unraveled only amidst the 2008–2009 financial collapse.

"What was the bezzle in 1719 Paris?" he asks the class.

"The French national debt?" a student responds.

"The French national debt and ... what was the scheme to reduce the French national debt?" he asks. "An equity-for-debt swap, right?"

France in 1715 was groaning under the debt incurred during the War of the Spanish Succession. Enter Scottish financier John Law, who soon became a trusted financial advisor to the French government under King Louis XV. Law created a company that became known as La Compagnie des Indes, acquiring the trade and development rights along the French-ruled Mississippi river. Through Law's connections, the company soon gained the right to collect taxes first in French North America and then around the world.

Then Law launched a plan to swap French sovereign bonds for shares in the La Compagnie de Indes.

"How did he persuade people to do that?" Chanos asks. "He inflated the prospects, to be generous to Mr. Law. The rivers of gold, the mountains of silver. Fields studded with emeralds. Friendly Indians. Soil that would grow anything."

Law offered shares in his company at 500 livres in January 1719, the French currency at the time, and they hit 10,000 by the end of the year. Peasants became phenomenally wealthy—until some of some of them actually began taking their profits. Company shares soon collapsed, the peasants were peasants again, and France entered a sustained economic depression.

Chanos goes on to briefly describe the Great South Sea Bubble and the land grant scandals that corrupted the construction of the United States' transcontinental railroads, via Crédit Mobilier. He also touches on the legendary Charles Ponzi, who claimed to be buying discounted postal reply coupons and redeeming them at face value in the United States And there were the financial manipulations of Ivar Krueger, the Swedish "Match King," who used a variety of tools, including the very first B shares, with lower voting rights and phony subsidiaries as part of his scheme, which collapsed in the Great Depression. Kreuger committed suicide in Paris, under mysterious circumstances, in 1932.

"Consistent stories, different stories, different technologies, but still the suspension of disbelief leading to disreputable people actually crossing the line and deceiving people," Chanos says.

Nothing, in other words, is to be taken at face value, in a changing world. That's a recipe for chaos.

Chapter 4

Einhorn: Contrarian at the Gates

The crowd at the Marriott Marquis Hotel was on tenterhooks as David Einhorn stepped up to the podium.

It was the Value Investing Congress, and the president of Greenlight Capital had set off fireworks at the same conference three years earlier, in 2007, using his accounting insights to dissect dubious risk management practices at Lehman Brothers, among other firms. That ended spectacularly badly for the storied investment bank—less than a year later it filed for chapter 11, ushering in the 2008–2009 financial crisis and great recession that followed. Einhorn soon ascended to a sort of demigod status on Wall Street.

Now, as the clock ticked toward noon on a cool October morning in 2010, the thin, boyish-looking Einhorn was set to unveil a new target—one that could mean millions in profits for the audience gathered in the soulless, burgundy-draped conference hall. The BlackBerrys were out as Einhorn, then 41, cleared his throat.

First came perfunctory disclaimers, and a round of thanks for his analysts' hard work. Einhorn, dressed in a dark suit, white shirt and patterned tie, added that the company he was about to talk about had declined to meet with him. The slide on the screen behind him read ominously: "Field of Schemes." Attendees were almost giddy with antic-ipation. Why shouldn't they be? They had front row seats to a Wall Street beheading.

"The topic of today is the St. Joe Company," Einhorn began, in his distinctive high-pitched tone. "The ticker is 'JOE' and the stock trades at about 24 and a half dollars a share."

In a flash, the audience was clicking away on their smart phones—and St. Joe shares, already down by double digits that year, went into free fall. Einhorn, who had built a hefty short position in the stock, then launched into a damning exposé.

St. Joe's tale was one of ambition gone awry. Once a sleepy lumber company owning tracts of Florida acreage, St. Joe was recast into a high-octane real estate developer under a former Walt Disney executive named Peter Rummell, whose previous credits included the entertainment giant's starchitect-studded planned community, Celebration, Florida (population: 7,427). Now St. Joe was aggressively building towns—though without the Disney cachet, and largely in Florida's downmarket Panhandle—the so-called Redneck Riviera. The two most prominent were Port St. Joe and WindMark.

Rummell was now out of the picture, having retired two years earlier, and Einhorn couldn't resist poking fun at him. He flashed a quote by the former CEO on the screen behind him from a 2007 St. Joe's earnings call: "This stretch of beach will be branded a national destination with the same kind of recognition as Nantucket, Hilton Head Island, or Napa."

Then, after posting lush, green photographs of Napa vineyards and the white sands of Hilton Head and the shingled cottages and vibrant blue surf of Nantucket, Einhorn clicked to the decrepit main streets of St. Joe and WindMark. There was an abandoned movie theater, vacant office space, and "For Sale" signs interspersed among forlorn and spindly palm trees—an almost derelict vision. "This is Port St. Joe and WindMark," he chuckled. "We visited it and took some recent pictures." The audience found the sorry depictions hilarious, exploding with laughter.

It was a great opener. Einhorn's homespun Midwestern disposition belies polished speaking skills. But it's really his contrarianism—the enthusiasm with which he goes against the accepted wisdom—that grabs investors' attention. The audience knew that his skill at parsing financial statements and accounting trickery—notable in that Einhorn never earned an MBA—had paid off time and again. He now launched into a full bore attack on St. Joe, displaying the kind of analytical firepower that so often turns target companies into Wall Street roadkill.

Einhorn's first point was really an obvious one, apparent to anyone flipping through recent company annual reports: While St. Joe's sale of vacant land had generated $724 million in profits over the previous 10 years, the company had lost $99 million building residential communities during that time. Simply put: Development was a money-loser.

Things were going from bad to worse. In 2008 and 2009, in the midst of the financial crisis, ballooning losses in the real estate business had swamped the parent company, resulting in overall pre-tax losses for St. Joe of $61 million and $205 million. The enterprise as a whole was also a shrinking asset. The sale of the cheap land had reduced total St. Joe acreage to 577,000 from 1,086,780 ten years earlier.

Powerful forces were aligned against Greenlight, as they are against virtually every short seller. In this case, a respected value manager, Bruce Berkowitz of the $10 billion Fairholme Fund had sunk a whopping amount of money into the company, building a 29 percent stake in St. Joe. Bulls had put a positive spin on the story. There was a sparkling new airport not far from Port St. Joe, Northwest Florida Beaches International. A New York conglomerate, Leucadia National, had purchased the old local airport in downtown Panama City with an eye toward developing the land. The price: some $57 million, or $80,000 for each of the old airport's 708 acres. St. Joe bulls argued that the 35,000 acres it owned around the new airport should enjoy an only slightly lower valuation, conservatively $60,000 an acre, or a total of $2.1 billion.

That figure was roughly equivalent to St. Joe's entire market capitalization. So by this rather simplistic sum-of-the-parts calculus an investor was getting the rest of St. Joe and its vast acreage, properties and planned communities, for free. What wasn't to like in this stock?

The key difference, Einhorn dryly noted, was that the old airport was smack in the middle of a bustling metropolis (Panama City had a population of 143,000)—not vacant scrubland like the new one. St. Joe itself had donated 4,000 acres to get the Northwest Florida airport built. Now, that same land deeded to the new airport was competing with St. Joe for commercial tenants: The Airport Authority was able to issue tax-free bonds to developers, giving it an advantage St. Joe couldn't hope to match. Indeed, the value of St. Joe's acreage was, if not worthless, close to it.

As his presentation gathered steam, Einhorn shot fleeting smiles to the audience—clearly enjoying himself. As an experienced high school debater, Einhorn knew firsthand that the best speakers always seem confident, affable. And he certainly did that afternoon. There was a lot of ground to cover and Einhorn labored to keep everyone amused, peppering his speech with tweaks at the company's marketing, mixing in a cartoon slide or two into the presentation, particularly with a sardonic eye for accounting matters.

There was better to come. Maintaining a measured pace, Einhorn zeroed in on the meatiest portion of his argument—backing it up with the meticulously detailed analysis, illustrated with photographs and embellished with on-the-ground reporting by Greenlight's team of field analysts. Though Einhorn didn't mention the word *fraud*, he cast a skeptical eye on the company's rose-colored accounting, especially its balance sheet.

The big issue for St. Joe was the lack of *impairments*, or markdowns on its properties. The year was 2010. Yet even after the greatest real estate collapse since the Great Depression, the company pretended as if the bust simply hadn't happened.

Exhibit A lay south of Jacksonville, in a landlocked St. Joe project called RiverTown. Here, just 215 of the planned 4,500 planned units had been developed, and of these, just 30 had been sold—less than 1 percent of the expected grand total. St. Joe had estimated it would cost $81,111 to develop the average lot. Yet, by August 2010, they were selling for a paltry $31,250, a theoretical loss of nearly $50,000 each.

Put another way, by the time Einhorn was giving his speech, the county RiverTown was located in had nearly nine years of housing inventory to work off, even without any new construction. Yet, St. Joe carried RiverTown residential lots on its balance sheet for $74.5 million or the equivalent of $400,000 per developed lot. In fact, the 185 remaining developed lots could plausibly be worth no more than their going price of $31,250, or a total of $6 million. "We believe there should be an impairment," Einhorn declared—a refrain he would repeat again and again.

Then there was a development called SummerCamp Beach, where St. Joe was carrying $41.8 million of residential real estate on its balance sheet. Einhorn valued it at $14.9 million. "There's nothing going on at the site," he said.

Finally, at WindMark, St. Joe had marked the residential portion of the development at $164.5 million. Einhorn pegged it at $17.8 million. "This is a ghost town," he said, clicking on a slide of an empty beach club and vacant retail space.

The upshot was simple: St. Joe's economics were disastrous—and there was no way out. "It costs more to turn raw land into a finished lot than the lot is worth," Einhorn said. "Joe needs to take substantial impairments and once you take that into account the returns are quite negative."

By Einhorn's calculations, the company's remaining 577,000 in rural acreage was worth $650 to $950 million, or $7 to $10 a share, with some additional value in 41,000 other acres that St. Joe had prepped for development. The irony was that St. Joe's then relatively high share price would preclude it from finding a buyer. "Joe is stuck, "Einhorn said. "It can't build, it can't sell and it can't generate the value to cover its operating costs."

As Einhorn thanked his audience, one attendee stood up to gleefully announce that the stock had already fallen more than $5. Shares closed that day at $20.03, down more than 10 percent. By November they were trading at $17. The company hired Morgan Stanley to find a buyer, but as Einhorn had predicted, the investment bank was unable to rustle one up.

St. Joe would prove to be no pushover. Soon, shareholder Berkowitz was scrambling to rescue his investment, first joining the St. Joe board, only to about-face, resign, and campaign to oust his former fellow directors—including the CEO. Berkowitz then took a formal role as non-executive chairman at the company. He lured a new CEO, and St. Joe slashed expenses 15 percent, curtailed new investments, and drafted a plan to draw retirees to its properties. Fairholme even released its own video seeking to burnish St. Joe's image.

What Berkowitz couldn't do was fix the dubious accounting. Einhorn's assessment on St. Joe's bookkeeping was spot on. In January 2011, the U.S. Securities & Exchange Commission (SEC) opened a probe into St. Joe's impairments. And six months later the SEC began a formal investigation that included Berkowitz. The stock hit a low of $12 a share in November 2011. That calendar year, the company racked up a loss of $330 million—this time including pretax noncash impairment charges of $377.3 million—the same type of markdowns Einhorn described as lacking. Shareholders sued St. Joe for fraud, based on Einhorn's analysis; the U.S. Court of Appeals for the 11th circuit in Atlanta threw out the case in February 2013, since Greenlight's presentation was based on information that was already public.

Einhorn's St. Joe campaign is emblematic of the deep dive research that most hedge funds use to justify steep fees but seldom produce. "He is 'ready, aim, fire' kind of investor, not a 'shoot, aim, ready' investor," says Marc Cohodes, the former managing partner of Copper River Partners, a now-defunct short-selling firm. "He is smart, he is ethical, he is hardworking, he is driven. There's no one else like him."

The campaign is also a classic example of Einhorn's investment process—one that has catapulted him to rock star status. Characteristically, his forensic work is meticulously and transparently sourced, based on public documents. These could be from the tax assessor's office or St. Joe's own SEC filings. Greenlight field analysts spent weeks fanning out across Florida, building the case. It sometimes takes years of gathering evidence before Einhorn will act on an investment. He and his colleagues drew on Freedom of Information Act requests, Airport Authority Board meeting minutes, myriad county appraisers' offices, and the fine print of municipal bond offering prospectuses. They pored over county residential surveys and specific property deeds. Greenlight, in its fourth quarter 2014 letter to shareholders, called the St. Joe Co. the fund's longest standing material investment. The stock traded at under $16 a share in early 2015.

The most ringing endorsement for Greenlight's process is the fund's own track record. Since its founding in 1996, the fund has returned more than 19 percent annualized versus 9 percent for the S&P 500 Index.

Over that span, Berkshire Hathaway's Warren Buffett, to whom some acolytes compare Einhorn, has generated a return of just 12 percent at his giant conglomerate.

Along the way, Greenlight assets, including borrowed money, have ballooned to $12.3 billion by early 2015—and would have surged higher had it not been for Einhorn's policy of shutting Greenlight to cash inflows when he feels he cannot profitably put cash to work. These days, Einhorn's takedowns are front-page material, earning him a prominent place in the short-selling canon with bets against such onetime stock market darlings as Allied Capital Corp., Green Mountain Coffee Roasters, Chipotle Mexican Grill, and most famously, Lehman Brothers Holdings. In May 2012, his questions about marketing expenses on a conference call for Herbalife, the nutritional supplement retailer later targeted by rival short seller and activist William Ackman, sent the shares plummeting 5 percent.

Despite this killer reputation, Einhorn has said he doesn't like being called a short seller. Indeed, Greenlight's bullish bets have been vastly more profitable than his shorts. Telling, these include wagers on the kinds of technology and computer–related stocks many classic value investors tend to steer clear of, among them Seagate Technology, Microsoft, Xerox, and Apple. It's a distinction that places Einhorn in a class by himself—and undermines the reflexive accusations by critics that shorts bet against stocks only for nefarious purposes. Greenlight always has more money riding on Einhorn's bullish bets than his bearish ones. The hedge fund term for firms like Greenlight is *long-short*. Even during the financial collapse that began in 2008, Greenlight maintained a net long position, though the fund escaped with a loss only in the high teens for the year, compared to a 37 percent fall in the S&P 500.

Nobody hits 1,000, especially in the world of investments, yet even some of Einhorn's failures burnish his reputation. In 2006, Einhorn pushed successfully to win a seat on mortgage lender New Century Financial's board. Greenlight had been an early investor in New Century, largely because of its status as a low-cost mortgage originator—it made the loans to dicey borrowers and sold them off quickly. But the company had changed course and began packing its own portfolio with the garbage loans it had made. Einhorn joined the board hoping to get the company to reverse course. After the fund manager left, New Century later filed for bankruptcy, yet Einhorn won praise for his role.

Not immune to the siren call of professional sports franchises, like such hedge fund managers as John Henry, Mark Cuban, and David Tepper, Einhorn in 2011 tried to buy a stake in the Mets baseball team. The proposed deal was a gobsmacker: He would reportedly pay $200 million for a one-third stake in the franchise with an option to purchase a majority position over the next few years. If the owners wanted to block him, they had to pay him back the $200 million but let him keep his minority ownership. Greedy? Perhaps. But boosters give this as an example of his tenacious negotiating skills.

Critics poured cold water on his public attempt in 2012 to push Apple, Greenlight's biggest holding at the time, into issuing a series of preferred stock as a way to return the mountains of cash it was accumulating, mostly overseas. The proposed new-fangled shares—which Einhorn waggishly dubbed iPrefs—would yield 4 percent. Warren Buffett himself doused the idea, saying if he were Apple CEO Tim Cook he would ignore Einhorn. But the iPhone juggernaut did ultimately agree to hike its dividend and start a $60 billion share buy-back plan. Apple shares surged, and the Cupertino, California juggernaut has since added to the buy-back program.

Nor does it hurt Einhorn's reputation that he is rumored by some to have been Buffett's first choice to help manage Berkshire Hathaway's stock picking—a role that was ultimately accorded to former hedge fund managers Todd Combs and Ted Weschler. (Like Weschler, Einhorn won a dinner with Buffett in a charity auction to benefit San Francisco's Glide Foundation). It probably helps that Einhorn's first cousin reigns as Silicon Valley royalty—Facebook's billionaire chief operating officer Sheryl Sandberg, author of the acclaimed book *Lean In: Women, Work and the Will to Lead* (Alfred A. Knopf, 2013) about her experience as a woman executive.

Einhorn peppers his investor letters with self-deprecating wisecracks, and they've become lore in their own right, embellished with quotes ranging from the empiricist philosopher Daniel C. Dennett to Seattle Mariners' centerfielder Ken Griffey Jr. to Lou Jiwei, chairman of the China Investment Corp., the sovereign wealth fund. Like Buffett, he's not afraid to be a bit corny. In early 2013, he acknowledged his soured bets against Green Mountain Coffee Roasters his unsuccessful campaign for the iPrefs. "Our coffee was too hot, our apple bruised," he wrote.

His fans—and Einhorn collects them up and down Wall Street—describe him as a throwback to an earlier era. Most weekday mornings, he boards the Metro North commuter train in Westchester County, New York, for the 40-minute ride to Grand Central Station in Manhattan. Navigating the Beaux Art terminal's marble passageways, Einhorn dashes across Lexington Avenue, and rides the elevator to a 24th-floor vestibule where indirect lighting casts an otherworldly, greenish glow.

Why the name Greenlight? Einhorn wouldn't start his own hedge fund unless his wife, former *Barron's* columnist Cheryl Strauss Einhorn, gave her approval—or a "green light" to the new venture. "When you leave a good job to go off on your own and don't expect to make money for a while, you name the firm whatever your wife says you should," Einhorn would later write.

Certainly, Einhorn makes an unassuming master of the universe. He drives a Honda Odyssey minivan, plays fantasy baseball with his brother Daniel, and generally manages to make it home for dinner each night with his wife and three children. The Einhorns have no Hamptons summer house. He has a reputation for working strange hours; generally he wakes up at 2:00 a.m. or so to answer e-mails and read. He supplements with a nap in the afternoon at the office.

On a rain-soaked morning in March 2013, Einhorn strides into Greenlight's office. After pausing to adjust his tie, inadvertently looped around the outside of his collar, he plops his wiry six-foot-one-inch frame into a high-backed leather chair in one of Greenlight's wood-paneled conference rooms—each one jauntily named for a common bookkeeping device used to dupe investors. There is the Gain on Sale Room, a reference to a legal but dicey accounting maneuver to boost sales; the Non-Recurring Room, a bow to common gambit to hide losses by declaring them one-time events, and the Penny Room, a wink at those companies that miraculously beat analysts' earnings per share estimates, if only by a single cent.

Einhorn, like Buffett, is careful in his media interactions. An interview with this author, for example, was not permitted to be taped.

Though he doesn't talk about it, Einhorn has reasons to be wary, as many short sellers do. Simply being pegged as a short seller can restrict an investor's access to company management. And the press can be unfriendly. the *Wall Street Journal*, in a 2002 opinion piece, called his first public short campaign, against Allied Capital, a "mugging." the *New York Times* described his criticisms of companies as "rabble rousing." And commentators widely berated him for his negative views of Lehman Brothers' accounting on the onset of a market downturn, likening it more or less to shouting fire in a theater.

There was also the kerfuffle surrounding a February 2010 *Journal* story about a so-called "idea-sharing" dinner attended by Einhorn, and assorted hedge fund representatives, including Soros Fund Management, SAC Capital Advisors, and others. One topic: the likelihood that the euro would weaken amidst the collapsing Greek economy. After the story was published, the Justice Department launched an investigation into some of the funds' trading. Why Wall Street investors discussing the markets would be suspicious is unclear.

Nevertheless, in Einhorn's letter to Greenlight investors that April he went nuclear, railing against the *Journal's* "Yellow Journalism," saying the paper's article suggested the discussion might have led to market manipulation. He called the reporting "shameful." The *Journal* stood by its story.

One instance of bad "press" was self-inflicted—whether a result of pushing the regulatory envelope or ignorance of foreign legal norms. Punch Taverns PLC in 2008 owned and leased out some 8,000 pubs. In addition to a United Kingdom–wide ban on smoking in such watering holes, the financial crisis and cheap supermarket suds combined to punish the shares. The big question was whether the leveraged company would be forced to issue new stock to shore up its balance sheet. "It appears the stock is under pressure because the market misunderstands PUB's debt structure," Einhorn wrote in his third quarter 2008 investor letter. Punch suspended its dividend to save cash and Greenlight used the opportunity to snap up shares at an average price of 2.83 pounds, or just four times estimated 2008 earnings, at one point building up to a 13.3 percent stake in the company.

In June 2009, Einhorn agreed to talk by phone with Punch management and one of its bankers—under the proviso that no nonpublic material inside information be disclosed. The pertinent term is "cross the wall" in financial-speak. By crossing the wall, an investor would be given privileged insight, but couldn't trade shares until after the news was disclosed. Einhorn absolutely wouldn't agree to that.

Still, a transcript of the call shows that he hadn't expected Punch's response to its tenuous predicament. Management, including its CEO, indicated it was considering a plan to issue equity within a week or so to retire debt. That meant Greenlight's position stood to be heavily diluted. "That would be shockingly horrifying from my perspective," Einhorn said on the call. He had specifically asked not to be "wall crossed," and confirmed that no definitive decision had been made on the matter. Within minutes of the conversation, Greenlight began selling shares, ultimately shedding 11.65 million of them over four days. When the deal was announced, Punch stock fell 29.9 percent. Greenlight avoided 5.8 million pounds in losses.

In February 2012, the U.K. Financial Services Authority fined Greenlight 3.7 million pounds for "market abuse." It said that Einhorn was not aware that what he had been told was inside information. "The market abuse was not deliberate or reckless," it said in its statement. It's strange language. In a public conference call, Einhorn railed against the decision. "This matter resembles insider dealing about as much as soccer resembles football," he quipped, clearly furious.

Einhorn is succinct in answering questions. How does Einhorn decide which of his investments he'll talk about publicly?

"It's if we think we have insight that will affect the discussion about the security," Einhorn responds curtly, making it clear earning money on his public shorts is not a subject he cares to dwell on.

Can he talk about its beneficial effects of short selling on the stock market? "I'm not going to answer that question," Einhorn says. "I'll leave it to others to make that argument."

Einhorn avoids speaking about specific numbers, dates, and examples when discussing stocks and investments, long or short. He has a philanthropic bent, having donated his own proceeds of one shortselling campaign against Allied Capital to a pediatric cancer charity. He often states that he speaks publicly about fraud and deception not to make money, but because it is "the right thing to do."

He told *Worth* magazine: "I do think there is a social value in identifying companies that are doing bad things and betting against them. I've seen the demise of a fair number of these companies and it's not because we bet against them, it's because these were flawed companies. And our country, our markets, our economy are better when companies that are flawed or cheating are replaced by better ones."

What is undeniable is that unlike hundreds of firms that claim unique insights into the market, under Einhorn's leadership Greenlight has developed a stock market discipline that sets it apart—not just from other firms that short but also from the entire tribe of value-oriented money managers and anybody else who trades in stocks for a living.

In its eerily quiet 24th-floor aerie, some three dozen Greenlight professionals hone a unique craft. All value investors by definition are on the hunt for inexpensive stocks. As Einhorn puts it: "They run screens looking for things that are cheap, say less than 13 times earnings, or under 6 times cash flow. Then they say, 'Go see if there's anything there'." The process understandably can lead to a herd-like mentality.

Some short sellers, though not all, argue this type of screening arguably works better for long investments since short-selling dynamics, particularly the risks and costs of borrowing shares, encourage an investor to cover and move on if overpriced shares don't fall soon after he or she takes a position. That's one big reason some make a case against a company publicly—it helps to get the message out and the stock falling. It's also why they talk to journalists, often on condition that what they say not be attributed to them.

Greenlight trawls for stocks in a different fashion. "We tend to flip that process around," Einhorn explains. The firm's dozen or so analysts begin by developing a thesis about why a particular security is likely to be trading at a price that does not reflect its true worth—"intrinsic value" in the lexicon of investing pioneers Benjamin Graham and David Dodd—on either the upside or downside. "We ask why is it that this stock may be mispriced?" says Einhorn. The answer might be rapidly evolving competition or industry fundamentals that Wall Street has failed to appreciate. There may be company-specific characteristics, regulatory changes, or accounting problems that aren't grasped by rivals. The market may totally flub advantages, or disadvantages, of a company's business model.

"We think there are dynamics that lead to mispricing," Einhorn says. "We develop a theory as to why [a security] is mispriced, misunderstood. When we find a big enough difference between what the market sees and what we see, then we may have an investible insight."

The process works for either bullish or bearish ideas. Einhorn and his analysts seek to find out whether a particular insight they stumble upon is widespread in the market. They query industry captains, customers, rival companies, analysts, suppliers, and even other investors for their opinions.

Einhorn uses his pulpit as a bullish one too. In 2010, for example, he used an investment conference to argue that Apple displayed the characteristics of a mispriced security, too—but the stock in this case was cheap, in part given the mountain of cash on its balance sheet that seemed to get ignored. More important, short investors at the time took the position that shares of rival hardware makers like Hewlett-Packard and Nokia were trading at well under three times book value and less than annual sales. Apple stock was trading at more than five times book value and nearly four times sales.

For Einhorn, the comparison was, well, apples and oranges. Apple's distinct, crash-resistant operating system, smooth graphics, and unique features like the Siri voice interface for its iPhone gave it superior characteristics to pedestrian hardware makers like Hewlett-Packard or Nokia. "It's a software company—that makes margins higher, and revenues are more recurring," Einhorn explains in his office. "We thought it was misunderstood." By the fourth quarter of 2012 it was Greenlight's largest holding, amounting to nearly 10 percent of fund assets.

Greenlight is different in more prosaic fashions, too. The portfolio is concentrated, with the top ten holdings sometimes amounting to more than half of net assets. The benefits of diversification in reducing volatility drop off sharply after the number of stocks in a portfolio surpasses eight stocks, according to academic studies. With just 20 or so securities—long and short—to focus on, the Greenlight analyst team can dive deeper. Accordingly, Einhorn is especially attuned to risk. His fund will on occasion buy put options, which give it the right to sell a stock at a particular price before a certain date. That, in some situations, may give him the opportunity to limit losses if he's wrong or establish a short position inexpensively.

There are subtler distinctions. Though hedge fund managers don't talk about it much publicly, most stock pickers in the industry, for lack of a better term, are really long-only managers in drag. That is, they are focused on buying stocks they think will rise and hedging those positions, typically by shorting index futures or industry-specific exchange traded funds, like energy or technology, thus reducing the portfolio's overall volatility. Some are pairs traders, buying PepsiCo and shorting Coca-Cola. In a bull market, of course, the portfolio's short positions on ETFs, on indexes, or on a pairs trade are an anchor, pulling down performance.

All this can arguably be viewed as disingenuous. Hedge funds, since the first one was started by former *Fortune* editor Alfred Winslow Jones in 1949, have typically charged 1 or 2 percent management fee and 20 percent of profits schedule by virtue of their mastery of long-short investing. By contrast, a pedestrian mutual fund charges, say, 1 percent of assets under management as a fee. Vanguard Group often charges expenses of 10 basis points, or hundredths of a percentage point, or less. So the short positions assumed by hedge funds are oftentimes simply a way to charge higher fees.

Some hedge fund managers simply opt to outsource a chunk of their portfolios to dedicated short sellers like Jim Chanos of Kynikos Associates or a dwindling number of others. Though most won't confirm it publicly, these managers have at times included hedge fund stars like Leon Cooperman of Omega Advisors and even Soros Fund Management, whose founder George Soros famously made more than a billion dollars—and history—shorting the British pound in 1992. Give them this: Such managers who farm out their short investments understand the distinct skills necessary to run such a portfolio.

Greenlight, sui generis, thinks differently. Einhorn's aim is to turn a profit on each of the fund's short positions, not mitigate market downdrafts. "We do not short to hedge," Einhorn emphasizes in his writing. "If we are uncomfortable with the risk in a position, we simply reduce or eliminate it." Einhorn and his analysts constantly probe and reassess positions in Greenlight's portfolio, revisiting numbers and keeping on top of a company's rivals, suppliers, and customers—the legwork of good investigative analysis.

The firm pays attention to investors on the other side of its trades—those that are long the same stocks Greenlight is short and vice versa. "We're constantly asking. 'Are we right?'" Einhorn says. "'Do they think what we think they think?'"

Greenlight is looking to ensure its analysis is at odds with that of its rivals. There is logic to that somewhat counterintuitive insight. After all, if most investors agree with Greenlight on fundamentals and therefore a stock's prospects, what kind of edge can Einhorn hope to have in the market? Not much.

There is no monopoly on truth in the stock market. Greenlight is open to rival arguments and sometimes swayed. In 2003, Einhorn was short Goodyear Tire & Rubber Co.—a classic rustbelt behemoth with a unionized workforce facing mounting competition from subsidized, lower-cost rivals overseas. The company hemorrhaged $767 million that year, its third of annual losses. The company's total stock market capitalization, the value of all its shares, had deflated to less than $1.4 billion versus $9.9 billion five years earlier. It had all the hallmarks of roadkill.

Some insightful investors, however, saw upside—or more specifically, the possibility that the storied American industrial hulk could find some way to rebound. Sifting through SEC filings, Greenlight analysts saw that distressed debt wizard David Tepper's Appaloosa Management LP had built up a substantial position in the tire company, betting on a turnaround that Greenlight saw no evidence of. It was confounding. The question was, "Why?" Einhorn picked up the phone.

The Greenlight founder says he doesn't recall details of the conversation—and does not seem eager to share what he does. Tepper, who describes his memory as "near photographic," says the conversation quickly turned to what in Wall Street–speak is sometimes called the "optionality" imbedded in Goodyear's stock.

Optionality is a common sense notion that works like this: Given Goodyear's formidable capital structure, there was plenty of money to burn through—any bankruptcy would be in the distant future, giving management a good shot at a successful restructuring or other opportunity to turn the business around. There were factories to shutter, acquisitions to make, even a possible sale. The Akron, Ohio-based industrial icon had $1.5 billion in cash on its balance sheet and an enterprise value of $5.7 billion. That kind of capital gave it a lot of time—and resources—to work through its problems.

Tepper, in an interview, says he thought it wouldn't take all that much to do so. "Basically we thought the stock had a lot of operating leverage and financial leverage," he says. "We looked at the size of the capital structure. They had a lot of runway. There were a lot of things that could go right." Einhorn, for his part, says that while he recalls not being entirely convinced, Tepper's arguments were sufficient to seed doubts in his mind. Greenlight soon covered the short position.

It was certainly the right move. Goodyear slashed capital expenditures in 2003 and suspended its dividend, among other things. Shares went on to rally, generating a fourfold return for investors from the start of 2003 through 2007. "We change our minds frequently," Einhorn says. Tepper chuckles: "I'm sure he pays more attention to optionality."

When bets do go wrong, Einhorn owns up, often highlighting them in his letters to investors. In 2008, Greenlight went long on Nyrstar NV, a Belgian zinc smelting company cobbled together from some cast-off business operations of Australian miner Zinifex and Umicore, a Belgian materials company—a *carve-out* in Wall Street parlance.

Greenlight's thesis was that fresh management would turn the company around quickly. "We thought this zinc-smelting carve out's new CEO would create a path to stable earnings, " Einhorn wrote in January 2010. "He didn't deliver and the stock cratered." Greenlight got in at 17.46 euros and sold at 7.03 euros. Einhorn doesn't sugarcoat his errors. He nevertheless looked on the bright side. "The good news is we didn't sell when the stock fell to 1 euro," Einhorn wrote.

Publicizing such blunders does more than just inform those who have entrusted their capital to Greenlight. It helps Einhorn avoid similar errors in the future. "When something does go wrong, I like to think about the bad decisions and learn from them so that hopefully I don't repeat the same mistakes," he says. Characteristically he deadpans, with a self-deprecating tone that investors and Wall Street fans have come to love: "That leaves me plenty of room to make fresh mistakes going forward."

That self-critical disposition—and willingness to change—prompted Einhorn to a wholesale reassessment of his approach to investing after the 2008–2009 financial crisis. Until then, Greenlight was a strictly bottom-up, fundamental value investment firm, albeit working both long and short books. The focus was on a portfolio company's balance sheet and earnings prospects, as well as its strengths and weaknesses relative to competitors. The overall economy, interest rates, and currency swings were of less concern—if Einhorn worried about them at all.

Like a lot of value investors of the period he was bitten—and badly, too. An early holding was MDC Holdings, a large homebuilder based in Denver with major operations in fast-growing markets such as Colorado, northern Florida, Las Vegas, Tucson, Salt Lake City, and Southern California. Greenlight had begun purchasing MDC shares the second day after the fund opened at under $6 a share and had ridden them as housing prices first rose, and then soared—especially in the white-hot markets MDC operated in.

The company's fundamentals were bullish. Unlike many rivals, MDC had a relatively strong balance sheet, with a debt-to-equity ratio of just 45 percent in 2005. And its business model provided it with a competitive advantage: the company owned far less land than rivals. It typically would not build without a firm order in hand, reducing risk and giving it operating flexibility. MDC management, under CEO Larry Mizel, was ranked top notch and owned more than a quarter of the company's shares to boot.

Greenlight hung on over the years: By mid-2005, MDC shares traded at around $70, and Einhorn gave a speech at that year's Ira Sohn Investment Research Conference lauding the company's prospects. His speech followed one by Stanley Druckenmiller, the founder of Duquesne Capital Management and former portfolio manager for Soros Fund Management's Quantum Fund. Druckenmiller's success—in contrast to Einhorn's—derived from prescient bets on macroeconomic factors on world interest rates dictated by such economic factors and GDP growth, inflation, trade balances and political change—things that drive currencies, government bonds and, yes, home building. All big-picture stuff. As a so-called macro investor, Druckenmiller used his speech to warn about housing.

Druckenmiller's insights fell on at least one pair of deaf ears— Einhorn's. "I ignored Stan, rationalizing that even if he were right, there was no way to know when he would be right," he said years later. "The lesson that I have learned is that it isn't reasonable to be agnostic about the big picture."

MDC finished 2008 at under $29 a share, contributing to Greenlight's flagship fund's double digit loss for the year, the only calendar year the fund finished in the red. The S&P 500 lost 37 percent. "Having my eyes open to the big picture doesn't mean abandoning stock picking, but does mean managing the long-short exposure ratio more actively, worrying about what may be brewing in certain industries, and when appropriate, buying some just-in-case insurance for foreseeable macro risks even if they are hard to time."

From there, Einhorn recalibrated, focusing on the Federal Reserve, and how its then-Chair, Ben Bernanke, was managing the financial crisis and its aftermath. It was hard not to, given the sharply increased correlation in the stock market. By late 2011, nearly all of a stock sector's price movement was due to the overall direction of the S&P 500. Many market players say it made less of a difference what stocks or industries an investor chose to invest in than it normally would have since the prices were largely determined by the direction of the stock market overall, which itself was unnaturally dependent on the Federal Reserves' easy money policies—"financial repression" to its critics.

In this environment, experts say, stock-picking skills were of relatively less utility. High quality or poor, it was not a stock's fundamentals that determined its price but investor perception of the Federal Reserve's next bout of quantitative easing—its policy of buying back massive amounts of bonds to keep interest rates low and credit flowing.

In addition to punishing fixed-income pensioners, whose income were tied to the near-zero interest rates on bonds in their retirement portfolios, Bernanke's policies effectively sidelined some veteran stock pickers—and mowed down dedicated short sellers wholesale. The only pertinent investment decision was whether to be in the market or not, depending on the consensus opinion of the central bank's actions—"risk on" or "risk off" in industry argot.

Einhorn reached back to his days as a government major at Cornell to help craft generally scathing assessments of the policies of Bernanke and former Treasury Secretary Timothy Geithner. He likened big banks to out-of-control teenagers who had partied wildly while their parental regulators were away. The banks, he declared, should have been left to pay for the mess they helped fuel. "The ATMs could have continued working, even with forced debt-to-equity conversions that would not have required any public funds," he said in 2009. "Instead, our leaders responded by handing over hundreds of billions of taxpayer dollars to protect the speculative investments of bank shareholders and creditors."

While continuing to invest in undervalued stocks, Einhorn steered Greenlight into a series of macro bets, informed by the gaping deficits that the central bank's policies were fostering. With the dollar at risk, by 2011 Greenlight held the second largest position in the SPDR Gold Trust. "Gold does well when monetary and fiscal policies are poor and does poorly when they appear sensible," he said in late 2009, adding that holds true whether the result is inflationary or deflationary. "Holding gold is better than holding cash, especially now where both earn no yield."

Einhorn bought long-dated call options on much higher U.S. and Japanese interest rates, giving him the right to profit if rates rose. By doing so, he pointed out, Greenlight limited the possible loss to what he shelled out to purchase the options. Shorting the underlying debt would have exposed him to the possibilities of steep losses.

This new direction dovetailed with Einhorn's enhanced profile as a pundit on global macroeconomic policy and regulation. In January 2009 he co-authored an op-ed piece in the *New York Times* with acclaimed author Michael Lewis. "Incredibly, intelligent people the world over remain willing to lend us money and even listen to our advice; they appear not to have realized the full extent of our madness," the op-ed said.

Soon Einhorn was developing a following among what might be called the "macroscenti"—at least those at war with Bernenke's quantitative easing. In May 2012, he penned a takedown of Bernanke's quantitative easing policy, then in its fourth year, for the Huffington Post, when GDP was growing at a sluggish 2.1 percent annualized. It read:

A Jelly Donut is a yummy mid-afternoon energy boost.

Two Jelly Donuts are an indulgent breakfast.

Three Jelly Donuts may induce a tummy ache.

Six Jelly Donuts—that's an eating disorder.

Twelve Jelly Donuts is fraternity pledge hazing.

The piece went viral. Wary investors—stung by the stock market losses of the 2000–2002 technology meltdown and then again during the 2008–2009 financial crisis—in fact resisted stocks until the financial repression of low interest rates made it too painful to resist. They began snapping up equities, arguably setting them up for the next downward leg of the cycle.

That kind of criticism has put Einhorn in an unlikely alliance with some of the Austrian school acolytes (they've been dubbed "austerians" in some circles) on the subject of Federal Reserve policy. "They do not understand or relate to the prime component of capitalism and a free market: Greed," Einhorn wrote, referring to the Federal Reserve. "And because they do not understand greed, they also do not understand fear, which presents a double whammy for making bad policy decisions."

Six months later he reiterated his conclusion at a conference sponsored by the *Economist* magazine. "We would be way better off if we did pretty much the opposite of the current monetary policy," he said. Nobel Prize–winning economist Paul Krugman, who argued that Bernanke should have done far more to stimulate the economy, coined a term for those opposed to the Fed's policies—"sadomonetarists." Name-calling aside, it's fair to say that Einhorn won't be on any short list for Treasury Secretary or Fed governor under any administration soon. But it does contribute to the enigma of David Michael Einhorn, a man whose DNA seemed baked through with matters of markets, balance sheets, monetary policy, and business from childhood.

Einhorn was born in 1968, spending the first seven years of a comfortable youth in Demarest, New Jersey, a prosperous suburb ten miles from Manhattan. His father, Stephen, helped negotiate the sale of the family business, Adelphi Paints and, enjoying the back and forth of the process, decided to try his hand as an independent investment banker, working out of a spare room.

To escape the financial pressures of metropolitan New York, the family set out for Wisconsin, where his mother Nancy had grown up. Together, with his brother, the Einhorn family, settled into Fox Point (2010 population: 6,100), a comfortable community on the shimmering shores of Lake Michigan, 10 miles north of Milwaukee.

The tight-knit Einhorn family was intimately engaged in money matters. At dinner, they on occasion chattered about business and the stock market. Facing off at family gatherings were two contravening forces: Grandpa Ben, on his father's side, was decidedly laissez faire. He distrusted the Federal Reserve, feared inflation, and advocated investments in precious metals and gold mining stocks. "Grandpa was a staunch libertarian who believed in the gold standard," Einhorn says. By contrast, his maternal grandmother, "Grandma Cookie" as Einhorn still refers to her, was an avid stock picker and fan of Louis Rukeyser's *Wall Street Week*, the PBS program. "I still remember the jingle," Einhorn laughs. Her focus was on the growth stocks of the 1970s and 1980s era: IBM, McDonald's, Nike, and Walgreens. Einhorn would eventually absorb both these influences into his worldview.

Einhorn's father toiled to build his mergers and acquisition (M&A) business, Einhorn & Associates. It was tough. Clients would backtrack on the fee his firm was owed on a deal—incensing his mother, who counseled him to demand full payment. Stephen Einhorn believed being flexible on fees would help build the business in the long term. David Einhorn opines that he mixes his father's long-term perspective and perseverance and his mother's negotiating toughness.

Today, Stephen Einhorn is also chairman of a venture capital fund, Capital Midwest, which he oversees with David Einhorn's younger brother, Daniel, and another partner.

Nicolet High School in Glendale, Wisconsin, was an impressive institution, producing a stream of overachievers destined for elite colleges. Alumni include Oprah Winfrey. Einhorn was unlikely to win popularity contests. He was focused and kept to a core group of close friends. "David had a personality where a group of people who really liked him, did," says Stacey Shor, a classmate who met him in third grade. "Other people didn't."

Einhorn wasn't the type to angle for mainstream acceptance. A math enthusiast, he wore button downs, not Aerosmith tee-shirts like some classmates, and projected a purposeful, serious air. "He was always a mature guy," says Shor. "There's always been an intensity to David. He was never spontaneous or light-hearted. "

In Einhorn's senior year, 1987, the four-person Nicolet debating team made it to the state championships. At the debate, Shor recalls Einhorn's confidence, quick wit, and use of reams of color-coded research material. He was an organizational whiz. She doesn't recall who won, but guesses it was Einhorn's team.

Einhorn and his wife in 2006 donated $1 million to bankroll the Milwaukee Urban Debate League.

With an impressive academic record, Einhorn was Ivy League–bound for Cornell University, in bucolic Ithaca, New York. Einhorn earned a B.A. in government and, once again, impressed his teachers. "He wasn't outgoing, but I liked him because he was so f--king smart," says government professor Theodore Lowi. "He was just the brightest guy around."

At Cornell his talent for deep research became apparent. After spending a semester in Washington, D.C., Einhorn had an idea for his honors thesis: examining the economic impact of airline industry deregulation. Lowi recalls criticizing the proposal, arguing that the subject matter was too big—and that as a government major, he wasn't qualified to analyze the financial ramifications of the subject. Einhorn produced a project report he had prepared during his semester in Washington. "I was absolutely amazed at the results," Lowi wrote in a confidential recommendation for Einhorn in December 1990. "What he had done was already the equivalent of most acceptable honors theses, and it possessed in addition to that a professional level of analysis that I don't see among economics graduate students."

Not that Lowi and his student saw eye to eye—and Einhorn's debating skills came into play. Lowi was a virulent critic of government backing of banks. "I thought the FDIC (Federal Deposit Insurance Corp.) was going too far," Lowi says. "I'm antagonistic towards how banks are assisted." Einhorn pushed back, Lowi recalls, besting him in arguments by pointing out the salutary impact of government help—a position somewhat at odds with his current views.

Ultimately, Lowi's entreaties for Einhorn to pursue an academic career came to naught. "I proselytized him to get him get to his Ph.D. in economics or political philosophy," Lowi recalls. In fact, Einhorn was rejected by several Ph.D programs. Years later, Einhorn, by then wealthy, bumped into his old professor at a campus dedication. "You son of a bitch," Lowi teased him. "You went off to get all that money."

Cornell wasn't all studying. It was there that Einhorn met his future wife, Cheryl Strauss, who would go on to work as an award-winning journalist at *IDD* magazine, *Barron's* financial weekly, and the television program *Inside Edition*. The two are active donors to the school's Hillel program, the Jewish cultural organization, along with Engaged Cornell, an initiative to encourage undergraduate community activism. The couple graduated in 1991, she magna cum laude and he summa cum laude and a member of Phi Beta Kappa.

Einhorn met with campus recruiters as he cast about for a career. He admits to being clueless on his future. One interview was with the Central Intelligence Agency. Wall Street was dusting itself off from the recession that followed the first Gulf War. The Dow Jones Industrials was climbing toward 3,000.

As the economy picked up, so too did M&A, securities underwritings, and leveraged buyouts. Einhorn met with a recruiter for Donaldson Lufkin & Jenrette Securities Corp., the pioneering firm founded by William Donaldson, Dan Lufkin, and Richard Jenrette. The investment bank was known for its top-ranked stock analysis—"the house that research built," as it was dubbed.

Einhorn told his interviewer that he was willing to work hard. He had no idea of the 100-hour weeks that he was expected to clock. Einhorn, though a diligent worker, soon came to loathe the investment banking culture.

"The attitude was, 'If you don't come in on Saturday don't even think of coming in on Sunday,'" Einhorn recalls. His father, running his own M&A business in Wisconsin, had usually made it home for dinner. At DLJ's merchant banking division, associates were expected to work through the night to satisfy the capriciousness of their bosses. "I just didn't like the way people treated each other," says Einhorn. "It was like having 200 bosses." Within three months, the gangly Einhorn lost 15 pounds.

Robert Medway, a DLJ colleague, recalls Einhorn being asked by a senior vice president to compile detailed one-page analyses of each station in a multioutlet TV broadcasting group that DLJ was considering buying—work that had no bearing on whether the firm would proceed with the deal.

"Why are we doing this?" Einhorn asked him.

"Because I said so," the senior vice president responded.

Opines Medway: "People had nothing better to do than flex their muscles."

Einhorn does credit DLJ with teaching him some Wall Street basics. "I learned some accounting," he says. "How to integrate a balance sheet with cash flow and income statements. Basic tools." After two years of sleep deprivation, humiliation, and make-work projects, Einhorn jumped when a headhunter called in 1993 to ask whether he was interested in a job at a hedge fund. "What's a hedge fund?" he recalls asking.

Einhorn joined Siegler, Collery & Company, a fund with $150 million in assets using a deep-value, bottom-up investment approach. The principals certainly had pedigrees. Gary Siegler had worked under corporate raider Carl Icahn, identifying cheap targets. Peter Collery had cut his teeth at Dillon Read & Co., a white shoe investment bank.

Siegler Collery did in pairs trading in one strategy. Under Collery's mentorship, Einhorn learned the precepts of value investing. He also developed the somewhat finer art of smelling out problems at companies—ambiguities in their financial statements that suggested dishonesty, ascertaining when management's interests were not aligned with those of shareholders, or simply when industry dynamics were unhealthy.

Einhorn would sift through SEC documents, interview management, analysts, suppliers, customers and rivals. What were the economics of the business? How were these reflected in the earnings? Then he would write up a report and supply pages of documentation to Collery, discussing what he had found. Overnight, Collery would read through Einhorn's research and arrive the next day with a list of questions—basically, what had been overlooked. "He taught me to ask questions—for example, 'Why was a stock misvalued?'"

At Siegler Collery, Einhorn spotted his first short sale—Homecare Management, a mail-order pharmacy selling drugs to organ transplant patients. Einhorn doesn't recall specifics but says Collery's focus on details stoked his skepticism. "The numbers didn't add up between revenues, the number of patients, and the profits," Einhorn says. Management evasiveness compounded his suspicions. "They said things that were inconsistent." Eventually, the CEO was sentenced to prison for fraud.

As 1995 drew to a close, two years after marrying Cheryl Strauss, Einhorn was at a crossroads. The U.S. stock market was on fire. Stocks were up 37.5 percent for the year, with the Dow Jones Industrials topping 5,117 for the first time. It was time to strike out on his own, or in this case, with a colleague from Siegler Collery, Jeff Keswin.

The two sketched out their hedge fund business on a paper napkin. Einhorn would manage money and Keswin market the fund. They secured a 150-square-foot office at a "hedge fund hotel"—an office building with space leased to start-ups like theirs run by a prime broker-age, in this case Spears, Leeds & Kellogg. Initial capital: $900,000, with more than half that from Einhorn's relatives.

At the outset, Einhorn decided against pairs trading, figuring that with superior research he could do better. The reason was that while one part of the trade, for example a big short on Delta Air Lines, might comprise a great opportunity, choosing a corresponding industry long, say, Southwest Airlines, might be only moderately attractive—if at all. Einhorn wanted to concentrate on his best ideas only and was willing to cope with industry risk or market risk by reducing exposures.

Greenlight started out with a bang. The fund finished its first year with a gain of 37.1 percent for the eight months it was in business in 1996 and $13 million in assets under management. The firm was bol-stered by gains in small cap companies—homebuilder MDC, retailer C.R. Anthony, and EMCOR, a mechanical and electrical contractor. Einhorn's focus on a handful of well-researched long and short positions was paying off. The next year proved even better, with Greenlight gar-nering a 58 percent return and assets surging to $75 million as word of Einhorn's investing prowess spread.

One early short, in 1998, was Sirrom Capital, a so-called business development company. BDCs, as they are known, have a gamey history. Overseen by the Small Business Administration (SBA), they bankroll small, mostly private companies that can't attract traditional bank financ-ing. BDCs often get free warrants to purchase stock in the small busi-nesses they lend money to—*kickers*, in Wall Street speak.

The lure for BDC investors is yield. They charged usurious rates. BDCs pay no corporate income tax and often yield 7 or 8 percent.

Einhorn saw a ruse. Greenlight analysts built a spreadsheet that tracked Sirrom's loans and warrant portfolio. Sirrom's rapid growth was obscuring the fact that over time, roughly 40 percent of its loans eventually went bad.

It also seemed to be dragging its feet in marking its portfolio down to fair value. Einhorn zeroed in on Sirrom's 1997 filings. The audi-tor, Arthur Andersen, had omitted a sentence that it had included in the prior year's opinion evaluating Sirrom's portfolio valuations. The deleted phrase read: "We believe the procedures are reasonable and the documentation appropriate."

It was a smoking gun. Greenlight initiated a short position and watched as Sirrom shares climbed to $32 a share in May 1998. Then, following the announcement of two serious loan losses in July, Sirrom shares collapsed, tumbling to $15 and then $10 when Greenlight covered its short position. The stock hit $3 in October. Business lender Finova Group acquired Sirrom in 1999.

Three years later, in early 2002, managers from a rival hedge fund contacted Einhorn. They asked for his insight into another BDC—Washington, D.C.–based Allied Capital. They thought the company was similarly mismarking its portfolio.

Einhorn assigned Greenlight analyst James Lin to construct a database, tracking as best he could costs and valuations of investments in Allied's portfolio over several years, much as Greenlight had done with Sirrom. Some price data was not available, but the pattern was similar. Allied was refusing to assign fair values to its myriad debt holdings, judging by market prices. It was issuing new shares and using proceeds to help pay out a fat 7 percent "dividend."

Other issues surfaced. Allied had embarked on a strategy two years earlier to obtain control of many of its portfolio companies by scooping up their stock. Then Allied would charge the companies for a variety of services—accounting, marketing, merger advice—effectively milking the companies for fees.

Einhorn arranged a conference call with Allied management in April 2002, taping the conversations. Upon questioning, the head of investor relations, Suzanne Sparrow, told Einhorn that the company did not write down loans even when warrants it held in the same company cratered. That, she said, was because the impairment on such a loan was not deemed "permanent."

If a loan does decline in value, Sparrow told Einhorn, Allied still wouldn't write it down because of the possibility it might rebound.

Then there was this sparkling gem, in which Sparrow explained the company's generous valuation policy. "That's the beautiful thing about a BDC as a vehicle," she enthused. "You don't have, you know, the bank regulators leaning on you to say you must write off this asset."

Lastly: Between 2001 and 2002, Arthur Andersen, Allied's auditor, had excised exactly the same language it used from its opinion on Allied as it had from Sirrom's three years earlier.

To anyone paying attention it was like a big, flashing neon sign reading: "Danger!"

It was certainly enough for Einhorn. He maneuvered a fat 7.5 percent of Greenlight's assets into a short position against Allied, then trading at $26.25. The Ira Sohn Investment Conference was scheduled for May, and Einhorn had been invited to speak.

Standing behind the podium, visibly nervous and with his name-tag comically askew, Einhorn joked about how he had put his wife to sleep rehearsing his presentation the previous night. He then launched into his fast-paced takedown. "What we have here is a closed-end mezzanine fund that is trading at two times net asset value," he declared.

In a speech lasting under 20 minutes, Einhorn went to town on Allied's loan portfolio. No, he couldn't determine the initial costs of many loans in Allied's portfolio because they were not disclosed, but Einhorn nailed down some choice atrocities. He pointed out that Allied was carrying bonds of telecom startup Velocita at 40 cents on the dollar while they were trading at 2 cents in the market. It hadn't written down its Startec Global Communications investment at all until the fourth quarter of 2001. By that point, the company had already filed for bankruptcy.

Einhorn waxed incredulous over the implications of Allied's valuation policies. These allowed the company to avoid writing down the vast majority of what he was sure were hefty losses. In 2001, Allied credit losses totaled just 1 percent of its portfolio. The previous year, by contrast, the default rate on high yield bonds was 12 percent, and over 5 years, 6 percent. It was crazy. "They must be great underwriters," Einhorn scoffed.

A 100 percent–owned Allied division, Business Loan Express, or BLX, which accounted for a big chunk of its profits, was paying Allied 25 percent interest on an $80 million loan. Allied was neither consolidating results of BLX nor eliminating the intra-company interest payments from its income statement. The effect was essentially counting as income money that merely passed from one of the company's pockets into another. BLX's business would eventually bring the entire Allied edifice crashing down.

First, though, Einhorn was drawn into a Kafkaesque odyssey in which he and Allied waged a public, at times scorched-earth battle in courts, with the regulators and the media—each accusing the other of disingenuousness, lying and fraud. Einhorn's recounting of the tale makes for a sometimes-gripping 426-page narrative, *Fooling Some of the People All of the Time* (2011, John Wiley & Sons, Inc.). It's worthwhile reading.

The day after the speech, Allied stock dropped almost 20 percent to $21 a share. Allied held a conference call. CEO Bill Walton and Allied executives hadn't heard or read Einhorn's speech and so skated over the issues that he had raised. For example, Sweeney said the reason Arthur Andersen had dropped the sentence endorsing Allied's valuations of portfolio securities was due to changes in an accounting industry audit guide. This proved to be untrue—there had been no such change. Walton ignored the question of why payments from BLX, a 100 percent-owned subsidiary, should be counted as income. He did talk about the value he saw in Velocita senior debt. Allied, in fact, held subordinated debt, which the company would write down to zero in a matter of weeks. And Walton opined about his confidence in the Startec investment, including a $10 million "money good" piece of secured paper that, again, was shortly written down to zero.

Einhorn shouldn't have been surprised, Allied's chief operating officer, Joan Sweeney, and chief financial officer, Penni Roll, had in February written and later posted on the Internet a white paper entitled "Valuation of Securities Held by Business Development Companies." They claimed that SEC regulations for valuing a security are not applicable to BDCs. And they suggested they followed different parameters, those set by the SBA.

Greenlight, working with another short seller, Jim Carruthers of Eastbourne Capital Management, began tracking down questionable loans made by Allied and its BLX subsidiary. Carruthers found court cases showing senior BLX executives were encouraging applicants to fill out fraudulent documentation to obtain loans from the SBA.

A key rainmaker for BLX was one Patrick Harrington. Greenlight hired Kroll Associates, the private investigation firm, to look further into BLX. Together with Carruthers, Kroll found millions of dollars in loans made to cheap motels, gas stations, and convenience stores. When businesses bellied up, BLX would often simply not write down the value of the defaulted loan. One reason: BLX executives got compensated based on the value of the loans they made, not on profitability or any other reasonable metric. BLX loans defaulted at three times the rate of other SBA-sponsored loans.

Allied didn't care. As a BDC, the SBA, not Allied, took almost all of the risk from the loans. Fully 75 percent of the loan was guaranteed against loss by the agency. Taxpayers were unwittingly subsidizing the charade.

More important was Allied's use of *gain-on-sale* accounting, which recognizes most of the income from a loan at the time of its origination. The likelihood of the loan being repaid was of small consequence from a profit and loss standpoint.

Some took note of the analysis proffered by Greenlight, which Einhorn posted on the company website. Notably, the indefatigable *Wall Street Journal* reporter Jesse Eisinger, now with the nonprofit Pulitzer Prize–winning ProPublica reporting website, bird-dogged parts of the tortuous saga.

Forces backing Allied stirred. Example: Deutsche Bank analyst Mark Alpert initiated coverage of Allied with a highly unusual "sell" recommendation in mid-2002. At the behest of Allied, the New York Stock Exchange launched an investigation into Alpert. By the end of the year, he no longer worked at Deutsche, which soon was picking up choice investment banking work from Allied.

The SBA expressed little interest in tackling Allied or BLX and defended their loan records. The much-criticized agency likely realized the dubious accounting reflected as poorly on its oversight as it did on Allied and BLX.

In March 2003, Greenlight received a subpoena from the New York State Attorney General Eliot Spitzer, whose publicity-generating pursuit of financial firms would soon propel him into the governorship. Einhorn was asked to answer questions about Greenlight's relationships with other hedge funds, such as Gotham Partners—run by William Ackman, another long-short manager.

Within the month, the SEC followed suit with its own probe. With the attending publicity—Spitzer's office leaked its investigation to the *Wall Street Journal*—Einhorn's wife was fired from her job as a columnist at *Barron's*, the financial newsweekly.

Ultimately, after days of back and forth questioning of Einhorn by an agency lawyer, the SEC did precisely nothing. The lawyer was later hired as a consultant by Allied. For its part, Spitzer's office, wisely, never followed up at all.

By the summer of 2004, Einhorn was hearing disturbing stories. The phones of *MarketWatch* journalist Herb Greenberg and others linked to the Allied story were being hacked by someone asking their phone companies to open an online billing account, a ruse known as "pretexting". The person had gotten access to all their phone records. When Einhorn asked AT&T whether someone had done the same thing to him, he was told they had.

Einhorn, infuriated, sent a March 2005 letter to Allied's board demanding an investigation into the pretexting. In a perfunctory fashion, Allied claimed it had looked into the matter and reported that the company had discovered no evidence of wrongdoing.

Einhorn continued to badger Allied, writing in a September 2006 letter to the company that "the board clearly has an obligation to investigate such illegal behavior." Again, Allied brushed off Einhorn's accusations.

Then, in February 2007 the company abruptly about-faced, issuing a press release stating: "Allied Capital has become aware that an agent of the Company obtained what were represented to be telephone records of David Einhorn and which purport to be records of calls from Greenlight Capital during a period of time in 2005." Einhorn testified before Congress on the subject of pretexting. It later turned out that Allied told the SEC that the lawyer it hired as a consultant was responsible for the pretexting.

It was a victory. But things had already begun to turn against Allied. In late 2004 the Justice Department had begun a criminal investigation into Allied and BLX's loan practices—though the company maintained it was merely a follow-on to Greenlight's accusations. In fact, in September 2005, Einhorn went to Washington, D.C., and presented federal prosecutors with a 50-page slide show, meeting with assistant U.S. attorneys and FBI agents.

With the government investigating fraud, Greenlight found a different way to make some money. Under a statute known as the False Claims Act, a private citizen who uncovers fraud against the government is entitled to a portion of the amount recovered, typically one-third or so. Given the scale of the losses that the SBA was likely to have suffered as a result of BLX's loans, this could amount to a sizable chunk of change.

As Einhorn's book lays out, Greenlight teamed up with a retired real estate developer who on his own was turning up dozens of sham transactions at BLX—particulary a raft of suspect loans to shrimp boat owners, part of an industry reeling from aquafarming and other competition. They filed a False Claims Act suit in Atlanta, in December 2005.

A big break for Greenlight came in late 2006. Allied, in its third quarter earnings statement, revealed that BLX was having trouble making loans and that the SBA Office of the Inspector General and the Justice Department had launched an investigation into the subsidiary and its Detroit office, which was soon shuttered. Nobody seemed to notice.

On February 28, 2007, Allied abruptly wrote down its investment in BLX by $74 million. In October of that year, BLX's Patrick Harrington, former head of the Detroit office, pled guilty to conspiracy and making a false statement to a federal grand jury. (In November 2008 he was sentenced to 10 years in prison).

Amazingly, throughout all this time, the share price of Allied Capital remained robust. Though it had tumbled from more than $25 a share to less than $17 in the months after Einhorn's initial speech, it soon recovered, hitting more than $30 by early 2004. Despite the mounting questions about the company's loans, its portfolio valuation, and the BLX write down, shares kept above the $30 threshold for most of 2006 and 2007. Investors were more interested in the Allied dividend than fraud.

In late 2007, the Office of the Inspector General of the SBA released a report on the agency's handling of the Allied and BLX case. It was so heavily redacted as to be nearly worthless—data was blacked out as well as entire passages, all at the request of BLX and the SBA general counsel. Indeed, three of the report's five recommendations were redacted entirely. A nonredacted version, disclosed by the *New York Times* in August 2008, showed that these recommendations called for better lending practices by BLX, a reduction in SBA guarantees until the improved practices were met and suspension of "preferred status" for BLX until the improvements were made.

The SBA later argued that it was worried about putting BLX out of business. By now the credit crunch was pummeling Allied's shares, as it could no longer maintain its dividends. In October 2008, BLX, which had changed its name to Ciena Capital, filed for bankruptcy, forcing Allied to use $320 million to backstop Ciena's line of credit. From there, as it slashed dividend payments, Allied's shares began a precipitous decline from well over $30 a share to under a dollar at the market low of March 2009.

In October 2009, the Department of Justice told Greenlight that it had reached a tentative agreement to settle its False Claims Act suit and wanted Einhorn to sign off. The case would be settled for $26.4 million, less than a tenth of the $336 million Einhorn felt appropriate. It was a disheartening victory: Ares Capital, another BDC, company, agreed within the week to acquire Allied for cash and stock worth $3.47 a share.

Greenlight's general partner donated its $6 million in profits from Allied to charity, including the Project on Government Oversight and the Center for Public Integrity. In his midtown offices, Einhorn waxes incredulous when this author asks him whether the end results of his Allied Capital campaign were worth the efforts he and his colleagues expended. "Certainly not," he says, "There's no investment that's worth that amount of grief."

It was a lesson that was to serve him well in Greenlight's history-changing campaign—one that, if it had been successful, might just have averted catastrophe and spared the world some of the worst aspects of the 2008–2009 financial crisis and great recession that followed: Einhorn's very vocal short-selling effort against Lehman Brothers. After all, if the storied investment bank's dysfunctional management, the Federal Reserve System, or the recalcitrant Treasury Department had acted to shore up Lehman's overleveraged balance sheet when Einhorn first raised his concerns, capital could have been injected in time to avert the disaster that followed, and an earth-shattering bankruptcy might have been avoided.

Einhorn pauses in the interview to emphasize a point that he thinks is sometimes overlooked—and it's one that he's not necessarily proud about. "There were people who thought there was a problem with the entire housing market early on," he says, then pausing for emphasis. "I was not one of those people."

One of the earliest inklings of the brewing storm came to his attention on August 9, 2007, when BNP Paribas announced it was suspending investor redemptions at three of its funds—Parvest Dynamic ABS, BNP

Paribas ABS Euibor, and BNP Paribas ABS Eonia. Earlier that year, two Bear Stearns hedge funds invested in mortgage-backed securities had collapsed spectacularly, creating a ripple of fear that quickly spread through the credit markets. But these BNP funds were conservative money market–like offerings and so should have remained unaffected. BNP, after all, itself had negligible exposure to subprime mortgages, which over the previous decade had been securitized into highly rated "structured products" such as collateralized debt obligations and their ilk. But the bank issued a statement explaining its predicament. "The complete evaporation of liquidity in certain market segments of the U.S. securitization market has made it impossible to value certain assets fairly regardless of their quality or credit rating," the bank said.

The news, from Einhorn's perspective, was both puzzling and ominous. If a French bank with minimal exposure to the U.S. securitized mortgage market was having trouble valuing assets, what could that mean for the hundreds of U.S. financial institutions whose opaque balance sheets and portfolios were loaded with all kinds of dicey subprime securities, not to mention derivatives and related toxic stuff?

Einhorn had a feeling that credit markets were about to turn ugly in a hurry—regardless of whether the CDOs and other securities carried AAA ratings from agencies like Standard & Poor's or not. It was, of course, an area Einhorn was intimately familiar with from his dealings with New Century—on whose board he had previously served. But he didn't have time to have his analysts churn through the customary mountains of research and documents to find the companies that were most at risk for a meltdown.

Einhorn gathered his seven analysts together and announced that they would temporarily ditch their rigorous and painstaking research process. Instead, they would work through the weekend to find the best list of names that, according to public documents, had the most exposure to the so-called structured finance market—including the kinds of CDOs and other packages of mortgages and debt that were seizing up. On Monday, they would begin the process of shorting them as they continued their research. "I saw the market unraveling," Einhorn recalls. "I didn't think it would be brief—I believed it was structural."

The initial "credit basket" of short candidates comprised between 15 to 20 stocks. Citigroup was in it, so was Bear Stearns, Morgan Stanley, a slew of commercial banks, Moody's Investor Services, and McGraw-Hill, which owned Standard & Poor's. Then, over the weeks, as more information poured in and analysts gathered more research on companies' structured debt exposure, they added new names and covered some of their shorts.

"Each of the positions was small," says Einhorn. "As we continued to do the work, we narrowed the list to those on which we had the most conviction—Bear Stearns, Lehman, Moody's, MBIA, Wells Fargo and maybe some others. That didn't make us geniuses for covering Citi and Merrill Lynch, which we did."

Einhorn became particularly interested in Lehman because of a quarterly earnings conference call he listened to on October 18, 2007. Management suggested that any credit-related problems were behind them. But Einhorn didn't like the back and forth between them and Wall Street analysts. "They weren't answering reasonable questions from reasonable analysts," Einhorn says. "So we dug into our work."

One particular new accounting rule was especially notable: Financial Accounting Standard (FAS) 159. When the value of Lehman's debt declined, the investment bank would book the decline as revenue. The thinking was that because Lehman could buy back the debt at the lower price, it wouldn't have to pay 100 cents on the dollar to retire the debt. It could, theoretically, pocket the difference. That means Lehman or any other bank could book it as revenue. Other investment banks did the same thing, but were very explicit about the numbers involved. Bear Stearns, Merrill Lynch, and Morgan Stanley broke the numbers out. Lehman did not.

Einhorn gave a presentation at the Value Investing Congress on November 29 addressing the issue. He wanted to know how much of Lehman's $1.2 billion in pretax income was due to FAS 159. He also pointed out the folly of FAS 159: Taken to its extreme, the worse a company's bonds performed, the more revenue it would book. Since compensation is often based on such revenue, the result is inescapable. "The most profitable and lucrative day in the history of your firm will be the day you go bankrupt!" Einhorn declared.

Investors didn't seem to care: Lehman shares rose $5 the next day.

There were, however, other warning signs. In conversations with Lehman executives, Einhorn got different answers when he asked how often certain illiquid assets were marked to market. Lehman also insisted that it hedged its exposure to mortgage-related structured debt. "They were saying they had seen the crisis coming," Einhorn says. "We looked at the balance sheet and asked how they could hedge that much risk? When you looked at what Lehman would have had to hedge, it was larger than the whole market."

When pressed on the details, Lehman executives couldn't even identify which instruments they were using to hedge.

In the spring of 2008, Lehman tapped a new chief financial officer—the lithe and photogenic Erin Callan, a protégé of Joe Gregory, chief operations officer but de-facto right hand man and chief confidante to CEO Richard Fuld. Gregory was a fierce loyalist—and an advocate of psychological paradigm called the Myers-Briggs Type Indicator, which grouped people into distinct personality categories. Ability was innate. The fact that Callan was a tax attorney with little experience in finance matters was of little consequence. Her ability would be enough carry the day.

Einhorn wasn't the only person, including some at Lehman, who thought she was in over her head. Yet Callan, in her short tenure as chief financial officer, had gained a reputation in some circles as being responsive to investors—dutifully pumping executives for more information when analysts requested it. A *Wall Street Journal* profile of her was entitled "Lehman's Straight Shooter." Einhorn, for one, didn't buy it.

At Grant's Spring Investment Conference on April 8, the Greenlight president told his audience bluntly: "There is good reason to question Lehman's fair value calculations." This was equivalent to calling the firm's financial statements hokum. He estimated that Lehman's ratio of assets to tangible common equity was an astonishing 44 times. "The problem with 44 times leverage is that if your assets fall by only a percent, you lose almost half your equity," he said. Lehman, in addition to recently buying back $750 million in stock as a way to goose its shares, had the week earlier raised $4 billion in new capital from investors. "The regulators seem willing to turn a blind eye toward efforts to raise capital before recognizing large losses," Einhorn said. "Some of the sovereign wealth funds that made these types of investments last year have come to regret them."

Lehman CEO Fuld, fulminating, blamed the mounting concerns about its accounting on short sellers. "I will hurt the shorts and that is my goal," he said in April. When the subject came to raising capital, he liked the idea of using money to buy back shares to squeeze the shorts as punishment—instead of shoring up the firm's balance sheet.

With the May 21, 2008 Ira Sohn Investment Conference approaching, Einhorn decided to try and nail down at least a few of the issues nagging him about Lehman. He questioned Callan on the discrepancies in so-called Level 3 assets—those that are particularly illiquid and tough to value—which had risen by more than $1 billion from the time of the earnings conference call and the filing of the firm's financial statements just weeks later. Their very illiquidity makes it easy to hide all kinds of portfolio problems in the category. In an hour-long phone call, Einhorn asked whether any such assets had been written up. Callan had responded categorically that they had not.

Most of Einhorn's Sohn speech was a summation of his Allied Capital campaign. He then turned to Lehman—and though not terribly long-winded, the Greenlight president was by no means gentle. Einhorn cited financial legerdemain that he attributed to Callan personally. Einhorn was especially focused on why an $8.4 billion portfolio of mostly corporate equities rose $722 million during a period in which the S&P 500 lost 10 percent.

There was also the fact that Lehman had $39 billion of exposure to commercial mortgages at year-end 2007. An index of such mortgages that were rated AAA fell 10 percent in the quarter. Lehman's portfolio was rated far below AAA and should have fallen more than 10 percent. Instead it dropped less than 3 percentage points. It was a sign of valuation chicanery. Einhorn called on SEC chairman Christopher Cox, Federal Reserve chairman Ben Bernanke, and Treasury Secretary Henry Paulson to act. "My hope is that Mr. Cox and Mr. Bernanke and Mr. Paulson will pay heed to the risks to the financial system that Lehman is creating and they will guide Lehman toward a recapitalization and recognition of its losses—hopefully before taxpayer assistance is required," Einhorn said.

He continued: "For the capital markets to function, companies need to provide investors with accurate information rather than whatever numbers add up to a smooth return. If there is no penalty for misbehavior—and, in fact, such behavior is rewarded with flattering stories in the mainstream press about how to handle a crisis—we will all bear the negative consequences over time."

Timed to start after the U.S. stock markets had closed, the Sohn speech sent when shares down less than 3 percent the next day, to $38.50. But after reporting a preliminary loss of $2.8 billion for the second quarter on June 9—the first since the firm went public in 1994—they plummeted. Three days later, Callan and Gregory both resigned and the stock slumped to $22.70.

In congressional testimony, Fuld said: "The n---d shorts and rumor mongers succeeded in bringing down Bear Stearns. And I believe that unsubstantiated rumors in the marketplace caused significant harm to Lehman Brothers." He claimed the alleged short campaign to be the work of a cabal. Some journalists backed up his claim, including Matt Taibbi of *Rolling Stone*. Surely, of course, a leverage ratio of 44 to 1 had something to do with Lehman's demise.

Lehman desperately searched for additional outside capital. Without backup or assistance from the U.S. government, which Treasury Secretary Paulson was adamant in not providing, nothing panned out. Bank of America opted to purchase Merrill Lynch instead, talks with Korea Development Bank never got serious, and ultimately British bank Barclays—the most serious contender—was overruled by U.K. regulators and eventually picked up Lehman's remaining post-bankruptcy assets for a song. The 158-year-old investment bank filed for bankruptcy on 1:45 a.m. on September 15, the largest in U.S. history, with more than $600 billion in assets.

It's certainly fair to say that Einhorn made financial history, although to lay blame for the disastrous outcome at his feet would be grossly unfair. Einhorn was the messenger—leverage and management hubris the culprits.

The crisis turned Einhorn into a keen Fed watcher, and he continued incorporate macroeconomic outlooks into his world view. He began a veritable campaign in 2012 to argue that the expansionary impact of former Federal Reserve chairman Bernanke's quantitative easing had dissipated, making it useless as a tool to goose growth. In an article in the *Huffington Post*, he then described a hypothetical episode of *The Simpsons* animated TV show mocking Bernanke's reasoning, with the evil nuclear power plant owner/operator Montgomery Burns standing in for Bernanke, bantering with his none-too-bright sycophant assistant, Smithers.

Burns: Don't you get it? A rising stock market allows people to feel wealthy. And a seemingly wealthy person is a profligate person.

Smithers: Profligate, sir?

Burns: Profligate. It means they spend money they don't have on things they don't need.

Smithers: So instead of enabling people to actually have more disposable income, we'll get them to spend more money by simply making them feel rich?

Burns: Exactly! Now how can we do that?

Smithers: Well, we can always encourage them to sell their bonds and buy stocks.

Burns: Now, how would we ever convince them to do something as foolish as that?

Smithers: Just set interest rates at zero indefinitely. Then no one can afford not to invest in the market.

Burns: Why Smithers, that's brilliant! This is exactly the kind of counterintuitive thinking we've been needing around here.

The imagined dialogue is classic Einhorn—logical, a bit hokey with more than a dash of wit and sarcasm. Even if you don't agree with this outlook, you ignore Einhorn's observations at your own risk. Market history has shown that time and again.

Chapter 5

Block: Playing the China Hand

T he white van careened along a narrow, two-lane road deep in the snow-covered He Bei province, 150 miles southwest of Beijing. In the back, Carson Block, attorney, entrepreneur, and capitalist adventurer, bumped along at 35 miles an hour on his way to visit Orient Paper and its upgraded factory, which, the company claimed, would allow it to sharply increase production of high-quality cardboard and other paper product lines. Beside him sat Sean Regan, a manufacturing expert and Asia hand with a specialty in supply chain management and quality control.

Both Block and Regan lived in Shanghai, graduates of the University of Southern California who had become close friends after bonding over USC football. On this blustery day in January 2010, they were on their way to visit a small, New York Stock Exchange–listed company, Orient Paper, at the behest of Block's father, William Block, who ran his own Los Angeles investment firm, WAB Capital. The older Block analyzed microcap companies and, if he liked them, published bullish research reports for a clientele of hedge funds and other money managers. The rub was that WAB got paid by the company—not investors—with warrants or restricted stock for the research and for introducing management to his investor clients. Some called him a stock promoter.

The previous night, the pair had scoured Orient Paper's U.S. Securities & Exchange Commission (SEC) filings—and grew skeptical of the company's claims to inventory turnover that was more than double that of rivals. There were also improbably high production figures, what looked like inflated asset values, a revolving door of top customers, and a list of suspect suppliers—at least one controlled by Orient Paper's own chairman.

Now, as the van approached the factory, something else caught their eyes—pavement. The road was not suitable for the volume of output Orient Paper claimed. "We figured they had to ship 100 trucks a day at maximum capacity," says Block. "Sean noticed that the road didn't have the kind of wear and tear you would expect."

Entering through a pair of battered gates, Block noted the paucity of workers or activity. There was a 20-foot-high pile of used paper outside, wet, which the company had described in an SEC filing as expensive feedstock for its operations—worth $4.7 million. Regan climbed the mound of scrap paper and shouted down to Block.

"If this is worth $4.7 million, the world is a lot richer than I thought," he said.

Inside the factory, the rolling machinery was antiquated. Water dripped onto a table where paper was to be folded. The air was thick with steam—a prescription for disaster in a plant that was supposed to produce high-quality paper.

Zhenyong Liu, Orient Paper's chairman and chief executive officer, greeted Block and Regan in his office and led them on a tour through the factory and workshops.

"How many tons do you ship?" Block recalls asking. Liu didn't know.

"Well, how do you define a good day?" Again, Liu demurred.

"What kind of metrics are you using, then?" Liu shook his head.

In fact, Liu was unable to answer even basic questions. Rather than the diamond in the rough that Block's father was hoping for, Orient Paper seemed a fraud. Liu rushed Block and Regan through the rest of the tour. "This is amazing," Block recalls thinking. "This is a zero. This is a sure thing."

Block himself at the time was bleeding cash—he was majority owner and manager of a struggling self-storage company in Shanghai and could ill afford the time and expense of this trip to He Bei. WAB obviously wouldn't be publishing anything bullish on Orient Paper. But on the flight back to Shanghai, Block and Regan discussed publishing a negative report via e-mail. Perhaps they could short the stock ahead of time and at least defray some of the cost of the research—$10,000 to $15,000.

Back in Shanghai, the two delved into their due diligence, calling Orient Paper's suppliers, customers, and competitors. Few of the numbers they turned up backed anything the company claimed. They compared the SEC filings meant for U.S. investors to information deposited with China's the State Administration for Industry and Commerce, or SAIC. The Chinese numbers were drastically less impressive. Total 2008 net assets, as disclosed to the SAIC, were less than half those in the SEC filings. Block determined that fiscal 2009 revenue was overstated by about 40 times.

Block and Regan admit to turning paranoid. They worried that the Chinese mafia—rumored to be entangled with fraudulent companies— was on to them. "I'm looking out for black sedans," Block says. "We started talking in code." He began carrying a heavy polycom phone handset with which he could defend himself.

The research report Block and Regan drafted would eventually total 30 pages—filled with every item they considered suspicious. They stated that Orient Paper had misappropriated $30 million in capital raised via private placements on machinery that did not meet the specifications the company claimed. The report detailed inflated revenue, turnover, and asset figures. "We are confident ONP is a fraud," the report stated. It included more than a dozen photographs illustrating the decrepit physical plant, and linked to videos of the tour they had taken.

Block waited for an alarm system to be installed in his Shanghai apartment before publishing. There were other delays: He needed a good name for his nascent firm to lend it some credibility. Block recalled a Chinese proverb. "Muddy waters make it easy to catch fish." He incorporated Muddy Waters LLC in Las Vegas, Nevada.

Then, through an online brokerage, Block and Regan located some $4,000 worth of put options, most with August expiration dates, that gave them the right to sell Orient Paper stock at a strike price of $7.50 versus the $8.50 or so the stock was trading at. It was hardly a precisely calibrated strategy. "I had no idea what the f--k I was doing," admits Block.

Block released the Muddy Waters report at 1:15 a.m. Shanghai time on June 28, 2010 via an e-mail blast to 75 investors, mostly people he had met in his earlier days on Wall Street. There were less than three hours before trading closed in New York, and Block remained awake long enough to watch the share price tick down at the end of the day, closing off 10 cents at $8.35. "I wonder if I did that," he said to his wife, a Vietnamese-American who had spent days formatting and paginating the report. (Block asked that her name not be divulged for security reasons.)

The next day, Orient Paper traded at $7.23, down 11 percent. The research report had gone viral overnight, and the stock price would fall below $5 before the company responded.

Orient Paper at first denied it was the company Carson had visited and accused him of lying and extortion. But the report gathered attention: The *21st Century Business Herald*, two weeks later, published an investigative report on the Muddy Waters research, an article that was later posted on Sinafinance.com, a popular website. Carson sold most of the options in mid-July for a profit of about $6,000, then went into the market a few days later to buy more—a move that backfired, wiping out his profit and then some.

Nevertheless, the Orient Paper trade catapulted Muddy Waters to the forefront of a small and contentious short-selling movement that has racked up a formidable record of unmasking fraud at United States– and Canada-listed Chinese companies—profiting as the shares of target companies crumble. Other research firms trolling the same pond include Citron Research LLC, founded by Andrew Left, and Alfredlittle.com, a website run by a long-time China investor named Jon Carnes.

They are not the only ones who have bet against the East's rising tide. Short sellers like Kynikos Associates' Jim Chanos have focused on China's bubble economy, awash in empty real estate and manufacturing capacity. That has left it to Block and his ilk to probe the underbelly of the dicey small-cap markets, where dubious accounting and outright scams flourish. The explosion in China-based fraud isn't difficult to explain: U.S. and other foreign investors face restrictions on buying A-shares listed in Shanghai and Shenzhen and so have scrambled to sink their money into Chinese growth story stocks, even those of dubious quality. Chinese operators are happy to furnish them. "So many people are being paid to manage China money right now," says Block.

The preferred medium for the dicey promotions are reverse takeover companies (RTOs in industry argot)—United States– and Canada-listed shell companies with no operating businesses that are bought by China corporations for the purpose of accessing North American capital. After the acquisition, the shell company typically changes its name to reflect that of its new owners and then proceeds to raise money, often via public equity or debt offerings. Orient Paper fit the description.

The benefits to RTOs are twofold. It's an inexpensive process, since listed shell companies can be purchased for a pittance—often in exchange for equity in the merged company. More importantly, for shady operators, reverse takeovers make it easier to avoid scrutiny by stock exchanges, the SEC, and other regulators, compared to a traditional IPO.

The number of United States–listed, China-based RTOs have climbed since 2007, according to DealFlow Media LLC. Most are traded on the New York Stock Exchange, NASDAQ and other marketplaces. Though most are legitimate or have only minor accounting problems, the area makes for fertile hunting ground for Block and his short-selling rivals.

The promotions have relied on an ecosystem of enablers. RTOs historically worked with a clutch of boutique investment banks, including Rodman & Renshaw Capital Group, Roth Capital Markets, and Global Hunter Capital Markets. These often underwrote stock offerings. Law firms providing legal advice to China-based RTO companies over the years include Loeb & Loeb and Pillsbury Winthrop. Accounting firms have included Frazer Frost LLP, Davis Accounting Group PC, and MaloneBailey LLP. "Everybody has a lot to lose—investment bankers, investor relations, the accounting firms, the law firms in the RTO world," says Block. "There is serious money at stake."

The degree to which such companies are entwined with China's political and economic elite is uncertain. Block suspects the worst.

"I think it goes to high levels," he says. "I believe local and national officials and their families have been involved with the U.S. listed frauds."

Block believes an organized network originates the frauds, taking the dubious companies and dressing them up for reverse takeovers and eventual listing. He cites an article by *Today's Fortune*, an economics newspaper, that alleges a sophisticated "Fraud School" matches sham enterprises with shady auditors who provide expertise on faking financial documents, tax receipts and bank accounts. For the occasional investor performing due diligence, the school furnishes the companies with phone numbers of fake customers who are given scripted answers to likely questions. If a factory visit is demanded, teams of "workers" are hired for the day and brought to empty factories where production equipment and bogus inventory has been shipped in the day before.

The ill-gotten profits are generated by selling shares to the public and then using those proceeds not channeled directly to management to buy machinery or properties at wildly inflated prices, with the kickbacks being distributed to scam artists.

Certainly, the risk of corporate fraud to investors outside of China's blue-chip, state-run enterprises is high. In 2011, Moody's Investors Service issued a report that looked for "red flags" that would signal possible problems at companies issuing high-yield debt in China. The flags identified problematic corporate governance issues like related party transactions, opaque business models, negative free cash flow, poor earnings quality, and suspect financial reporting. Of the 23 non-property related high yield issuers Moody's looked at, the average number of red flags tripped for each company was 7.5. Hong Kong's Securities & Futures Commission charged Moody's with fraud over this report in December 2014.

Accountants signing off on the financial statements are part of the problem. The SEC has sued Chinese-based affiliates of the United States' Big Four accounting firms for withholding documents as it investigates fraud cases at nine China-based companies that trade in the United States. The four—Deloitte Touche Tohmasu CPA Ltd., Ernst & Young Hua Mong LLP, KPMG Huazhen, and PricewaterhouseCoopers Zhong Tian CPAs Ltd—along with BDO China Dahua Co. all deny wrongdoing and say they are only complying with Chinese accounting rules that prevent them from turning over documents to foreign regulators.

With the audits suspect, investment banks co-opted, and the Chinese government often supportive of fraudulent companies, uncovering corruption has fallen to the likes of Muddy Waters, Citron, Alfredlittle.com and GeoInvesting LLC, a Skippack, Pennsylvania, firm that pursues both short and long investment ideas.

The business is increasingly nasty, litigious and dangerous. Citron has been sued for defamation at least three times by Chinese companies, including Qihoo 360 Technology Company, a software manufacturer that it accused of accounting irregularities. Kai-Fu Lee, founder of Google China and Internet gadfly, began the website Citronfraud.com challenging Left's research. A lawyer for Alfredlittle.com was pistol-whipped in August 2011 by police from the Ministry of State Security as the firm conducted research on China New Borun, a New York–listed alcohol maker. After the website questioned production figures of Silvercorp Metals, a Toronto Stock Exchange–listed mining company with operations in China, police from the same organization arrested Alfredlittle.com analyst Huang Kun, who served prison time on charges of "criminal" defamation.

And Alfredlittle.com founder Jon Carnes himself was investigated for, among other things, publishing inaccurate information in a Silvercorp research report, not by Chinese authorities, but by the British Columbia Securities Commission, which accused him of fraud. A commission panel cleared him in May 2015.

Block himself receives periodic death threats via e-mail, and Muddy Waters' website is regularly hacked. "The campaign against the shorts is at a fever pitch," says Dan David, vice president of GeoInvesting. "Somebody's going to get killed."

Regan, for one, decided the pressure was not for him. Married to a Chinese citizen and with ongoing business interests that bring him to China, he asked Block to not include his name on research reports following Orient Paper, and left Muddy Waters altogether in early 2012. Regan cites another Chinese proverb for his decision, one that bluntly advocates making an example of one person to intimidate another: Kill the chicken to scare the monkey. "I figured I would be the chicken," Regan says.

Block too, though publicly defiant, packed up and moved his base to San Francisco. Muddy Waters' staff, 30-somethings who pool their capital, are spread between the United States and Asia. Block will not disclose their names or any office locations and won't divulge personal information like travel plans.

Nevertheless, Block polishes a kiss-off bravado. Despite a wardrobe of bespoke suits, he has a penchant for gangster rap and peppers conversations with choice profanity. Muddy Waters' earlier website showed two dapper models posing under the letterhead for a fictional brokerage firm, "Churnham & Burnham." Research reports—enlivened with quotes from hip-hop stars like Notorious B.I.G.—tend toward the incendiary. One title: "Is 'Independent' Verification in China Better Than Toilet Paper?"

Despite e-mail threats, Block vows not to be pushed around by what he describes as a "thugocracy" of China's business and political elite. Born into a family of renegades, Block's contrarian tendencies trace back to childhood. One key role model: his father, William A. Block, a polio survivor who still has issues with the establishment. "I hate authority," says William Block. "So does Carson."

The elder Block's Wall Street career is a worthy tale in its own right. Shortly after graduating from USC in 1966, he landed a job as a junior analyst at Tri-Continental Corp., a venerable closed-end stock fund run by J.W. Seligman & Co. It was terrible fit. "The investment committee was made up of stodgy, blue-blooded a------s," the older Block says.

Block had a penchant for picking small-cap winners—and getting his ideas shot down. His first year on the job, Block recommended McDonald's—the great growth stock story of the decade. "Who would want to buy this company?" one committee member demanded. "All they do is sell hamburgers!" Other picks included Health Corporation of America, H&R Block, and what became Tenet Healthcare. The committee usually ignored him. "I didn't think they knew s--t," he says. "They didn't like me either."

In 1971, Block quit. An avid athlete, he started a squash club in Chatham, New Jersey. In the late 1960s, he met his future wife and married her in 1974. Carson was born two years later. The family moved from New York City to Summit, one of New Jersey's wealthiest suburbs, where luxury cars, swimming pools, and country club memberships determined the social pecking order. Among its famous residents was former Goldman Sachs Group CEO Jon Corzine, who went on to become a New Jersey senator and then governor.

The Blocks definitely did not fit in. William Block drove a battered grayish Chevrolet Nova with a cracked window shield, its bumper
secured with duct tape. The Blocks separated when Carson was six, his
father taking a townhouse in the adjacent town of Chatham. Over the
years, as their interests became more aligned, Carson gravitated more
and more towards his father.

The separation was tough on Carson—and both parents compensated. An only child, Carson pined for a dog, so his mother bought
him an African Basenji named Wysches, which tore apart Carson's
mother's house.

Disillusionment fed into an early rebelliousness. In elementary
school, Carson was suspended and banned from field trips for his
backtalk. Along with his best friend, Daniel Devroye, Carson began
a campaign to undermine the school "safety patrol," which was what
the well-behaved children joined. "Carson and I thought there was
something fascistic about it," says Devroye. "The kids were being
co-opted."

By 1982, the older Block returned to Wall Street, this time as
analyst for a progression of sell-side brokerage firms specializing in dicey
small caps—Rosenkrantz Lyon & Ross, Triad Securities, Buckingham
Research Group, and M.H. Meyerson & Co. Carson, always interested
in his father's work, constantly peppered him with questions about
the markets.

Amidst his campaign of hit-and-run rebellion, Carson by middle
school had moved in mostly full time with his father. He would binge
on junk food, engage in petty shoplifting, and have pizzas delivered to
classrooms at school. Once, the police detained Carson and Devroye
for loitering at the local mall. "I was terrified," recall's Block's friend.
"Carson just played it cool."

William Block tried his hand at discipline, but his heart wasn't in
it—something Carson picked up on. Their relationship was more like
that of siblings than father and son—competitive, bickering, yet intensely
close. Secretly, William admired Carson's nerve, confidence and growing
poise. "He is what I'd like to have been," he says. "He was always very
savvy. He's always been attractive to women."

For years, the fathers running the local Little League blackballed the
crusty, Chevrolet-driving William Block from managing a team. When a

manager dropped out, they relented. The Lions' uniforms were mismatched, the players spontaneously changed positions in the field, and the team finished dead last. The kids loved it.

Carson was of two minds about the Summit social scene. On the one hand, he felt it extremely provincial. "The parents felt they were raising their kids in this safe environment," Block says. Instead, it was the kind of highly pressurized social scene that often results from living in a bubble. For teenagers, including Block, booze was one escape. "It was party at my place, party at your place," Block recalls. "It wasn't really a party. It was more or less the same people sitting around getting drunk." A so-called "funnel club" included members who used a funnel to pour straight vodka down each other's throats. Block was not a member.

Summit High School ran a sister city exchange program with Toyomashi, Japan. Fulfilling a boyhood dream, Block took a horizon-expanding trip there, in the summer between his freshman and sophomore years. The experience got Block thinking about global markets as they toured metal workshops and factories. "I'd say, 'Imagine you're the guy selling Pepsi in China,'" Block says.

His father bought him a copy of *Security Analysis*, the definitional tome on value investing by Benjamin Graham and David Dodd. "Unlike Warren Buffett, I didn't read the whole thing," Carson says. Still, his interest in markets grew. He accompanied his father to Wall Street, where he learned how to build spreadsheets, with columns for revenues, expenses, and profits. "He was curious, he was intrigued," says William Block. "He liked the idea of making money and the lifestyle Wall Street offered."

Block passed his Series 7 securities broker exam at age 18. Ever precocious, Carson even called clients about stocks, once convincing a fund manager to buy 100,000 shares of Anchor Gaming.

Applying for college, Block steered clear of Ivy League and other highly competitive options, targeting party schools like Tulane University, Notre Dame, and USC. His essay for USC was a personal one: How much he admired his father.

Envisioning a career in Asia, Block headed west to USC with its Pacific Rim campus and big Asian-American student body. He was soon immersed in the culture and languages of the Far East. With its bright sunshine, Mediterranean-style architecture, and palm trees, it was a welcome change from New Jersey.

His first roommate was Jason Tsai, a native of Taiwan, with whom he shared his aspirations. "He said China would be the next big thing," says Tsai, who helped Block with his Mandarin and got him hooked on ma la kuo, a spicy Chinese stew.

At Tsai's suggestion, Block joined the Asian students' association. Later, after Block returned from summer school in Beijing, Tsai recalls his business idea to introduce Chinese companies to U.S. mutual funds.

Block had promised his parents he wouldn't pledge to a fraternity. But he pointed out that the business fraternity, Alpha Kappa Psi, was a great way to further his commercial contacts. Adding to the fraternity's interest: It was nicknamed Asia Kappa Psi, as a majority of the members were of Asian heritage. Block won an election as pledge class party planner, campaigning on his credentials as a licensed bartender.

In junior year, he was a member of the Alpha Kappa Psi team competing in USC Business School's inaugural business case study competition. Most of the rest of the team blew the project off, leaving it to Block and a friend, Arvind Mishra, to keep the fraternity from looking bad in front of the school, and the team from looking bad in the eyes of the fraternity.

The case study involved a struggling laundromat, which was presented with three business opportunities from which participants had to select one. Based on the financials furnished, all the alternatives were terrible. "We knew all three options sucked," says Block.

At the presentation, Block and Mishra explained as much to the judges, walking them through the poor economics of the options. They then presented a list of better ways to employ the capital. First—buy an army of penguins and put on a show.

"That will make money because everybody loves penguins," Block said.

Second—buy O.J. Simpson's Heisman trophy.

"That will certainly increase in value," Block deadpanned.

Block continued through eight more alternatives, like a late night TV comedian.

The judges were silent for a minute before bursting into applause. The Alpha Kappa Psi fraternity won the competition—and one judge offered Block and Mishra jobs.

In his senior year, Block wrote a letter to Jon Corzine, then at Goldman Sachs. He was interested in investment banking and though he had slim hopes of landing a job at the firm, he had been friendly in high school with Corzine's son, Josh, and could use some insights into the business.

Corzine, who with his neatly trimmed beard and wire-rimmed glasses had a professorial look about him, graciously welcomed Block to the firm's gray granite monolith headquarters at 85 Wall Street. They talked about the investment banker career path. Typically, a new hire with an undergraduate degree would join as an analyst in the investment-banking department and, after two years, leave for business school. After earning an MBA, a different bank would typically hire him or her as an associate. Yet a few of the analysts would become associates without leaving to get their MBA. Block's question was why Goldman insisted analysts return to business school for their MBAs and whether that could be avoided.

"If we don't feed the business schools, we will lose our recruiting privileges," Corzine responded. "Merrill Lynch and Salomon Brothers would keep theirs." It was a lesson in the riptides of hidden interests that churned beneath the surface of the business world. "That was an 'a-ha' moment," Block says.

Ultimately, Block realized his goal was to head east—with the cushion of cash he built helping his father, he booked a flight to Shanghai to find his fortune.

Block settled in, planning to follow through on his plan to write research reports about Chinese companies for foreign investors. He networked with expatriates, hanging out at a watering hole on Mao Ming Road called The Stock Bar.

There was a gold rush mentality to the city. To Block's amazement, a local operator gave lectures at the Stock Bar on how to manipulate stocks, which he explained was part of company policy. The idea was to invest on Monday morning and wait until promoters hyped the stock over the next two days, then dump shares late Wednesday. Companies not only approved, they participated—buying alongside the manipulators. With the profits companies reaped they could report earnings surprises and goose the stock further.

"I came to the conclusion there were no companies that were investable," says Block. "The stock market was really a policy tool—it gave people the ability to dream about becoming rich. It kept them from protesting in the street." In fact, the government wouldn't list good companies at the time, because doing so would throw a light on how poorly the public ones actually were.

In 1998, Block headed back to Los Angeles to take a position at CIBC World Markets as an investment banking analyst. It was a small office of seven bankers; the work was uninspiring and the hours grueling. He nevertheless learned skills. Analysts were required to create all the pitch books, including graphics. Block also became proficient in building financial models with balance sheets, cash flow, and income statements. All this would come in handy when he turned to researching and publishing on his own.

The next year, Block announced to his father that he wanted to work at WAB Capital. William Block hated the idea, but when Carson told him he had already quit CIBC, there was not much to debate.

WAB's dicey business model—being paid by small companies to generate research in exchange for stock or warrants—worried Carson. It was an era when institutions were slashing commissions, and plenty of analysts were casting about for new ways to make money. "We felt we were managing the conflicts," Carson says, pointing out that if a company didn't pass muster, WAB simply wouldn't publish.

WAB took a hit with Rent-Way Inc., a company it covered that leased electronics and computers to a low-income clientele. It turned out the chief financial officer was understating expenses in order to inflate profits. The stock plummeted and WAB was left awash in losses. "I said 'F--k this,'" Carson recalls. "I don't want to be in equity research anymore."

Block decided it was time to get serious about starting his own business and resolved that a law degree would provide him the tools he needed. He enrolled in Chicago-Kent College of Law, expecting to suffer. "I'm here to learn what I need to become a business person," he recalls thinking. Instead, he found himself fascinated by the law, and not just the corporate-related subjects. "Lo and behold, I really enjoyed law—criminal law, torts, constitutional law," he says. In addition to making law review, he was named to the moot court honor society and became president of a law school honor fraternity, Phi Delta Phi. Block also married his wife, who he had met at USC. He asked that her name not be published for security reasons.

Block was suddenly hot law firm property. "Because I enjoyed law, I thought I will practice law," he says. He soon jetted off to Hong Kong and Shanghai, upon arrival cold-calling managing partners at major law firms. Jones Day, the global firm with headquarters in Cleveland, Ohio, hired him in the summer of 2005.

It was interesting work for 15 months—Block's business background helping him work on the proposed leveraged buyout of construction giant Xugong Group Construction Machinery, at the time China's biggest—although his client ultimately lost. Then, the businessman in Block began to get the upper hand. "I was getting the itch to be a financial entrepreneur," he says. "I figured to help the Chinese manage their wealth outside China."

Block registered his new wealth management company in Singapore—Yi Bao Sheng Ptl Ltd, or YBS, which means "easy to attain treasures." The plan for YBS was to focus on the burgeoning capitalist class that was growing up in China's so-called third- and fourth-tier cities, places like Wenzhou and Nanking with growing economies that bigger players like Goldman Sachs and UBS had yet to target.

As he began laying plans to get YBS off the ground, two other projects presented themselves. He and a businessman with a China background collaborated to co-author an installment to the wildly successful *For Dummies* series, *Doing Business in China for Dummies* (John Wiley & Sons, Inc., 2007). The book, a primer for prospective entrepreneurs, belies its low-brow title, humorously dispensing smart advice on the protocols of declining duck tongues at business banquets, the proper way to behave when addressing high government officials, and the etiquette of business meetings. It also carries sharp guidance on hiring and terminating employees, negotiating contracts, and interacting with the Communist Party, local government, and People's Liberation Army.

An acquaintance named Zhao roped Block into a new venture bankrolling China's first self-storage facility. Block intended to be a passive investor, but he could see the opportunity: With the growth of Shanghai's wealth and increasingly expensive real estate, the business made sense on a number of levels. An uncle of Block's had run a self-storage business in the United States and regaled Block with tales of the 50 percent cash on cash returns it generated, not including real estate. As a kicker, Zhao agreed to let Block use office space at the new self-storage company for YBS.

The venture was a slow-motion disaster. From his original passive stance, Block soon agreed to help build the company with Zhao and then retreat into the background. He put his plans for YBS on hold, and then abandoned them altogether. With Zhao, he named the company Love Box Self Storage, and leased a 14,000-square-foot space near central Shanghai. The plan was to build top-line growth as a way to generate investment interest and then move the storage business into ever more economical locations. Zhao soon lost interest and Block bought him out, bringing his investment to nearly $400,000.

Building the physical facility, though, was a nightmare. "Nothing they said would be done was done," says Block. "Construction quality wasn't there."

The build-out was as tortuous as it was time consuming. "We had a 45-minute conversation about what kind of screws we would use in our partitions," says Block. "It was an epiphany. Companies are not driven by financial models. It gave me an appreciation of what went into running a company." Ultimately, the steel container units were ordered from and manufactured in the United States.

By early 2010, Block was being hit up routinely for bribes by contractors—which he wouldn't pay, not just on principle, but because it would jeopardize his standing as a United States–qualified lawyer. While the contractors were a problem, the landlord was worse. It turned out the holder of the property was not precisely who the lease suggested it was. His landlord had presented itself as a subsidiary of a state-owned enterprise. Instead it was privately owned, and Block discovered it owed millions of dollars to the local government and private contractors. That rendered his lease problematic, so Block withheld rent until his landlord resolved its government problems. "They threatened to shut down utilities and ban us from the premises," Block says. "It was going to be an extinction-level event."

Block rented a generator, installed gates on the windows, and brought in air mattresses and provisions. He lobbied the local government. "We were prepared to hang banners out the window," he says. At the 11th hour, following a call from a local Communist Party's secretary's office, the landlord relented. Nevertheless, Love Box was a costly lesson. "We sold it for $125,000 net in August 2012. It cost me $600,000,"says Block. "It was payment for my Ph.D. in Chinese business." The tribulations of Love Box also steeled him for his new career as a short seller.

It also fomented Block's go-for-broke attitude. "Having nothing to lose: there's a real power in that," he says.

Indeed, Orient Paper responded to Muddy Waters' report two days after it was published by flatly denying virtually every negative assertion. It claimed that that Block and Regan had researched the operating subsidiary of an entirely different company. Five weeks later Orient Paper published a more comprehensive rebuttal, 11 pages long—essentially reiterating its claims concerning production, capital spending, feedstock, and financials. On November 29, Orient Paper presented the findings of an independent committee comprised of Loeb & Loeb LLP, Deloitte & Touche Financial Advisory Services Ltd., and TransAsia Lawyers, exonerating the company on all counts.

The market didn't buy it. The stock hit a low in August 2010 of $4.08, before rallying to close out the year at $6.36. By late 2012, it was trading at under $2.00. In early March 2015, Orient Paper traded for 95 cents.

The days and weeks after the Orient Paper research report were a flurry of activity. Muddy Waters issued follow-up reports, and the often-somnolent Chinese news media began to investigate Orient Paper. Meanwhile, Block found himself in demand. "I learned this was the tip of the iceberg," Block says. "People are e-mailing, calling, Skyping. This company is a fraud, that company is a fraud. It was investors, funds, short sellers."

Some communications were less welcome. "Bullets to the brain can be quite painless," read one anonymous e-mail message. A blogger posted his father's address in Los Angeles—suggesting a group visit by Orient Paper investors.

Though Block ultimately lost money on the deal, he knew he had stumbled on a business opportunity, but needed to decide how to proceed. Should he sell his bearish research by subscription? Or publish it for free on the web? Should he perform contract research for U.S. investors? "I was discussing it with friends and family, talking to fund managers," Block says, "It was an exciting time. I was on the cusp of a new career."

One burning question was whether his new career would let him remain in China. To Block's thinking, he was protected to some degree after Orient Paper in that if anything should befall him, the police would have a single and obvious prime subject to pursue. Anybody thinking of harming him would be keenly aware of that. If Muddy Waters began publishing multiple reports, the pool of motivated suspects would grow, providing some safety to a potential predator. Regardless, Block began pulling together a team of researchers and analysts. "We always look for particular skill sets," says Block, who declines to identify any of his colleagues. "They have to be true believers. We are punishing the wrong-doers."

Among the flood of tips proffered was one concerning RINO International Corp., a manufacturer of flue gas desulphurization equipment, which scrubbed pollutants from steel plant emissions. Based in Dalian, China, and listed on the NASDAQ Stock Market, there were a series of warning flags in its presentations and SEC and SAIC filings. As was the case with Orient Paper, no single line item in the compendium of evidence proved decisive. Instead, Block says the accumulation of questionable income and balance sheet items combined with kick-the-tire research convinced him the company's credentials didn't pass muster.

The balance sheet, for example, showed a preponderance of paper assets: As of June 30, 2010, the company reported tangible operating assets of $17.4 million, just 8.3 percent of total operating assets of $209 million. This was particularly strange for a manufacturing company like RINO. Industry rivals reported tangible operating assets of more than 60 percent of the total. "Document forgery is so prevalent," says Block. "We thought so much of this could be faked."

Next, Muddy Waters analysts zeroed in on raw materials in relation to revenues. Sales, earnings, and cash flow figures are relatively easy to massage and sneak by inattentive auditors; raw material balances, by contrast, are more difficult to fake and remain one of the best ways to measure a manufacturer's production. From 2007 through 2009, contract revenues at RINO grew more than fourfold, to $187.5 million. Yet raw material balances had risen little more than 33 percent, to $246,798. That pointed to another suspicious ratio: Contract revenues totaled more than

750 times raw material balances at the end of 2009. At competitors, that figure was in the low to mid teens. Either RINO was astonishingly more efficient than its rivals or something wasn't right.

Again comparison to rivals turned up questions—if no smoking guns. The company told Muddy Waters Research that gross margins on desulphurization gear, which accounted for 70 percent of RINO's total revenue, were 35 percent or more. Two larger competitors, by contrast, reported margins of 20 percent and 11 percent. That made no sense.

Block consulted an engineer at the in-house research institute of one of China's biggest steel companies, Baosteel Group, to evaluate RINO's technology. The expert—who requested anonymity—told him RINO's system had a relatively low sulfur reduction rate and had higher operating costs because it took longer, used pricier chemical additives, and had a bigger physical footprint than its competitors' equipment, amongst other things.

A Muddy Waters analyst, claiming to represent a steel mill in the market for a flue desulphurization system, surveyed nine steelmakers that RINO executives listed as customers in an investor presentation it gave in March 2010. Five of them outright denied having bought RINO gear while at a sixth steelmaker the executive in charge of such purchases claimed to have never heard of RINO.

RINO, like many RTO companies, was structured using something called a variable interest entity, or VIE. This complicated structure was designed to allow management to tap offshore capital while retaining technical ownership, as required under Chinese law in many restricted industries, like the Internet and, in this case, steel. The VIE, controlled by management, ran and technically owned the operating business. But through a series of legal contracts, all profits, liabilities, and legal powers, like the power of attorney, are supposed to be channeled to the foreign-owned entity, which is typically domiciled in the Caribbean and traded on a North American stock exchange—in this case, RINO. To Block's amazement the money was flowing in the opposite direction—from the operating company, RINO, to the VIE, controlled by RINO CEO Dejun Zou and his wife, chairwoman Jianping Qiu.

The most vexing issue in dissecting RINO was its tax situation. The company in its SEC filing reported paying no income taxes in 2008 or 2009—though it should have been paying at least 15 percent, according to Muddy Waters calculations. Then there was the Value Added Tax (VAT) reported by RINO. Virtually all companies in the Peoples Republic of China pay a VAT of 17 percent. However, the amount reported by RINO over the course of several years implied that RINO was underreporting its revenues by large amounts—62 percent for 2009. In fact, they were reporting real revenues to the tax authorities and false ones to investors. Block did notice that RINO had been through four chief financial officers in three years.

RINO traded at $15.52 on November 10, 2010. Block had no problem borrowing shares to short. He won't disclose how many shares he shorted, nor whether he bought any put options. Block does say he entered some limit orders to lock in profits if the stock tanked.

The truth was that RINO shares were already under pressure, as several analysts had downgraded shares citing rising competition in the flue desulphurization market: The stock had fallen from a high of $31.25 in early January to $15.52 the day before the Muddy Waters research report was released on November 10. Shares began to tumble, closing the day at $13.18, and RINO's chief financial officer was quoted saying the company was considering legal action. The company scheduled a conference call to address the Muddy Waters report for a week later. (Block later admitted in a 2014 *Wall Street Journal* article that he had sold a copy of his RINO report in advance to an investment firm before releasing it).

Block decided he wasn't going to wait around to hear what management had to say. Breathing a sigh of relief, he settled back into a hired minivan and headed out to Shanghai Pudong International Airport with a one-way ticket, an assortment of bags, and his two cats, leaving behind Love Box and his dreams of a life as a Chinese businessman. "I had to get the f--k out of China, especially with that report out," he says. Block still grouses about the $1,500 in excess baggage fees he coughed up to United Airlines. Upon arriving in Los Angeles, he called his brokerage firm to find out where the stock closed. All the limit orders had been triggered.

The next week, at 7 p.m. New York time on November 16, the RINO call was set to begin. Shares had closed at $7.15. The conference moderator announced a delay of 10 minutes—and then abruptly cancelled the call altogether. The next day, shares fell to $6.07, and the

company filed a statement with the SEC quoting CEO Dejun Zou saying that two of the six flue desulphurization contracts pegged as likely
shams by Muddy Waters were "problematic." On November 18, RINO
filed a second statement saying its three previous quarters' financial statements should not be relied upon—insofar as they included data from
2008 and 2009. Its stock was suspended and reopened on the pink sheets
on December 8, declining to $3.15. By year-end, shares RINO traded
at $4.04 and in March 2015 for under a penny.

From the safety of San Francisco, Carson Block directed the
campaign against his next target, China Media Express Holdings, a
company that sold advertising over video monitors installed in intercity
buses traveling between major Chinese cities like Shanghai, Shenzhen,
and Beijing. Investors began badgering Block to investigate China
Media Express Holdings shortly after Muddy Waters published the
Orient Paper reports. The years building financial models and analyzing
balance sheets had instilled in him a sensitivity to the kinds of business
characteristics that signaled problems. "I read the numbers, read the
story," Block says. "It just smelled."

The premise for the China Media Express business model was indeed
on the surface somewhat questionable. The demographics of intercity
bus riders in China are unattractive. With an impressive air route system, world-class high-speed trains, and a fast-improving highway system,
intercity buses are typically filled with farmers and low-paid factory
workers. Not a choice customer base—and one that Block doubted
could generate the $290 million in annual revenues the company claimed
for 2009.

Nevertheless, China Media Express's biggest shareholder was C.V.
Starr & Co., the insurance agency overseen by former American International Group. CEO Maurice "Hank" Greenberg, a seasoned China
hand. A Starr executive sat on its board. China Media Express's auditor was no second string bean counter, either, but the China affiliate of
Deloitte Touche LLP, the Big Four juggernaut.

In its investor presentations and SEC filings, China Media Express
cited copious data and analysis it commissioned from CTR Media
Intelligence, a Chinese market research firm, to back up its claims
regarding its network, viewership, and demographics. If Muddy Waters
could establish that the information CTR was generating wasn't

accurate, Block would have a powerful basis for questioning China Media's fundamentals.

Block instructed one of Muddy Waters' analysts to approach the China Media Express sales department and describe himself as a clothing designer looking to buy advertising time. That's legal, but ethically debatable. In business parlance, misrepresenting one's identity to gain information is referred to by a benign-sounding term, *pre texting*, which certainly sounds better than, say, *lying*.

Block makes no apologies. "Pre texting is entirely justified because we are investigating criminal activities," he says. "You have to use measures that go beyond walking in the front door." With a certain disdain he adds: "That's what sell-side analysts do."

Regardless, the Muddy Waters analyst, whom Block declines to identify, turned up incriminating information by scrutinizing the China Media Express advertising kit he was e-mailed. For example, China Media Express's press releases claimed that over 27,200 buses plied its intercity network of routes. The ad kit it furnished to Muddy Waters claimed the company had less than half that amount, only 12,565 buses.

A China Media Express salesperson confirmed the doctored numbers in a taped phone conversation with the analyst. "When we reported the details to the stock market regulator, we didn't report the number of vehicles we quoted you. The number we reported is times two, or doubled," she said.

The largest client mentioned in the CTR report, Shanghai Ba-Shi (Group) Industrial Co. Ltd, upon questioning by Muddy Waters, said it did not have a business relationship with China Media Express. Among the buses purportedly in the China Media Express network equipped with the proper gear, fewer than half were actually airing the advertising. Block dispatched an analyst to Shanghai's central bus terminal and showed that mostly they were airing DVDs of current movies provided by travelers themselves or commercials produced by the local government to drum up interest in local events.

Muddy Waters analysts surveyed six major buyers of outdoor digital media in China: None had heard of China Media Express. The company claimed that three of its top ten advertisers were China Mobile, Master Kong, and Coca-Cola—all of which were represented by media buyers who claimed they had never heard of China Media Express.

Lastly, in December 2010 China Media Express had launched what it described as an online shopping platform and had claimed that Apple Inc. or its distributor were among the companies that had signed on as participants. Upon questioning by Muddy Waters, Apple denied that was the case.

Block points out that Muddy Waters' research didn't show China Media Express was a total fraud, only that it was vastly overstating its business and revenues. For example, Block pegged 2009 revenues at no more than $17 million versus the $95.9 million China Media Express reported. And if the financial statements were to be believed, there was a fair amount of cash on China Media Express's balance sheet: about $170 million. All told, Muddy Waters' report valued the stock, trading at $16.61, at $5.28. Block thought the value would be much lower if the cash wasn't there.

As Block and his colleagues wrapped up their research, it became apparent that other shorts had taken an interest in the company. Andrew Left of Citron Research, for example, was growing increasingly skeptical about the scale of China Media Express's business. On January 30, he published a scathing note about the company—observing in particular how major advertising surveys in the country failed to make mention of what he called "the phantom company." Another short seller, John Hempton of Bronte Capital, had also posted negative comments about China Media Express. Block began borrowing shares in the last week of February—as apparently did other investors. Short interest as a percent of China Media's free float had risen to nearly 25 percent from 10.2 percent three months earlier.

When Block released his report, the effect was devastating. Shares fell 33 percent in a day, tumbling to $11.01 from $16.61 a share.

Unlike RINO, which essentially folded in the face of Muddy Waters' accusations, China Media struck back—for starters castigating Muddy Waters for releasing the report at the outset of the Chinese New Year. In a press release a week later, the company quoted its CEO, Zheng Cheng, denying any inaccuracies in its numbers, pointing out that Deloitte had audited them.

Others facilitators fell in line. On February 17, Ping Luo, an analyst at Global Hunter Securities issued a report on China Media Express saying that she had reviewed contracts, tax filings, and bank statements and found nothing remiss. Luo claimed to have met with bus company executives and confirmed the number of buses under contract with China Media Express. She also met with advertising clients who, once again, confirmed their relationship with China Media Express. Luo reiterated her $26 price target.

Bloggers disparaged Block. One website posting claimed to be filing a class action suit against him. China Media Express shares seesawed between $11 and $14. Block again declines to reveal specifics of his short position.

On March 14, China Media Express announced that Deloitte Touche Tomatsu had resigned. So too had the company's chief financial officer. At Muddy Waters' offices, it was fist bumps all around. "It had been a really bitter battle, with numerous nasty things put on the Internet about me," says Block. "It felt absolutely great." NASDAQ halted trading in the company's stock. When they opened 35 days later on May 19, they fell to $2.16. Block won't say what Muddy Waters' profit was on the trade except to say that it exceeded the profit for RINO.

Muddy Waters was making a name for itself—challenging the financials of not just Orient Paper, RINO, and China Media Express but with varying degrees of success a smattering of other dubious prospects too: It accused Duoyan Global Water, Inc. of forging audit documents; Spreadtrum Communications of aggressive accounting; and New Oriental Education and Technology Group of claiming to own its entire network of schools while, in fact, it franchised some of them.

Newspapers in the United States, Canada, and even China itself had begun portraying Block as the "go-to" guy for RTO fraud. Investors, including rival short sellers, would call in regularly with tips. And in mid-2011, Block picked up the phone and began talking with an investor who was skeptical about Sino-Forest Corp., a timber company based in Hong Kong and Missewea, Ontario, whose shares were traded on the Toronto Stock Exchange.

Sino-Forest was no run-of-the-mill penny stock. It purported to be a major harvester of timber, which it turned into a variety of products, including plywood, veneer, and wood chips for China's burgeoning construction industry. Over five years, earnings had surged 28 percent annualized on sales growth of 41 percent.

With a market cap of $4.2 billion dollars, it was worth four times Orient Paper, RINO and China Media Express combined—and it had some $2 billion in debt outstanding. While Sino-Forest went public via a reverse takeover in 1994, since then Morgan Stanley had underwritten shares in 2004, giving it a respectable imprimatur. Credit Suisse and Dundee Capital Markets had also sold shares. And unlike other RTOs, whose auditors were China-based, Sino-Forest relied on Ernst & Young Canada.

Adding luster to the Sino-Forest story, three of the biggest shareholders had gilded reputations: John Paulson of Paulson & Co., the hedge fund firm that had made $4 billion wagering against the housing market in 2008; Fidelity Investments; the giant mutual fund firm; and Singaporean sovereign wealth fund Temasek Holdings.

Muddy Waters's research was extensive—one requiring more than two months of work by ten analysts, who panned out to five different cities. Muddy Waters retained four different law firms as outside counsel. The analysts plowed through tens of thousands of pages of SAIC documents—noting dozens of red-flags, accounting discrepancies and questionable transactions on numerous whiteboards in their Hong Kong offices. Every couple of days, an analyst would come across an incriminating piece of evidence. "Oh my God!" he would shout. "I found another one!" They found more than a dozen serious issues.

It was an exhilarating paper chase. "The smoking guns were all in the SAIC files," says Block. "We ran out of whiteboards."

The problems lay in Sino-Forest's byzantine corporate structure. It relied on six so-called "Authorized Intermediaries" to handle essentially all of its forestry business. The shadowy A.I.s, as they were known, would buy the timber, process the wood, and sell it. In so doing, they were acting as both suppliers and customers to Sino-Forest.

Sino-Forest itself, however, would book the revenue and profit, reimbursing the A.I. for expenses. The critical point was that the A.I.s were responsible for all tax payments, including the VAT, the invoices for which in China are key to tracking down fraud. The country has controls in place to prevent money laundering, and a massive tax bureau is actively engaged in doing so. The identities of the A.I.s, with the single exception of one headed by a Sino-Forest executive, were secret, allegedly for competitive reasons.

Without VAT invoices, there was no paper trail to verify Sino-Forest's revenues or profits. The company could claim what it wanted. Muddy Waters calculated that the company was booking several times more timber from Yunnan province than was allowable under government quota limits for the entire province. Even if Sino-Forest could produce the kind of timber product volumes it was claiming, the road network in the remote region was far too primitive to support it. In sum, by Muddy Waters's estimates, timber assets in the region were overstated by about $900 million.

There were moments of levity. Muddy Waters analysts found what they believed was an obviously forged bank reference letter from HSBC Holdings with fractured English that was a dead giveaway. Overall, though, the scale and hubris of the operation were shocking. "They didn't have to forge VAT documents, they had the A.I.s deal with that," he says. "It was stunning." Block says that ultimately, the vast majority of gross profit simply never passed through the company's bank accounts.

Block met with a Sino-Forest executive at an investment conference in Hong Kong, pre texting, in this case, that he was a slow-witted mutual fund analyst, brushing his hair forward to make himself look like a rube. "I tried to appear disheveled, 'Dumb & Dumber' kind of look. I asked dumb questions and then a leading one, say, on how they dealt with currencies."

The high trading volume of Sino-Forest shares kept the cost of the borrow low, initially. Muddy Waters by this time had its own dedicated trader—Block won't disclose where.

Once again, Block worked late into the night before pushing the button on the 39-page research report, laying out Muddy Waters' findings.

The stock was trading at $18.21 when the report was released. Block had set some limit orders to begin covering positions if the stock began to fall. He got into a cab and called his trader—only to discover that the shares had plunged below the limit order prices on their way to closing out the day at $14.46.

The company responded in 24 hours. "The allegations contained in this report are inaccurate and unfounded," CEO Allen Chan said in a press release, and soon promised a full-throttle investigation to be completed in two to three months. That was later postponed to the end of 2011. Shares fell to $5.23.

On a June 13 conference call, Chan cut off an analyst asking pointed questions about Sino-Forest's cash balance. A high-pitched feedback sound drowned out another query and the analyst was disconnected from the call. Shares tumbled to $3.36 from $4.98. "It seemed as though because we had lifted the veil, investors were now listening to the company and thinking, 'These guys don't sound like business geniuses who created billions of dollars of investor value,'" Block says.

On June 18, 2011, the *Toronto Globe & Mail* published a lengthy article that among other things questioned Sino-Forest's ownership of swaths of Yunnan province forestry property. "They corroborated our conclusion about the overstatement of timber purchased in Yunnan province," says Block. "That's when I breathed a large sigh of relief."

As with RINO, some brokerages rallied around the timber purveyor. One Dundee Capital Markets analyst accused Block of shopping the research report to hedge funds in the weeks leading up to the release. And some investors piled in, seeking to profit from an expected rebound. Wellington Management LLC snapped up beaten-down shares, buying a 7 percent position. Paulson, notably, did not, dumping his entire position for a peak to trough paper loss of nearly half a billion dollars, with the actual hit a fraction of that.

Within a week, the Ontario Securities Commission (OSC) opened an investigation, and in late August it accused Sino-Forest executives of inflating revenues and misrepresenting timber holdings. The OSC suspended trading in Sino-Forest shares and later referred the case to the Royal Canadian Mounted Police for criminal prosecution.

Chan resigned that month. When Sino-Forest released its own report in mid-November, the company's independent directors said that they had verified the company's cash balances and confirmed its rights to timber assets whose book value it also vouched for. "We can categorically say Sino-Forest is not the 'near total fraud' and 'Ponzi scheme' as alleged by Muddy Waters," the report said.

Nevertheless, the company defaulted on a convertible bond debt payment later that month. The Toronto Stock Exchange de-listed Sino-Forest on May 9, 2012. Block declines to disclose Muddy Waters' profit on Sino-Forest.

By then, however, the window for betting against China-based U.S.-listed companies was closing fast in the wake of the negative short seller reports. As their share prices dived en masse, China Development Bank Corp. began financing management buyouts of companies like Harbin Electric, Focus Media Holdings, Fushi Copperweld, and China Security and Surveillance Technology. All told, the state-run bank committed more than $1.5 billion in financing to pull them off the U.S. exchanges. Roth Capital estimated 27 Chinese companies with U.S. listings announced plans to go private through management buyouts in 2012, up from 16 in 2011. About 50 mostly small Chinese companies "went dark" or deregistered with the SEC, meaning they needn't file public disclosures.

On the other hand, local Chinese authorities revved up their repression of short sellers—or anyone else getting curious about corporate financials. Local city offices stopped furnishing the SAIC and other filings so helpful in identifying frauds. Those requesting them face harassment—or worse. "China has gotten harder in the sense that the government has really taken the side of the fraud," Block says. "The government is working with a number of these companies to try to conceal records that are public. That is one of the reasons we're not that interested in China anymore."

In November 2012, Carson Block—at the inaugural Sohn Conference Foundation investment forum in London—launched into a new campaign, this time alleging the target company, a trading firm backed by blue chip Asian institutions, had embarked on a capital expenditure and asset purchasing "binge" that threatened its very solvency. Block detailed a series of accounting missteps. Before the packed audience of hedge fund managers in Grosvenor Square, he compared the firm to Enron and said the company should be valued on a liquidation basis, since it was unlikely to survive. Particularly notable was that the company—commodities juggernaut Olam International—was based not in China, but Singapore. (Temasek back stopped Olan and eventually purchased a majority stake in May 2014.) "We are done with companies that operate in China," Block declared.

Easier said than done for the China hand. Less than a year later, on October 24, 2013, Muddy Waters released a research report on NQ Mobile, a maker of mobile Internet services, including security, search and games as well as enterprise-focused products. It alleged 72 percent of the company's security revenue was fictitious, that its antivirus software was unsafe, and its cash balances were unlikely to be real. American Depositary Receipts of the company, based in Beijing and Dallas, fell to $10.63 from $20.10 before the report. NQ Mobile called the allegations false and threatened legal action. ADRs traded in May 2015 at $3.81. For Block, apparently, fishing in the murky tidal pools of one of the world's fastest growing economies is to hard to resist.

Chapter 6

Fleckenstein: Strategies and Tactics

B ill Fleckenstein slammed the door to his black BMW 740i and
rode the elevator to the 4th-floor offices of his most famous
client, Paul Allen's Vulcan Capital, the private firm that oversaw
the Microsoft co-founder's $5 billion fortune. Fleckenstein, whom
friends call Fleck, was there to see Vulcan president Bill Savoy. In late
1999, the end-of-millennium Internet bubble was inflating at mach
speed, generating billions for technology stock investors like Vulcan. By
contrast, it was open season on Fleckenstein's eponymous bearish firm,
which had nearly been wiped out over the previous two years as wagers
against market darlings like Micron Technology, Compaq Computer,
and Gateway hemorrhaged cash.

Intel was trading at a price-earnings multiple of 80. An analyst had
just hung a $450 price target on a money-losing online retailer called
Amazon.com. And the stocks of personal computer makers were spiking, even as the price of desktops fell below $1,000. The very name of

Fleckenstein's own hedge fund mocked him—RTM, for Reversion To the Mean.

There was no reversion—only surging stock prices as investors bet their life savings on something called the *new economy*. Now, in Savoy's office, which looked out onto shimmering Lake Washington, Fleckenstein told his favorite client he was ready to quit.

"I'm thinking about throwing in the towel," he said. "I need to maintain my sanity."

Savoy held a Louisville Slugger baseball bat, taking practice swings as they talked. He looked Fleckenstein in the eye and told him to hang tough—that the hedge his fund RTM provided was critical for firms like his. Fleckenstein's insights were invaluable. The market would turn.

"You've got to stay in there," Savoy said.

"But I can't keep losing money for people," Fleckenstein said. "I've got to stop doing this."

"No, you've got to keep on, Bill, you're our insurance policy," Savoy said. The two discussed strategy changes for RTM, anything to relieve the unrelenting pressure. "Do what you have to do," Savoy concluded. "But closing the fund is not any option."

Savoy kicked in an additional $15 million—a lifesaver for his beaten-down fellow investor.

Fleckenstein needed it. The next quarter, as he worked to revamp his trading methodology, the NASDAQ Composite Index surged another 24 percent to its all-time peak of 5,048 on March 10, 2000. Staunch bears packed it in: Loews Corp's Larry Tisch covered the last of the company's short positions on the Standard & Poor's (S&P) 500, locking in a stunning loss of $2 billion. Julian Robertson's vaunted Tiger Management hedge funds, which had bet heavily against tech stocks, packed it in.

RTM turned in a stomach-churning first quarter loss of more than 30 percent for the quarter. Without Vulcan's capital injection, it likely would not have survived.

Then, as they always do, the markets turned. The NASDAQ index began a vertigo-inducing fall that would eventually vaporize 75 percent of its value, equal to $5 trillion of market capitalization. RTM cashed in as its bearish bets began to pay off, scoring a 58.1 percent gain for the last three quarters of 2000, versus an 11.9 percent decline for the S&P 500.

The next year, RTM notched a 33.1 percent gain as the index tumbled another 11.9 percent, and in 2002, RTM posted a further 17.3 percent profit while the S&P 500 dropped 22.1 percent.

Fleckenstein's resolute stance during the Internet bubble made him a legend among short sellers—and sealed his reputation as a steel-nerved contrarian seer. "It was strength and conviction," declares Fred Hickey, editor of Nashua, New Hampshire newsletter *Hi-Tech Strategist*, and an outspoken bear at the time. "It takes confidence, but not so much that you're arrogant."

From there, triumph just followed triumph. By late 2003, Fleckenstein was already warning of galloping speculation in the housing market. "The Fed and government have attempted to bail out the aftermath of our giant stock bubble with a leveraged real estate bubble," he wrote. "This will end in disaster."

Fleckenstein, spot on, wagered against subprime lenders and mortgage insurers—including IndyMac, Countrywide Financial, and MGIC. But as the bubble deflated in 2008, he began to target economically sensitive technology companies, a favorite being what was then called Research in Motion, the Canadian maker of the BlackBerry mobile phone, as well as banks and brokers such as Washington Mutual and Lehman Brothers.

Though the market declined during that period, the Federal Reserve's efforts to manage the crisis, as well as other government intervention, such as bailout legislation and the ban on short selling financial stocks, provoked violent rallies, making the lives of short sellers like Fleckenstein difficult. The ban on shorting financial stocks, absurdly broad, included International Business Machines Corp. and Winnebago Industries, two stocks RTM was short.

Nevertheless, in 2008, as the mortgage-fueled credit bubble deflated, bringing the world financial system to the brink of collapse, the fund gained 41 percent versus 28.4 percent for the average short-biased hedge fund and the 37 percent drop in the S&P 500.

He nailed it again in March 2009, shuttering RTM within weeks of the stock market low. A student of the crash of 1929, Fleckenstein reasoned that in the kind of deep recession he foresaw, Federal Reserve chairman Ben Bernanke would flood the economy with money, pumping liquidity into the stock market. That would generate a gale force headwind for any dedicated short fund. "There was no way I was going to fight that battle," says Fleckenstein.

Today, short sellers are on the run—and not just because of the central bank's loose monetary policy, though that of course remains the most important factor. Far too many investors are sifting the same fundamental data to identify profitable short sale candidates. The signs they look for are well known—compressed corporate profit margins, increased account receivables versus sales, and high "days sales outstanding," the average number of days a company takes to collect revenue after a sale has been made. All are bearish signals and all can be sussed and sorted out with a click or two of a computer mouse.

"There are just a lot of guys looking at the same predictive indicators," says Claudio Chiuchiarelli, a partner at Banyan Securities of Greenbrae, California, which caters to short sellers. "There's too much money chasing too few poor-quality companies, especially when you include the short books of the long-short managers."

The competition has inflated the cost of borrowing shares. The rate, known as the "borrow" in short-selling argot, tops 40 percent annualized for hard-to-locate shares like Sears Holdings or Netflix, double what it was before the financial crisis.

Macro funds managed by firms like Bridgewater Associates and Brevan Howard Asset Management have surged in popularity, partly because their returns do not track those of stock markets, though their performance has turned lackluster of late. Such funds use currency, bond, and commodity futures to wager on global economic trends. Of course, with less skin in the equity markets, investors are less interested in hedging their stock positions.

With the exception of 2011, when they eked out a 0.35 percent gain, short-selling hedge funds have bled money every year since 2008, according to Hedge Fund Research. The number of such funds tracked by the firm has fallen to just 17 at year-end 2014 from 50 in 2009. Assets under management are just $5.8 billion, down from $7.8 billion in 2008.

"Practicing short sellers are an endangered species," says Harold "Fritz" Garrecht, former president of East Shore Partners, a brokerage in Hauppauge, New York that was known for generating short-selling ideas. "There are as many of them as pandas bred in captivity."

As for Fleckenstein, today he manages a $70 million "go-anywhere" fund, Fleckenstein Partners LP, that he invests as he sees fit—longs, shorts, or anything else. "I run it for friends, family, and a few like-minded souls," he says. In 2012, for example, it was heavily invested in precious metals, both the raw commodities and mining stocks, both of which should benefit as the world turns away from the dollar as its reserve currency. "I'm not expected to do anything specific," he says. "And I don't have to explain what I'm doing."

Fleckenstein, who has shoulder-length gray hair and favors brightly colored shirts, has always charted an independent course—and kissed off convention as he does. He advocates a return to the gold standard, dismisses reflexive bulls as "U4ians," and refers to CNBC, the business news channel, as "Bubblevision" for its relentless stock market cheerleading.

When *Mad Money* T.V. host James Cramer before the 2008-2009 crisis began recommending Apple, Google, Amazon.com, and Research in Motion to viewers, dubbing them the "four horseman" of the technology sector, Fleckenstein rechristened them the "four horseflies" for their high risk and high valuations. For Fleckenstein, sell-side analysts are mostly "dead fish" who unthinkingly issue buy recommendations on stocks they don't know particularly well.

One Fleckenstein proposal—renaming the U.S. dollar the "Xera," a word he invented by combining *Xerox*, the copying machine brand, with *lira*, Italy's former, notoriously hyperinflated currency. "'Xera' sounds like 'zero,' which is ultimately where the dollar is heading," Fleckenstein wrote.

Fleckenstein churns out contrarian opinions on his website, fleckensteincapital.com, and wrote a weekly column for *MSN Money* for 10 years as well. His 4,000 website subscribers and MSN readers have helped bolster his position as an informal spokesman for what might be called Bear America, a cadre who believes the Fed's bouts of quantitative easing—buying back mountains of Treasuries and other bonds to keep interest rates low—combined with a willingness to print money are undermining the dollar, pumping up stock prices to dangerous levels, and fueling a global, debt-fueled super bubble that will end in disaster.

Affable and self-deprecating, Fleckenstein turns scathing on the subject of the Federal Reserve, especially its former chairman, Alan Greenspan. "People don't understand what a completely reckless and incompetent fool Greenspan was, even to this day," he snaps. "In addition to a financially corrupt two-party political system, the biggest problem we have is the Fed."

In an act of catharsis, Fleckenstein wrote a best-selling book on the topic: *Greenspan's Bubbles: The Age of Ignorance at the Federal Reserve* (McGraw-Hill, 2008). In it, Fleckenstein trawls through transcripts of the Federal Open Market Committee from 1996–2002 (these are kept secret for five years) and compares them to the public statements of Alan Greenspan at the time. "I remember seething as I read through the transcripts," he says. The book details contradictions, mistakes, and what Fleckenstein sees as Greenspan's utter indifference to the rampant speculation of the era.

Fleckenstein blames the Federal Reserve chairman's loose money policy for the Internet and housing bubbles. He slams Greenspan for not tightening margin requirements, for ignoring evidence of a housing bubble, and for lax regulatory oversight, including the abolition of the Glass-Steagall Act, which until 1997 separated commercial lending from riskier investment banking activities. "There is no debate: Greenspan was no 'Maestro;' he was the master of the United States' descent into financial turmoil," Fleckenstein's book concludes. "The evidence speaks for itself."

Whether you agree with Fleckenstein's arguments or not, *Greenspan's Bubbles* was an act of market-timing genius, published at the cusp of the credit crisis. It has been translated into a dozen languages, including Russian, Chinese, Bulgarian, and Thai.

"Bill made the case as bluntly as anybody that this Fed chairman was doing enormous harm to the economy," says James Grant, editor of *Grant's Interest Rate Observer*. "It was a work of great passion and great power in terms of its impact on Wall Street."

In early 2015 Fleckenstein says that the Federal Reserve has "done it again but only bigger" and produced not only another bubble in stocks but also one in bonds. Current equity valuations as measured by market capitalization to gross domestic product have only been exceeded in a couple of quarters at the zenith of the subprime-fueled bubble. "When these markets exhaust themselves and finally begin to decline, the ensuing financial disaster will be worse than in 2008," he says, though it will also be different. So Fleckenstein has readied plans to launch RTM 2.0, a new fund, and will return to the short side once again as soon as he feels the time is right.

For all his focus on the U.S. central bank, the public track record speaks equally to Fleckenstein's acumen as a bottom-up accounting sleuth—making him one of those relatively uncommon investors who can claim both great micro- and macroeconomic expertise. What he unearths in SEC filings, balance sheets, and footnotes informs his short positions, since he seldom bets against broad market indexes.

In 1998, Fleckenstein began shorting Gateway, a maker of budget personal computers that he felt would suffer as prices fell through the floor. "I had a jihad for that company," he admits. "It was just a commodity."

In October 2000, Fleckenstein dug into new SEC filings, zeroing in on the sharp growth in the balance sheet item called "other assets." Fleckenstein was sure this reflected the increased financing Gateway was providing customers to bolster computer sales—a bright red flag that the business was in trouble. Four weeks after his post on the subject—"Fudgement Day"—the company announced it would miss estimates and its shares lost nearly a third of their value. "It was a complete bottoms-up detective case," Fleckenstein says.

Another perennial Fleckenstein short was Dell. In July 2004, the company raised earnings guidance by two cents, to enthusiastic market response. Fleckenstein, who trained as an actuary, crunched the numbers and found a rounding error in the company's calculations. The mistake, it turns out, permitted Dell to trumpet improving profitability. In fact, a lower tax rate was largely responsible for the bump in earnings. The Securities & Exchange Commission (SEC) subsequently investigated Dell's accounting. Its results have not been made public. Dell went private in a management-led leveraged buyout in 2013.

All in all, Fleckenstein's successes have made for a heady redemption since the overwrought days of the Internet bubble. Even as the markets pushed him to the brink of financial ruin, he was under near constant attack for his contrarian outlook—and for his readiness to talk publicly about it.

E-mails and anonymous phone calls were vitriolic, message boards sometimes worse: "total loser," "pinhead," "complete Bozo," and "the village idiot of the technology sector" are some examples. One accused him of making up numbers. Another compared him to cult leaders Jim Jones and David Koresh.

"I even had subscribers to my website sending me hate mail," says Fleckenstein.

On television, anchors mocked Fleckenstein for questioning stock valuations and advocating that investors avoid companies like Compaq, Hewlett-Packard, Dell, and Gateway. "If I had followed your advice and sold this market short at any point in the past three to five years, I would have lost my shirt, and you sir, I believe, lost money last year," sniped Stuart Varney on *CNN Moneyline* in February 2000. "What do you have to say to that?"

Characteristically unflappable, Fleckenstein responded that so-called new economy valuations seemed to have no relation to profits. "I'm no technophobe, but we've lost all sense of reality," he said.

Like a lot of short sellers, Fleckenstein says an ethical impulse was underpinning his advocacy at the time. "In the 1990s, I could see that people were being led like lambs to the slaughter," he says. "I wanted to warn people."

Says Fleckenstein's younger sister, Mary Fleckenstein Simpson: "He just wants to be right. I asked why he sat there and took it and he just said, 'I'm going to be right and they'll remember.'"

That didn't make it easy. "To see one's neighbors getting rich by doing the wrong thing is unbearable," says Grant. "His interrogators were pounding shivs of bamboo under his fingernails."

Today, Fleckenstein works from a Mediterranean-style home in the Madison Park district of Seattle; his spacious office faces east, toward Mercer Island, from which direction light floods in on a bright September morning. Unlike most successful hedge fund managers who buy lavish apartments or estates, Fleckenstein rents, in keeping with his bearish outlook when he moved in. "I said, 'I'm not going to buy a house in the middle of a bubble," he chuckles.

The room is dominated by a five-foot-ten-inch-tall stuffed upright black bear—a gift from a fellow short seller, now retired. The bear—who has no name—wears a baseball cap emblazoned with what became a sort of a mantra in the early years of the Internet bubble: "Dow 10,000." Initially, it was a sign of the euphoria overtaking the financial system, since the Dow Industrials traded at around 8,000 in 1996. When the index surged past the 10,000 milestone in 1998, it became a slogan for bears who foresaw a day of reckoning. The Dow peaked at 14,000 in 2007, and hit its nadir on March 2009, at 7,400. In March 2015 it traded at 18,000 again.

Facing the big picture windows is a wall of Bloomberg terminals and other computer screens. The decor speaks to the occupant's relentless Fed-watching. On the walls are caricatures of Greenspan—a bit obsessive, you might say. In a first floor bathroom hangs a signed copy of a Statement to Congress from October 17, 1979, by former Fed chairman Paul Volker, who Fleckenstein admires for his campaign to rein in galloping 18-percent inflation during his tenure. At their leisure, visitors can ponder Volker's handwritten missive: "Monetary policy can only be part of the overall framework."

Despite his dark economic worldview, Fleckenstein is upbeat. He talks quickly, zipping from subject to subject. Fleckenstein will make near-instantaneous connections between, say a balance sheet footnote in a 10-K filing and a Financial Accounting Standards Board (FASB) regulation that would take a normal investor half an hour to figure out. On occasion, that will result in a lightening quick trade. "It's surprising how quickly he goes from premise to thesis to action," says Grant. "That's Bill—decisive."

At five feet, ten inches and 165 pounds, Fleckenstein looks 10 years younger than his 60 years. He has been married to the same ex-Wall Street analyst for 30 years; the couple has two daughters.

Fleckenstein plays national tennis tournaments, does CrossFit, and helicopter skis. He collects white Burgundies, which he ages, one favorite being Corton-Charlemagne. From the bouquet alone he can identify a wine's varietal blend, maker, and vintage. Fleckenstein is an enthused audiophile, and a high-end stereo system is in the corner. He prefers vinyl LPs to digital alternatives, has two turntables, and keeps CNBC anchor Maria Bartiromo on mute as he blasts British 1970s-era rock, including the Rolling Stones, David Bowie, and the Who. "Bill is all-in on anything he does," says one high school friend. "He is never half-hearted."

One morning in late summer, Fleckenstein sprawls on his office sofa, dressed in a long-sleeved green T-shirt and worn gray sweatpants. He's scheduled to play tennis later that day, and friends say his athletic disposition helped him endure the pressures of short selling. Fleckenstein and most of his ilk describe the short business as a more taxing investment discipline than other varieties, especially when managing other people's money. "You have to be even more willing to stand against the crowd," he says. "You've got to be disciplined and flexible at the same time."

Finessing that contradiction has been key to Fleckenstein's success. The discipline is embodied in the rigorous fundamental analysis he does when valuing a security. However, market dynamics require that today's short seller cover positions quickly or find ways to cut risk when a trade doesn't pan out or goes awry—hence the requirement for flexibility. "My firm belief is that research is not enough," says Fleckenstein. "It's tactics."

It was Fleckenstein's meeting with Savoy that emboldened him to reassess his trading methodology—and go in a very different direction. A truism of the business is that short sales generate most of their profits in only relatively brief periods. "You make money in a small amount of time," he says. "Stocks fall much, much more quickly than they rise." Hence the Wall Street adage: escalator up, elevator down.

Fleckenstein's research pinpointed when those sudden downdrafts are most likely to occur—for example, when the Federal Open Market Committee is meeting, because that is generally when interest rates are raised or lowered. Or during the mid-quarter "pre-announcement period," when companies signal to analysts whether their earnings estimates were too high or too low. Or during earnings season itself. "It didn't take catalysts to get people to buy stocks," Fleckenstein says. "It sure took catalysts to get them to sell."

Fleckenstein worked with a technical portfolio manager, Dave Davidson, to sort through volume and price patterns to identify the best times to initiate a trade. Fleckenstein calls the strategy "tactical short."

"My thinking was, 'I'm not going to be short all the time,'" Fleckenstein says. "I was going to be short when it made sense."

Fleckenstein abandoned his strategy of maintaining near-constant shorts on April 1, 2000—a fortnight after the stock market turned. It was in fact superb timing. Though in retrospect, many people recall a freefalling stock market from the peak, in reality there were several violent bear market rallies, like the three-week period in September 2000 when the NASDAQ Composite surged 20 percent. Fleckenstein's tactical short strategy largely sidestepped those surges.

When stocks began to rebound from their nadir in late 2002, Fleckenstein was again able to avoid steep losses, even turning a profit in 2005, when the S&P 500 rose 5 percent. "If you were a jihad short seller you would have gotten your face ripped in 2003 and 2004 and 2005," says Chiuchiarelli. "Fleckenstein's strategy will lose you less when the market is going against you and make you more when the market is going down."

Tactical short selling is proving transformational for some in the industry, allowing select short sellers to flourish even during an era of continual central bank easing—which is now happening in Europe as well. Fleckenstein, characteristically, is sanguine about his achievement. "I'm proud of the fact that after getting beat up in the market mania, I was able to revamp my strategy," he says.

William Alan Fleckenstein was born in 1955, the youngest of four siblings, in what is today the capital of value investing—Omaha, Nebraska. His mother, Shirley, kept house; his father, William Russell Fleckenstein, served in the National Guard with Warren Buffett before landing a job at Mutual of Omaha, the insurance company, where he rose to assistant controller.

Both of his parents were Depression-era babies, born in 1926, and a frequent topic of conversation was the Crash of 1929 and the Great Depression that followed. It helped inculcate the notion in the boy's mind that things do go wrong. "My Mom said there was just no money," Fleckenstein says. "I asked, 'How could there be no money?'"

In 1967, the elder Fleckenstein quit the insurer after it refused to address what he considered a conflict of interest. The family decamped for the Seattle area, where the older William took a job at what is now Milliman Inc., a consulting firm, rising to chief financial officer.

The young Fleckenstein excelled at sports—especially skiing—and showed an innate propensity for mathematics. At the all-boy Seattle Preparatory School, Jesuit fathers taught him the meaning of discipline—or at least tried to. There was frequent back and forth, for example, about his rebellious demeanor. "I kept trying to grow my hair longer than I was supposed to," says Fleckenstein.

Nor did the fathers appreciate his unorthodox opinions. "He was a dissenter back then," says a high school friend. "He knew more than was presented by the fathers and therefore came to different conclusions."

By his sophomore year, Fleckenstein was chafing under the Jesuit fathers' discipline and lobbied to transfer to a high school closer to home—one with a broader curriculum. The fathers made the decision easier by expelling him. He graduated from Newport High School, in Bellevue, after acing a class in accounting—a rare subject for a U.S. secondary school. Fleckenstein hoped to follow in his father's footsteps.

From there it was off to the University of Washington—and what became his beloved fraternity, Theta Chi. "Everybody says their fraternity was like 'Animal House,' but ours really was," says Fleckenstein. Expulsions, suspensions, and dropouts had reduced the number of students in the frat house to 15 from 90 two years earlier. Among his extracurricular activities: beer, namely four-person pony keg drinking contests.

Fleckenstein's unlikely passion (at least for a partier) remained accounting, which put his intuitive math skills to practical use. "It was all about how the pieces fit together," he recalls. "It was fascinating." Fleckenstein helped work his way through school, hawking subscriptions to the *Seattle Times*, doing underwater construction in the Puget Sound, and—mostly—crunching numbers in the accounting department of Milliman.

Rolling into his senior year, he found another practical outlet for his mathematical skill sets: computer programming. In particular he mastered the high-level ALGOL programming language used by Burroughs Corporation in its popular mainframe computers. "I thought, 'This is really cool,'" says Fleckenstein. "This is better than math."

Fleckenstein picked up his B.A. in mathematics from the University of Washington and persevered toward his ultimate goal—to follow in his father's footsteps. Actuaries are business professionals certified in the techniques for modeling and managing risk—crucial to insurers, accountancies, and some money managers. To become an associate actuary, Fleckenstein needed to pass ten tortuous, math-heavy tests administered by the Society of Actuaries covering subjects such as probability, financial mathematics, and corporate finance.

Perhaps the Theta Chi kegs tripped him up. "You needed a six to pass," Fleckenstein recalls. "I got a five, twice."

Dejected, Fleckenstein went hunting for his first full-time work. The local Burroughs office was looking for a salesman. "The branch manager was blown away that I knew ALGOL," he recalls. Fleckenstein joined and basked in his newfound independence. "I was getting paid well, $800 a month," Fleckenstein says. "I remember thinking, 'If I could get $1000 a month, I'll be set for life.'"

Fleckenstein picked up a book: *Psychology in the Stock Market* by the now acclaimed value money manager David Dreman. It was his introduction to investing. The takeaway changed Fleckenstein's life. "You didn't have to be an expert in any industry to be a successful investor," he says. "You just had to recognize that unanimity in the markets pushed prices to extremes. My 'a-ha' moment was that in any price is embedded risks and fears."

Fleckenstein was soon devouring other investing works—Benjamin Graham and David Dodd's *Security Analysis*, John Train's *The Money Masters*, and the annual reports of Berkshire Hathaway.

Investing might have remained a hobby had it not been for a way-laid jet at Los Angeles International Airport in 1980, when Fleckenstein found himself sitting next to George Froley, a bond fund manager with Pacific Investment Advisors. Froley recalls being impressed by his seat-mate's Wall Street savvy. "I said, 'You're ready to go into the stock business,'" Froley says. He referred Fleckenstein to Kidder Peabody's Seattle office where a friend was branch manager.

Kidder Peabody, an innovative firm at the time, seldom hired rookies, but the branch manager took a flier on Fleckenstein—and was soon glad he did. "He brought in more accounts and did more business than anybody they'd ever seen," says Froley.

It was the maw of the 1977–1982 bear market, during which time the S&P 500 lost 48 percent. "If you had survived that drought you had to be pretty savvy," Fleckenstein says, recalling that the predominant product of the day was neither equities nor bonds but certificates of deposit. "Nobody wanted stocks. It was all about CDs."

The Kidder Peabody greybeards fostered a collegial environment and looked after their longhaired rookie broker. "I was always bombarding them with questions," Fleckenstein says. "They always had time for me."

After running the New York City Marathon in 1981, Fleckenstein developed a passionate interest in something aside from the markets—Melody Miller Johnson, a blonde Kidder Peabody stock analyst in New York who covered copier companies Xerox and Savin. "She was a tech person who believed in rapid growth," Fleckenstein says. "I was a value guy. We butted heads."

Though Kidder Peabody policy forbade analysts from taking phone calls from brokers, she accepted his. It flowered into an enduring romance. The two were married in 1984.

At Kidder Peabody, Fleckenstein showed entrepreneurial flair. While keeping a roster of retail clients, he also tried his hand, unofficially, at research, penning a white paper on an Apple disc drive clone maker called Standun Controls. Confident as always, he sent it to Warren Buffett, mentioning his father's connection to the Oracle of Omaha. Buffett wrote back that he remembered Fleckenstein's father but didn't comment on individual stocks.

Fleckenstein also developed a distinctive line of business. Using his mathematical background, he measured the risk, volatility, beta and Sharpe ratios of different institutional portfolio managers, positioning himself as matchmaker for pensions and directing them to the managers best suited to them. "I thought, somebody has to evaluate the money managers," he says. "If I can hook them up, maybe I can get a piece of the action."

One of the firms on Fleckenstein's roster was three-year-old Olympic Capital Management, a value-oriented shop in Seattle. "When he asked questions, you could just see he knew his stuff," says Olympic founder John Crowl. "He had a good analytical mind." When Crowl asked Fleckenstein to join him in 1982, he jumped at the chance to get into the money management business.

By that time, Olympic Capital had $2 billion under management and Crowl decided to cull its client roster, limiting it to those with $5 million or more to invest. Fleckenstein would run an internal fund—Fleckenstein Capital—that would handle smaller accounts with a minimum of just $250,000. "It was a way to help me out, keep the number of clients low, and stave off competition," he says. When Crowl merged Olympic into Sirach Capital Management in 1996, Fleckenstein set off on his own.

The former head of the investment division of New York–based Bankers Trust Corp, Crowl became a mentor to the still-green investor. "He just understood how the world worked," says Fleckenstein. "He would synthesize things."

Crowl constantly drove home to Fleckenstein how the changing market dynamics determined the catalysts driving stock prices. "There are times when macro doesn't matter. There are times when it's all that matters," says Fleckenstein. "John taught me you had to know both bottoms-up stock picking as well as the macro view."

As the bull market began to gather steam in the mid-1980s, Fleckenstein plowed ahead with a voracious reading schedule: 10-Ks, *Barron's*, *Forbes*, *Fortune*, and *Financial World*. He was particularly fascinated by the stock market crash of 1929 and the subsequent Great Depression, and his favorite books included *Only Yesterday* by Frederick Lewis Allen, *Economics and the Public Welfare* by Benjamin Anderson, *Modern Times* by Paul Johnson, and *The Crash and Its Aftermath* by Barry Wigmore.

By mid-1987, Fleckenstein saw stock markets getting frothy. The U.S. dollar was under pressure, and bond markets were weakening. Equities were spiking upward, rising 27 percent in the first half of the year. Ominously, investors were throwing money at a newfangled product called portfolio insurance—an invention of the Berkeley, California firm of Leland O'Brien Rubenstein Associates. The idea behind portfolio insurance was simple: For a fee, Leland O'Brien would hedge an investor's stock market exposure in the event of a crash by furiously selling stock index futures as a way to limit losses. The firm's book of business covered portfolios worth an estimated $60 billion, a lot of money at the time.

"I knew that would be a disaster," Fleckenstein says. "Everybody can't get out at the same time." More importantly, portfolio insurance meant pension funds, foundations, and endowments felt inured to the risks they were taking on as stock prices rose. They weren't shifting money into cash as they normally would in a surging market. Why should they? Portfolio insurance would protect them.

Olympic Capital built a 30 percent cash position by October 1987, sidestepping a big part of the 24 percent one-day sell off. While Fleckenstein believed the meltdown would trigger a recession, Crowl thought not. He argued, correctly it turned out, that since there hadn't been a major misallocation of capital, the economy would shrug it off. "I didn't understand that at the time," Fleckenstein says. He was learning to think big macro thoughts.

The next year Fleckenstein turned his attention to Japan, where, in addition to galloping real estate prices, stocks like Sony Corp., Japan Air Lines, and Toshiba Corp. were trading at multiples of 80 times trailing earnings or more. "They were insanely priced," Fleckenstein says. One key problem for a bear was that it was virtually impossible to borrow shares on Japanese markets to sell short, and the American Depositary Receipts of Japanese companies that traded on the New York Stock Exchange were sufficiently illiquid as to be vulnerable to short squeezes.

Fleckenstein found an arcane yet useful instrument to help him bet against the Japanese market—a series of three put warrants on the Nikkei Stock Index issued by Salomon Brothers beginning in June 1988. The warrants gave the holder the right to sell the benchmark index to a counterparty at strike prices of around 28,000, 31,000, and 33,000, respectively, and expired between August 1990 and April 1992. The cost? As little as $4.50. When the Nikkei, which was trading at 35,000 as Fleckenstein began buying the warrants, tumbled to 20,000 by April 1991, he was able to garner a twelvefold payoff on his investment. "It's not the analysis that will get you to the Promised Land, it's the tactics you employ," says Fleckenstein.

Fleckenstein was less interested in size—the biggest his fund ever got was $170 million—and more focused on being right. "I think $50 to $100 million is a good size; you can move in and out quickly. I don't have trouble finding options, which is part of my strategy," he says. "I don't want to be the richest man in the cemetery."

By 1996, however, Fleckenstein was growing increasingly skeptical of Greenspan's easy money policies. In 1994, with GDP growth accelerating to 6.5 percent, the Fed acted to dampen inflationary worries, raising its target rate six times over 12 months to 6 percent. Growth throttled back to 3.2 percent by early 1995. Wall Street, the media and politicians lauded the chairman for navigating this economic "soft-landing" that forestalled a recession. Greenspan would later call the maneuver "one of the Fed's proudest accomplishments during my tenure."

Fleckenstein took a dimmer view. To his mind, following the soft landing, the Fed chairman ignored the speculative bubble building in stocks, especially the technology-heavy NASDAQ Composite, which rose 22 percent in 1995. Worse, he began cutting rates again in July of that year, just six months after his last rate hike, and repeated cuts twice more over the next eight months. The NASDAQ index spiked 22 percent in 1996. "He was serving more punch to the party," Fleckenstein wrote. "Greenspan thought of the stock market as one giant applause meter."

In Greenspan's book, *The Age of Turbulence: Adventures in a New World* (Penguin Press, 2007), the Fed chairman writes that he held off tightening because of his suspicion at the time that technological changes were in fact fueling productivity growth in an unprecedented fashion. "What if this wasn't a normal business cycle?" he wrote. "What if the technology revolution had, temporarily at least, increased the economy's ability to expand?"

In other words, despite his famous 1996 admonishment warning of "irrational exuberance," Greenspan was himself buying into the fantasy about an Internet-enabled new economy—and persuading the Federal Open Market Committee (FOMC) as well.

Needless to say, Fleckenstein thought that was claptrap. And he parried the prevalent notion that technology was increasing productivity growth, when even Greenspan conceded there was no evidence to suggest that it was.

While Fleckenstein blames Greenspan for starting the bubble, human nature played its own role. One early example: the 74 percent one-day rise in Netscape Communications shares at its initial public offering in April 1995.

The Federal Reserve, combined with crowd psychology and a confluence of factors set the stage for disaster. An aging baby boomer population approaching retirement with insufficient savings; the introduction of the Microsoft Windows 95 operating system, which greatly increased the ease of communications—and fired up the public's imagination as to the power of the Internet; the advent of cable channel CNBC, a relentless cheerleader for the bull market; and companies themselves, who, enabled by Wall Street analysts and bankers, hawked dubious "accounting" measures of profitability—price per eyeballs, clicks and so on—if not promulgating outright fraud.

Set against Greenspan's backdrop of loose money, this cauldron of indomitable forces led Fleckenstein to think a traditional Dodd & Graham approach to picking beaten-down, out-of-favor stocks would be a hopeless slog. "I knew the value business was going to be impossible going forward," he says. From 1995 through March 2000, growth stocks more than doubled the gains of value stocks, returning 32.7 percent annualized versus 14.9 percent.

Fleckenstein kicked off RTM in 1996, marketing it as a short fund—one that would bet continuously against the expanding bubble. One of his first investments as an independent firm, however, was a long investment in silver. At $3 to $4 an ounce, the metal was priced at the cost of production or lower. "I knew silver was going to have a big move," he says.

The best way to profit from rising precious metal prices is often through beaten-down mining company stocks, which because of their fixed costs are leveraged to the price of the commodity. Among the cheapest was Pan American Silver Corp., a Vancouver-based producer with a mine in Peru and an appetite for acquisitions. Shares were trading at $4.50, and Fleckenstein figured they would quadruple on even a modest rise in silver prices. He held the position until 2007, when silver hit $12.75 an ounce—and Pan American shares $44.

"It was something that took a long time to evolve," he says. "With value investing you're combating apathy. With a short sale there is no apathy. It doesn't matter if you're right, it only matters when the market agrees with you."

Although by 1996 rampant speculation was inflating sectors ranging from telecommunications to banks, Fleckenstein focused on a shifting portfolio of 15 to 30 computer hardware stocks. That's largely because of their interconnectedness: Computer sales drive chip sales, which in turn drive sales of semiconductor equipment. "They are all suppliers and customers of each other," he says. "You get a pretty good idea of what's going on in the whole mosaic."

Micron Technology, America's largest maker of DRAM chips, was a perennial on Fleckenstein's short list. The stock in December 1997 traded at some 30 times trailing earnings. The prevalent view was that as the Internet continued to make over the world economy, there would be a shortage of DRAMs that Micron would benefit from. Fleckenstein thought Micron's chips were commodities, looked at the DRAM manufacturing capacity that was slated to come on line and predicted a glut. Moreover, Micron's principal competitors, Samsung and Taiwan Semiconductor, were subsidized by their governments.

Computer makers Hewlett-Packard, Compaq, Dell, and Gateway, also made the list. At year-end 1997, their price earnings multiples were at what Fleckenstein considered to be nosebleed levels, too. Conventional wisdom was that the Internet would foster year-over-year unit sales growth as buyers annually traded in their old models for new, faster ones. Fleckenstein argued that computers had plenty of power already. Plummeting PC prices would pressure margins no matter how many they sold anyway.

Intel was a case in and of itself. It traded at 80 times earnings and, together with Microsoft, constituted the half of the Wintel cartel that provided the brains of the personal computer. Intel, however, with rare consistency failed to meet its own earnings projections. Midway through the quarter it would hold a conference call for analysts to *pre-announce*, in the argot of Wall Street. That meant guiding earnings and sales targets lower. "They were terrible at knowing their own company," says Fleckenstein. RTM would be short Intel before the pre-announcements—and made money 70 percent of the time.

"With bubbles, people believe a false set of assumptions," says one former Fleckenstein Capital investor. "Bill basically looks at those assumptions and says they're wrong."

Indeed, Fleckenstein in August 1999 had a new and bully pulpit from which to voice those opinions. Fleckenstein began writing a column for Seattle-based Go2Net Inc., sounding off on stocks he was buying or shorting and commenting on the markets and economy in general. "I felt strongly that Greenspan's policies were going to have terrible repercussions," Fleckenstein says. "I wanted to warn people."

Beyond that, Fleckenstein admits to enlightened self-interest. "In my own selfish way, I wanted to be in the camp of those who saw problems coming," he says. "I thought the investment world would be sorted into two piles—those who saw the problems and those that didn't."

In 1998, Fleckenstein moved his column to Jim Grant's investing website, www.grantsinvestor.com. When that folded in 2001, he moved to what was then called TheStreet.com, and later to *MSN Money*, owned by Microsoft.

"Bill has never been shy about giving people his opinion. I don't think it's an ego thing," says Hickey. "He wants to educate them."

The NASDAQ rose 22 percent in 1997, yet Fleckenstein Capital's RTM Fund managed to turn a profit. The next year would prove far tougher.

In August 1998, Russia unexpectedly defaulted on its sovereign debt, triggering a global rout of hedge funds that had been betting that spreads between emerging markets, like Russia, and developed ones, like the United States and Germany, would narrow. Instead, they exploded.

The biggest casualty was Long-Term Capital Management LP, a $4.7 billion fund run by former Salomon Brothers trader John Meriwether. In addition to employing two Nobel Prize–winning economists, the Greenwich, Connecticut–based LTCM was distinguished by the more than 25-to-1 leverage it employed in making its myriad bets worth over $125 billion. LCTM's derivatives exposure reportedly topped $1 trillion. Much of the borrowed money was imprudently furnished by Wall Street's biggest banks, including Goldman Sachs, Merrill Lynch, Morgan Stanley, and UBS, many of which were also investors in the ill-fated fund.

As word of LTCM's collapse spread in August, world equity markets began to unravel. The S&P 500 dropped 19 percent peak to trough.

Greenspan rushed to cut rates, slashing three times in the space of two months to 4.75, once in an emergency meeting on the Friday before options expiration. "I went absolutely apoplectic," Fleckenstein says. "That was the moment they really got drunk. They had no concept of the damage they were doing with a monetary policy that was drastically too loose."

The markets, as Fleckenstein puts it, "got the wink-wink"—and began their relentless rocket to the moon. Over an 18-month period, the NASDAQ Composite would more than triple to 5,048 from 1,428. RTM, which had been up more than 30 percent going into September 1998, finished the year with a loss. Fleckenstein, already suffering, was entering a new world of pain.

Each morning, he would wake up at 4:30, read the papers, and drive to his 33rd-floor office in downtown Seattle. There, in the predawn darkness, the markets would open on the East Coast, and soon his computer screens would begin to glow green—signaling another up day for technology stocks. "The lights would start up and we would scramble to play defense," Fleckenstein says.

Chapter 7

Kass: Nader's Raider Hits the Street

Doug Kass's journey into short selling began at a harness-racing track at the Lycoming County Fair in in Williamsport, Pennsylvania. Going into the home stretch he was in the lead, driving a three-year old standardbred horse, Bacon, under sunny skies. Kass, a New York money manager, describes himself as obsessed with the sport of kings, hooked on the speed, excitement, and of course, the magnificent horses themselves. "I owned them, I bred them, I raced them," Kass says.

That July morning in 1990, danger lurked. The leather collar that held up Bacon's head, called a martingale, had worn thin. As the two neared the finish line, it snapped and Bacon stumbled, overturning the sulky and spilling Kass, then 44 years old, onto the track into the path of trailing horses and their drivers.

Bacon escaped injury. Kass did not. The tumble and trampling collapsed Kass's liver. It shattered his left fibula and tibia and broke seven ribs and nine vertebrae.

Kass was airlifted to New York and Mount Sinai Medical Center in Manhattan, the start of a two-year convalescence in a full body cast. His agonizing recovery gave him time to ruminate about life as well as investment ideas—more to stave off boredom than to turn a profit. "I had to do something because I was going crazy," he says.

By early 1992, still in a cast, Kass had turned his attention to a white-hot market darling—newly public Marvel Entertainment, the comic book publisher whose characters included Captain America, Spider-Man, the Incredible Hulk, and the Silver Surfer. It was the age of the hostile takeover, and Ronald Perelman, serial raider and corporate acquirer, had snatched up Marvel three years earlier for a pittance: $82.5 million from New World Entertainment. The previous July, Perelman's holding company, MacAndrews & Forbes Holdings, sold 4.2 million shares to the public at $16.50 each—the stock shot up, tripling by the time Kass began to research it.

Here's what he saw: Marvel shares were trading at 46 times trailing earnings, 6.4 times revenues, and 17 times shareholder equity. In fact, its $786 million market capitalization was almost twice the entire comic book industry's annual sales. Could that possibly make sense? Although the IPO proceeds were to have been used to pay down debt, MacAndrews & Forbes had instead helped itself to a $37.2 million special cash dividend, on top of a $10 million one-year dividend note.

That left Marvel leveraged, with $57 million in debt and other liabilities and just $43 million in equity.

As Kass dug into Marvel's quarterly reports, he realized the stock was at nosebleed levels—the question was what would cause it to tumble. Confined to a wheelchair, Kass cold-called comic book stores around the country, talking to dealers who told him that Marvel was repeatedly raising prices, to as high as $2.95 an issue. Customers were starting to balk. Together with his caregiver, he hired a van to take him to retailers, where he saw for himself how boxes of *X-Men* and *X-Force* issues were stacked high. "This was the top of the comic book cycle," Kass recalls thinking.

Marvel's promotional efforts, Kass felt, smacked of desperation: The company printed its third quarter annual report in comic book format. That seemed gimmicky. Marvel hired celebrity sports anchor Frank Gifford for its board. Kass didn't see what he added. Kass learned that many of Marvel's best writers and artists were leaving, sometimes to upstart rivals like Malibu, Viz, Innovation, and Valiant, which were generating buzz.

Kass wrote a draft research report and resolved to personally show it to his favorite business writer, Alan Abelson of *Barron's*, the financial news weekly. Though the two had never met, the acerbic columnist was required reading for Wall Street cognoscenti, especially those with a bearish disposition, since he exulted in debunking market shibboleths—blue chips as well as red-hot trend stocks. "I had like a man crush on Alan Abelson," says Kass. "I thought he was a journalistic treasure. I just loved his skepticism, his cynicism."

Kass's aide wheeled him to Abelson's office on the 16th floor of the Dow Jones & Co. headquarters at the World Financial Center. His leg was full of rods, making him look like an Erector Set. The receptionist told him he needed an appointment. Just then, Abelson returned from the men's room.

"What the f--k do you want?" he asked.

"Well Mr. Abelson, I love your journalism," Kass gushed, by way of introduction.

"Get to the chase, kid," Abelson replied. "I'll give you four minutes."

Wheeling himself into Abelson's office, Kass handed him his analysis of Marvel Entertainment. Abelson raised an eyebrow.

"Look over there," he told Kass, gestured to his conference table. There was a Marvel prospectus on it.

"I f--king hate Ronald Perelman," Abelson declared. "Why don't you leave this with me and give me a number where I can reach you?"

That Saturday, *Barron's* ran Kass's research report as a bylined story. "High-Flying Marvel Comics May Be Headed for a Fall," the deck ran. Kass playfully sprinkled the terms "Pow!" "Smash!" and "Ker-plash!" throughout the piece. Come Monday, Marvel shares crashed.

Perelman sued Kass for $20 million for his "inflammatory" research—though he was later forced to reimburse Kass for legal fees. Kass and Abelson went on to write five follow-up items for *Barron's*. Just 18 months after the initial article, Marvel Entertainment filed for bankruptcy.

Thus Kass says he found a métier as a professional bear. "My reputation as a short seller and as a kind of protégé of Alan Abelson was made," he chuckles. Abelson died in May 2013.

Investors took note of Kass's penchant for sniffing out losers. The stock research department he took over at First Albany Corp. earned some credibility for incisive, sometimes bearish calls. Kass soon fled the chilly Northeast and signed on as head of sales research and trading at J.W. Charles Securities, a Florida brokerage firm. Though Kass flogged plenty of small-capitalization stocks, many of which flamed out, the firm was soon known for its sell recommendations. He was dubbed the "Bear of Boca"—a sobriquet Kass relished. He later worked a stint at Leon Cooperman's Omega Advisors hedge fund, ultimately launching Seabreeze Partners Short LP in 2005.

The dedicated short fund notched an impressive record over a five-year history: According to investors, it gained 11 percent in its first year versus a return of 4.9 percent in the Standard & Poor's (S&P) 500. In 2006, the fund lost 5 percent when the index surged 15.8 percent and mustered a 7 percent gain in 2007 versus a 5.5 percent rise in the S&P 500. In the cataclysm of 2008, it surged 18 percent versus a 37 percent loss for the benchmark. And amidst a rebounding S&P 500 in 2009, during which the index jumped 26.5 percent, the Seabreeze Short LP lost just 6 percent.

Kass continued to manage the $300 million Seabreeze Long-Short Fund LP until a bout with cancer prompted him to close the fund and focus on managed accounts. He remains Mr. Media. The hyperkinetic money manager's experience at *Barron's* fed into a passion for broadcasting his views across the spectrum—television, the Internet and print. After Marvel Entertainment, Kass kept Abelson abreast of his fund's picks and pans, maintaining an almost worshipful affection for the man he calls his mentor. In 1998, Kass began writing for what was then called *TheStreet.com*, becoming friendly with its fast-talking, ebullient, and bullish founder Jim Cramer, who is now a TV show host on cable news channel CNBC.

Distinguished by home-styled argot—pricey stocks are "Snapplesque" and beaten-down companies are "schmeissed"—Kass is also a regular on the channel, counterbalancing relentless boosterism from many of its contributors with regular cold-water dousings on the prospects for the stock market and economy, always delivered in his

Long Island accent. Kass calls his outspokenness a public service, especially when it comes to his bearish outlook.

Privately, some friends say his penchant for punditry undercuts his ability to gather assets, as investors prefer their money managers to keep their views to themselves, especially when they are so relentlessly bearish. "Being publicly acclaimed means more to him than the wealth that comes with managing more money," says one. "He has a yen to be known as a great financial prognosticator."

For the record, he's done okay on that count, calling the market bottom in 2009 and sporting an impressive record in his annual list of likely surprises for the coming year. Kass comes from a potent intellectual milieu, the son of a multi-instrumentalist jazz musician who, according to Kass, jammed with the likes of Benny Goodman and Billy Holiday. One of Kass's sisters, Deborah, is an celebrated conceptual artist. The other, Barbara, is a psychologist. His cousin, Sandy Koufax, is the great former Brooklyn Dodgers southpaw, the youngest player ever elected to the Baseball Hall of Fame. Kass's older son, Noah, is a psychotherapist and contributor to *TheStreet*, as it is now called, and MSNBC, while his younger son, Ethan, is an award-winning playwright.

Hooked on stocks from his early teens, Kass nevertheless can claim a distinctly antiestablishment track record. He's prone to reminisce about Jimi Hendrix's legendary rendition of "Hey Joe" at the 1969 Woodstock Music Festival. In 1970, Kass helped organize the student anti-Vietnam War march on Washington. Later, he worked with consumer activist Ralph Nader to take on Wall Street cronyism, co-authoring an exposé of what was then known as Citibank. He was toiling on a Ph.D. in philosophy at Princeton University before suddenly switching gears to earn an M.B.A. from the Wharton School and pursue a life on Wall Street. A lifelong Democrat, he repeatedly interjects in any discussion of politics to emphasize that he's "to the left of Obama."

Sitting on a sofa in his den in East Hampton, New York, Kass is dressed in jeans, a T-shirt, and a dark blue cardigan. He is five feet nine inches tall and weighs 205 pounds, having shaved off 10 pounds after a recent operation for prostate cancer. Though little over a month out of surgery, Kass bubbles with energy, first leading a visitor into the basement to see a poster-size photograph of him from his harness-racing days, jumping up to print out a stock chart or a bottle of water, or rolling up a trouser leg to show off his scars.

Kass has a full head of salt-and-pepper hair and a beard to match. He dotes on his wife, Nanette, as well as their four dachsunds—Bella, Oliver, Cousette, and Sebastian, who at age 16 is deaf, blind, and dumb and sleeps soundly beside Kass throughout a two-and-a-half-hour interview on a cold winter evening. Unlike a lot of bears, Kass projects relentless optimism, sprinkling his conversation with jokes, asides, and humorous anecdotes. "I'm not miserable the way some short sellers are," he says. "I'm not downbeat about the secular world. I don't think the world is coming to an end—I just think some companies are coming to an end."

The investment discipline Kass hones is based on an independent outlook and sometimes tacks sharply against common short-selling wisdom. "The real function of a short seller is to develop a variant view," Kass declares. "You try to find companies whose business models are changing for the worse and then develop a projection of earnings that's far lower than the consensus estimates."

The approach is rooted in common sense. The kind of business-disrupting change to which Kass is attuned is often related to technology and in particular the Internet. A classic example is the destruction of the newspaper industry, which Kass bet heavily against beginning in the 2000s. Later in the decade, Sea Breeze successfully wagered against Regal Entertainment Group, the movie theater chain undermined by streaming video; American Greetings Corp., whose birthday and other cards were upended by the growth of free e-cards; and coupon publisher Vallassis Communications, undercut by the likes of Groupon. Kass bet against them all and won.

Where Kass begins to differ from some other investors is that he won't wager against a stock based on its valuation, as measured by such common metrics as a high price-to-book value, earnings, or earnings growth ratios. "It is not a catalyst for a short, because an inflated stock often moves even higher," says Kass. "It's arrogant to believe that one can determine whether something is fully priced on a valuation."

That stance redounded to Seabreeze's benefit most obviously during the technology bubble of the late 1990s. Shares of companies like Cisco Systems, Oracle, and EMC were trading at outrageous levels, yet continued to rise higher, some topping out at more than 150 times trailing earnings in early 2000, by which time they had wiped out an entire generation of short sellers who had bet against them.

By contrast, Kass steered away of such companies, as well as the sea of profitless dot-com ephemera of the era like Pets.com and theglobe.com. "There was no way of evaluating the intrinsic value of these companies," says Kass. "It was totally a function of emotion, and the best thing was to stay clear."

Unlike rival shorts like Bill Fleckenstein and David Tice, Kass eschews gold as a hedge or alternative to a weakening dollar. That's partly because while bullion prices tend to rise in low-interest-rate environments, the attraction dissipates as rates begin to rise. "It has no intrinsic value," Kass says. "So being totally a function of demand and supply, that means that if gold goes from 1800 to 900, I wouldn't be able to assess what that really means."

Kass admits to a streak of paranoia, living in fear of a short squeeze—in which opposing bullish traders buy shares of a company targeted by shorts with the aim of pushing its share price higher. As they do so, the short sellers are forced to cover, buying shares to pay back those they've borrowed, goosing prices further. It's the short sellers' worst nightmare.

He keeps an eye on two simple ratios. First, Kass won't make a bearish bet if the short interest in the stock—that is, the total shares being shorted, divided by the average daily trading volume—exceeds 7 days. Likewise he'll steer clear if the total number of shares being shorted, divided by a company's share float, exceeds 8 percent. Both metrics warn of the danger that too many shares have been shorted, leaving a short seller vulnerable. "I simply don't want to get caught in a short squeeze," says Kass.

There are other ways to limit downside—specifically by creating so-called *synthetic puts*. If a stock seems susceptible to a positive surprise, Kass is likely to construct a trade that caps possible losses if the market turns against him, by purchasing call options, which give the holder the right to buy a set number of shares at a given price by a particular date. So, when shorting 10,000 shares of, say, Herbalife, at $40, he will simultaneously purchase 100 call options for $2 apiece, giving him the right to buy 100 shares of Herbalife for, say, $45. Kass will still make money if the stock falls, but his loss is capped at $7 a share, since if the stock rises past $45 he'll be able to exercise his $45 options at $2.

The synthetic put neutralizes one of the most of daunting of challenges for a short seller—the prospect of unlimited losses when a bet goes awry. "What that does for me is it defines my risk," says Kass. "That's kept me alive."

Nevertheless, Kass's market success is rooted in a deep aversion to the bullish mass psychology that overwhelms otherwise sober investors. "Doug is very smart," says Jerry Jordan, chairman of Hellman, Jordan Management Company, Inc., an investment firm and a former colleague of Kass's from Putnam Investments. "He has a very, very strong bearish bias, which lets him make money shorting stocks when others can't."

Cocky and precocious, even as a child Kass had a way of impressing those around him, including fellow elementary school students who dubbed him "the professor" when growing up on the South Shore of Long Island in New York. That's where Douglas Allen Kass was born in 1948, just in time to catch the early post-World War II wave of New Yorkers fleeing the city for the bucolic suburbs, among them Rockville Centre, a comfortable, multiethnic town 20 miles east of Manhattan. It was a prime destination point for beneficiaries of the G.I. Bill, which amongst other things provided cheap mortgage financing for ex-servicemen.

His mother, Selma Koufax, taught elementary school. His father, Saul Kass, worked by day as a dentist, but was known as Dr. Hip in New York's illustrious jazz community for his ability to play virtually every instrument likely to find its way into a combo—clarinet, alto saxophone, piano, trombone. Radio station disc jockeys knew it was Dr. Hip calling in during "Name That Tune" contests because he would often nail the song after just two or three notes. Arriving home from school, his father would be in the den drinking Johnny Walker scotch with jazz greats like Benny Goodman, Gerry Mulligan, Illinois Jacquet, and Billie Holiday. Saul Kass taped high-quality recordings of jazz performances on a Wollensak reel-to-reel machine—color coding, rating, and writing reviews on the cardboard boxes. Columbia University offered $15,000 for the collection in the 1960s.

"Dougie," as he was known, tried his hand at various instruments—saxophone and clarinet among them—but eventually stopped playing in high school as his tastes turned to 1960s era rock 'n' roll, the lyrics from which he still sprinkles throughout his market commentaries. Besides, Kass was more interested in collecting baseball cards, following the Brooklyn Dodgers, which his Cousin Sandy would soon join, and studying, at which he excelled.

In 1958, Kass appeared on the junior version of the television game show *Tic-Tac-Dough*, in which host Jack Barry quizzed contestants on a variety of subjects.

"Name two of the New York daily newspapers," Barry asked.

"*Daily News* and *New York Times*," the young Kass responded.

"Tell me the name of Popeye the Sailor's girlfriend."

"Olive Oyl."

Kass was on for five consecutive shows, winning a color television set. The eight-year-old flamed out on the subject of holidays.

"The Sunday before Easter is given the name of a tree. What is this Sunday called?"

"Dogwood? Redwood?"

Barry teased the fourth grader about it. "But Mr. Barry, I'm Jewish," Kass wailed.

Kass's maternal grandmother, Jeanne Koufax, was an avid stock market enthusiast and instructed him to use a notebook to keep track of what products he was interested in and then track the share prices of the companies that made them in the newspapers. "We would talk about stocks," he recalls. Among the names he remembers tracking were Arkansas Gas & Electric, Harvey Hubble, IBM Corp., and various airline stocks. A local Merrill Lynch branch in Merrick, Long Island, had a real-time ticker and Kass would go over to watch the changing prices, like other kids watch movies. Classmates thought he was weird.

At South Side High School, Kass earned mostly As. "I was smart—I excelled in math, history, everything," Kass says. "I was an over achiever." From there, it was off to Alfred University in the rolling hills of western New York State, a school known for its liberal politics—it was one of America's first racially integrated schools—and home to a world-famous ceramics program.

Money was tight. One semester, Kass slept in his car to save on room and board. His grandmother, who ran a successful chain of children's clothing stores in the Bronx called Koufax Youth Center, helped with tuition. "Thank you very much for the clothes," Kass wrote her. "I'm having a fantastic time at Alfred. Everything is great."

The focus at Alfred was on learning, not class rank or competitiveness. "It was bucolic, serene, and low pressure," he says. Kass was enthralled by existentialists like Friedrich Nietzsche, who pioneered the concept of the overman and rejected contemporary Christian values as life-defeating, and embraced the concept of the Dionysian man. He loved Søren Kierkegaard, who in books *Fear and Trembling* and *The Sickness unto Death*, argued for a personal interaction between the individual and God. An even greater influence was Martin Buber, a quasimystic philosopher and author of the definitional text, *I and Thou*. He posited two kinds of relationships between humans and indeed between the individual and God himself—an authentic comprehensive embrace known as the "I–Thou" and the pedestrian, cursory "I–It."

Kass was definitely of his times. He teased his hair into a "Jew-Fro," a bushy style reminiscent of an Afro that was popular with leftist Jewish Americans. He wore denim overalls, attended the Woodstock music festival in Bethel, New York, and protested the war in Vietnam. "We were galvanized in an important theme to stop the war," he says. "It wasn't about being a partner at Goldman." Yet Kass kept his interest in the markets. He used some of his bar mitzvah money to wager $1,000 on the conglomerate Teledyne, which initiated a series of buybacks and earned some $2,000, which he used to purchase a Triumph T4 convertible.

Kass graduated Alfred with a double major in philosophy and economics, earning his degree in three years rather than the typical four in order to save on money. His father, at age 47 died of a stroke in 1971, likely brought on by his late-night jazz gigs and fairly heavy partying. Money became even tighter.

Kass headed to Princeton University with plans to earn a Ph.D. in philosophy. The subject of his thesis would be a Buber quotation: "As I become I, I say I–Thou." It referred to the personal journey to an authentic existence and relationship to God and the world. Kass already had his future mapped out after earning his Ph.D. "I could teach philosophy in a small girl's school and trade stocks on the side and make millions of dollars," he chuckles. "It would be a great life."

His advisor at Princeton was noted for his work on the philosophy of science: Thomas Kuhn, author of *The Structures of Scientific Revolutions* which argued that technological progress did not occur in a steady linear fashion but in sudden and sporadic leaps and bounds. Kuhn coined the term "paradigm shift" to describe the process.

The cold breath of economic necessity was breathing down Kass's neck, however. A *Time* magazine story on job prospects for Ph.D.s put a chill on his plan for a career teaching philosophy. Among all subjects, it ranked dead last.

Kass about-faced and applied to the Wharton School of the University of Pennsylvania and Harvard Business School in Boston, choosing the former not just because of the economic aid it offered but because it allowed him to start in the January semester. He was eager to get out in the real world. His favorite professor was Dan Rei, who dressed like a Hell's Angel and often digressed into conversations about extrasensory perception.

Like thousands of college graduates at the time, Kass sent his resume in to the Center for Responsive Law, the consumer advocacy group established by Ralph Nader with money he won in a suit he brought against General Motors Corp. The carmaker had hired a group of prostitutes to discredit Nader after he published *Unsafe at Any Speed*, an exposé of safety problems with the Chevrolet Corvair sports car. Kass heard nothing for six months, until his phone rang at 5:45 a.m. one Saturday morning.

"Mr. Kass, this is Ralph Nader," the voice said.

Kass thought a friend was ribbing him.

"Ralph, you can call me Doug."

Kass went to work for Nader, commuting every Thursday by Metroliner to Washington, where his officemates included Mark Green, the future New York City public advocate and mayoral candidate, as well as a cherubic film buff named Michael Moore, who went on to direct such documentaries as the scathing anti-General Motors broadside *Roger & Me* and the anti-gun diatribe *Bowling for Columbine*.

"Anybody who worked on these projects got a huge dose of self confidence," says Nader. Other former Nader's Raiders included columnist Michael Kinsley and talk show host Jimmy Fallon.

Kass ultimately contributed three chapters to a book-length exposé—*Citibank: Ralph Nader's Study Group Report on First National City Bank*—focusing on the conflicts between the money management side of Citibank's business and the lending side, particularly about the lack of a Chinese wall between the two. He tackled the conflicted nature of interlocking directorates and the lack of investment in poor neighborhoods from which Citibank drew deposits. "We were 40 years ahead of our time," chuckles Kass.

Citibank CEO Walter Wriston was not happy, and summoned Nader to New York. "They were nervous," says Nader. "They had never had a book length exposé on them." The bank launched a response: an 80,000-word report entitled "Citibank, Nader, and the Facts," seeking to rebut Nader's claims.

Nader keeps in touch with Kass and views his short selling as a public service. "In the Pollyanna-ish world of gung-ho investment promoters, he basically recast the function of the short seller in the manner of 'This is a critical appraisal,'" says Nader, "He said the short sellers in this situation are realists. He has an antenna into the speculative side of Wall Street."

Ultimately, the Citibank report allowed Kass to kill two birds with one stone: His three chapters formed the basis for his MBA thesis and he was able to graduate Wharton in just 13 months, saving big-time on the $3,000-per-semester tuition.

Upon graduation, the Wall Street job offers rolled in. Kass's heart was set on Goldman Sachs. "The job I wanted was in arbitrage," he says, but after seven interviews he was eventually passed over by risk arbitrage co-head L. J. Tenenbaum for another candidate. In 1972, Kidder Peabody was rebuilding its equity research department under a new director, Johann Gouws, an alumnus of H. C. Wainwright & Co. who had gained some notoriety for his 70-plus page research ticklers.

Gouws was looking for new, uncorrupted thinkers and says he took an instant liking to Kass. "He would look at a situation and see things other people wouldn't," says Gouws. Hired as Kidder Peabody's housing analyst, Kass plunged into an in-depth analysis of the mobile home industry, the hottest part of the market that brokers loved to pitch. Kass issued a deeply negative report on the sector—and Gouws backed him up.

Like a lot of analysts, though, Kass really wanted to manage money. An opening for an analyst's position at Boston-based Putnam Investments—a prestigious yet tradition bound money management firm—offered a foot in the door to the buy side.

Research director Lawrence Lasser hired him as part of a campaign to transform the sleepy mutual fund giant into an aggressive, risk-oriented competitor to up-and-comers like crosstown rival Fidelity Investments. "It had been a savings-oriented industry," says Lasser. "There was a change in the business. Doug exemplified that."

Lasser rode Kass hard, he says, partly because portfolio managers, superior to analysts in the rigid Putnam pecking order, were sometimes put off by Kass's cocky self-confidence. He would send off scathing, typewritten criticisms to employees; Kass dubbed them "Lassergrams." One constant was Lasser's laser-like focus on communication—the best research is useless if the portfolio managers don't understand its value. "The job of an analyst is to engender confidence in the portfolio manager," Lasser says.

Kass excelled at that. In 1978, Argonaut, a property and casualty insurance subsidiary of Los Angeles-based conglomerate Teledyne Inc., posted a surprise loss. "Everybody wanted to sell," says Kass. He persuaded them not to, and the stock rose twentyfold over the next 10 years. Kass calls Lasser a key mentor. "He was a perfectionist," Kass says. "I copied him."

In 1979, top Putnam management issued strict new personal investing limits on traders and analysts—curtailing their freedom to manage their own accounts. However noble, the new guidelines were a deal breaker for investment talent, who loved buying and selling stocks. Soon, Kass and a bevy of other investing professionals, including Jeffrey Tabak, Larry Laverty, and Jerry Jordan, left Putnam, either for other firms, as in the case of Kass, or to start new ventures, in the case of Tabak, who launched the options powerhouse Miller + Tabak + Hirsch Inc., and Jordan, who built an investment firm with former Lehman Brothers chairman Warren Hellman.

Kass was eager to head back to New York. After talking to Sanford C. Bernstein and Oppenheimer & Co. in 1978, he opted for a tiny, family-owned business called Glickenhaus & Co., specializing in municipal bonds with just $5 million or so in assets. It was run by family patriarch Seth Glickenhaus. Kass helped rack up an impressive record investing in deep value stocks, and assets under management rose to $500 million as institutional investors like the State of Oregon, Xerox Corp., and Blue Cross Blue Shield became clients.

By 1983 Kass was ready for a new challenge. He hooked up with partner John Jakobson to start a hedge fund, which closed within a year following poor performance. Kass then struck out on his own, founding his own firm, DAK Securities, managing a pool of money from First Executive Corporation, the Los Angeles-based insurance firm run by Fred Carr. Kass had been introduced to Carr by Drexel Burnham Lambert junk bond pioneer Michael Milken. First Executive, a huge buyer of Drexel Burnham Lambert–underwritten junk bonds, would file for bankruptcy in 1991 amidst the collapse of the high-yield bond market that year.

Kass wound down DAK while convalescing from his horse-racing accident. In 1991, with money running low, he took a call from CEO Allen Goldberg of First Albany, a well-regarded regional brokerage firm in upstate New York that was looking for someone to run its equity research and asset management divisions. Kass, his leg still held together by external metal rods, liked the idea of not enduring painful commutes to midtown in bumpy taxis. He lived during the week in Albany and commuted back to Manhattan on weekends. Over two years, he built the firm's research department and asset management group in conjunction with the ubiquitous Hugh Johnson, the company's equity strategist.

The weekly Amtrak commute eventually weighed on Kass and he quit in 1994. The next year, he got a call from Marshall Leeds, the CEO of J.W. Charles Securities, a scrappy brokerage firm in Boca Raton, Florida. He was looking for someone to head sales, trading, and research. Kass jumped at the chance: He loved the Florida weather and lifestyle and relished the chance to run a research department the way he saw fit.

With just five analysts, Kass kept a tight rein and made sure that sell and buy recommendations were balanced 50/50. Most brokerages, then as now, overwhelmingly tilt toward buy recommendations. Kass also banned the wishy-washy "hold" recommendation, to which analysts default when they don't want to offend the management of the companies they cover. "We had a hard-hitting research department," he says.

Kass was building his public persona. With his witty quotes and contrarian market views, journalists loved him. After J.W. Charles slapped a sell recommendation on virtually the entire brokerage industry, a writer for the *Wall Street Journal*'s influential "Heard on the Street" column in late 1993 dubbed Kass "The Bear of Boca." The next year, brokerage stocks turned in a terrible performance, pummeled by a series of interest rate increases by Fed chairman Alan Greenspan.

A lot of J.W. Charles's recommendations were cited by *USA Today* columnist Dan Dorfman, a friend of Kass's who was later tied to a dicey stock promoter named Donald Kessler, who plead guilty to securities fraud. A 1996 *BusinessWeek* article eviscerated Kass, highlighting some of his firm's bad calls. Kass says it comes with the territory. "One of the risks of being a person in the media is you become a target," he says.

By that time, however, Kass had moved on to work on Omega Advisors, the famed long-short hedge fund run by former Goldman Sachs Asset Management chairman Leon Cooperman, who had recruited him to work as a senior portfolio manager. Cantankerous and demanding, Cooperman parceled out the different names in the portfolio at Omega among portfolio managers, with each keeping track of a group of positions and on call to endure Cooperman's withering interrogations. "It was a tough job for two years," Kass laughs. "He basically fired me."

That was okay, though. Kass, who remains friendly with Cooperman, was eager to return to Florida, where he had bought a house, and start up his own investment firm, with money from an insurance firm. He ran Kass Partners until 2003.

Kass launched a hedge fund under the Seabreeze Partners moniker in 2001, eventually allocating capital between Seabreeze Partners Long-Short LP and, from January 2005 to August 2009, to the short fund called Seabreeze Partners Short LP, which he shuttered after the Federal Reserve got its quantitative easing program underway.

In early 2003, Kass oversaw short positions for 12 months at a market neutral fund for Circle T Partners LP, a New York hedge fund run by Seth Tobias, a fellow CNBC talking head who had a house in nearby Jupiter, Florida. Circle T later imploded. Tobias was found dead in mysterious circumstances in September 2007.

Today, buffeted by the warm Caribbean tradewinds, Kass runs Seabreeze from posh Palm Beach. The fund is housed in a red terra cotta–roofed guesthouse that overlooks Kass's swimming pool. The walls are festooned with laminated press clippings, and sunlight pours into the offices. Aside from Kass, there are a head trader, three analysts, and an administrator.

The typical Seabreeze research initiative is informed by what Kass learned from Johann Gouws at Kidder Peabody and Putnam research director Larry Lasser—exhaustively enumerate every issue, large or small, that may bear on a company's share price. Kass is often prone to warm over plenty of well-known observations, almost burying the new insights that he brings to the analysis. "I'm old school," says Kass. "I don't shoot from the hip."

In early October 2001, though, Kass did what most any introductory book on investing will advise: He simply read the footnotes to AOL Time Warner's 10-Q filed with the Securities & Exchange Commission (SEC) and traded on it.

To be sure, Kass was a long-time skeptic toward AOL's business model well before it had purchased Time Warner in a $180 billion all-stock deal in January 2000, having profitably shorted it on several occasions. The previous May, for example, as the economy headed into a tailspin, Kass bet against the merged company's shares based upon, among other things, decelerating ad sales growth. Second quarter earnings results proved him right, and the stock fell 9.7 percent.

More fundamentally, by late 2001, Kass was worried that AOL Timer Warner's market was increasingly saturated. Subscriber growth, by his calculation, was on track for its third straight year of decline. While Wall Street analysts were forecasting 25 percent long-term earnings per share growth, Kass pegged the number at half that amount, give or take. It would be Kass's "variant view" versus the consensus.

Plowing through AOL Time Warner's filings, Kass stumbled upon a surprising footnote in the 10-Q. It had to do with AOL Europe, the company's 50.5 percent–owned subsidiary, which was struggling against such rivals as Tiscali and T-OnLine—a sideline to the bigger issues, but involving a potentially huge amount of money. What had escaped much notice at the time was that AOL, shortly after agreeing to buy Time

Warner, had entered into a put-call arrangement with Bertelsmann, the German publishing giant that owned the other 49.5 percent of AOL Europe. As the footnote spelled out, the agreement valued AOL Europe at between $13.5 billion and $16.5 billion.

AOL Europe was in fact hemorrhaging. Kass estimated it would lose $300 million on $700 million in sales for the year and pegged the value of the subsidiary, in what was now a post -technology bubble market, at just $2 billion. The key was that the put-call agreement gave Bertlesmann the right to sell 80 percent of its stake to AOL-Time Warner for $5.3 billion by January 31 of 2002, and the remaining 20 percent for $1.45 billion the following June. At least $2 billion of the payment had to be in cash, of which AOL Time Warner had just $1.3 billion on its balance sheet. "That was a 'what the f--k' moment," says Kass. "I couldn't believe what I saw."

He called Abelson, and told him about the put-call agreement that everybody seemed to have overlooked.

"It can't be right," Abelson erupted.

"Alan, would you like me to fax you the report?" Kass responded.

Abelson wrote up Kass's analysis in the "Up & Dow Wall Street" column. Kass began shorting the shares at $70, which is about where they traded before the article appeared. Shares fell to $65.54 the first day after *Barron's* published. As the footnote stated, AOL Time Warner was forced to buy the balance of AOL Europe for $6.85 billion and issued billions of debt to finance it. By June 30, 2002, AOL Time Warner shares had tumbled to little more than $30, the price at which Kass covered. Though he won't give a dollar amount for the profit Seabreeze notched, the gain on the position was more than 50 percent. "It was one of the great finds ever," Kass says of the footnote. "The company was symptomatic of the avarice of the time."

Kass concedes that no matter how thorough his research, sometimes markets don't cooperate. "Doug remembers when he is wrong," says Herb Greenberg, of Pacific Square Research. "He makes bold calls and 'fesses up when he doesn't get it right."

His history with Washington, D.C.-based Danaher Corp., a manufacturer of auto parts, power tools, and medical equipment, stretched back decades. In the early 1980s he had purchased a 10 percent stake in its predecessor company, Diversified Mortgage Investors, a money-losing real estate investment trust (REIT) with a market capitalization of $15 million, on behalf of Glickenhaus and some of its clients.

The REIT owned a motley assortment of assets, ranging from a motor home park in upstate New York to an underground refrigeration facility in Kansas City. Its lure was $125 million in tax loss carry forwards. "I thought, this thing is worth more dead than alive," recalls Kass. His plan was to take control of the firm, sell off its holdings and merge profitable businesses into the REIT to take advantage of the tax losses.

Kass got as far as ousting management, but was impatient to leave Glickenhaus. With no one to oversee the REIT investment, he agreed to sell it to brothers Steven and Mitchell Rales, who eventually changed the name to Danaher Corp. The Rales executed Kass's strategic plan, building sales to $4.6 billion by year-end 2002 by rolling up manufacturers across a range of markets—including test tools, electronic motors, and dental equipment.

It was this last segment that interested Kass in mid-2003, as he sifted through the market looking for short candidates in the dental equipment sector. Familiar as he was with his late father's line of work, Kass knew dentists in tough economic times postpone buying equipment. Some 25 percent of Danaher's revenues derived from the sector.

As Kass dug down into Danaher's SEC filings, evidence began to mount that the company would make a good target on a number of counts. Like a lot of short sellers, he was suspicious of serial acquirers, such as Tyco International, because of the ease with which they can engage in accounting obfuscation. "They set up reserves," Kass says. "There are all kinds of accounting gimmickry." More than other companies, roll-ups are dependent on the vagaries of external market forces, which may pump up prices of target companies or, alternatively, reduce their access to financing.

Right off the top, Danaher's stock was expensive for a conglomerate, trading at 22.5 times trailing earnings, the upper range of its historical price-to-earnings ratio (P-E) and well above industry bellwether General Electric, which traded at 19 times trailing earnings. Danaher used its high market valuation to good effect. It bought mid-sized companies at prices equivalent to about one times their annual sales while Danaher shares themselves traded for 2.4 times sales. This meant paying $100 million for a company with a like amount of sales would generate a $240 million rise in Danaher's market capitalization—the dynamic is seductive yet is also a classic warning sign for investors.

That's because the high P-E multiple was based on the investor assumption that the company could wring all kinds of synergies out of its acquisitions and integrate them smoothly. The Seabreeze analysis showed this wasn't happening. Internal sales—that is, excluding acquisitions—had shrunk 4.5 percent in 2002. Kass was forecasting a further 3 percent decline for 2003. That suggested Danaher was having trouble making its purchases work, the very reason for its high P-E in the first place. Kass figured that once investors were convinced of his variant forecast, the premium would revert to that of the overall market, and shares would decline 25 to 30 percent.

For the t-crossing, i-dotting Kass, that wasn't good enough: He drew up a list of 18 reasons why the stock was overpriced and likely to post disappointing earnings going forward. These ranged from its low dividend payout of 10 cents per share to brisk competition and high production costs. Two accounting analysts, he noted, were also critical of the quality of its earnings, which benefited from nonrecurring gains, a sliding tax rate, and special restructuring charges.

Seabreeze began accumulating a short position in Danaher in May 2003. Shares were trading at $17.35 the day Kass published the analysis in his column on *TheStreet.com*. Critical to Kass's game plan, he figured Danaher management itself would provide a catalyst for a sell-off when it would be forced to lower 2003 earnings guidance in the next few months. The consensus analyst estimate was $3.20 earnings per share—Kass thought $3 seemed more reasonable.

Things didn't work out. Five weeks later, during its second quarter earnings call, the company confirmed that it expected to post 2003 profits of between $3.25 and $3.15 per share, essentially on target. Danaher stock, which had traded down to $16.55, the previous day, closed at $16.93, finishing off the week at $17.40. At year-end the stock closed at $22.94.

Seabreeze was sufficiently deft to close out its Danaher position with a loss of just 5 percent or so, but Kass says there are lessons to be learned.

What he did not pay sufficient attention to were the problems besetting two far larger diversified manufacturers. Tyco was still digging itself out from ex-CEO Dennis Kozlowski's wide-ranging accounting fraud, and General Electric was being hammered by a portfolio of souring small business and real estate loans. Institutional investors were looking toward Danaher as the remaining market leader—and were prepared to stand by the stock.

"Psychology is often as important as fundamentals," says Kass. "One lesson in short selling is that you have to leave your dog at the doorstep. You've got to be flexible and when the market ignores, you move on."

The stumble on Danaher did not prevent Kass from shorting conglomerates. He bet against it again in 2007 with similar results. And in early 2008, he turned his attention to Berkshire Hathaway, the Omaha-based juggernaut lorded over by Warren Buffett. For decades Berkshire Hathaway investors rested easy in the knowledge that its fortress balance sheet and AAA credit rating made it a bear market tank—as safe a place as any in collapsing markets. There was confidence to be derived from its varied business mix, with subsidiaries focused on power generation, homebuilding materials, machine tools, and ice cream, to name a few. The company's massive insurance portfolio was comprised of huge stakes in some rock-solid blue chips, including Coca-Cola, Johnson & Johnson, and Procter & Gamble. Berkshire Hathaway's balance sheet coffers swelled with $37.7 billion in cash—part of an almost unfathomable war chest under the command of the world's undisputed master of asset allocation.

The key for Kass, once again, was developing that "variant view." What was the consensus missing that could be the basis for a negative take on Berkshire Hathaway?

It started with valuation: The $134,000 price on those shares as of March 2008 seemed rich. Kass crunched a sum-of-the-parts valuation comparing Berkshire's various businesses to their peers and assumed a P-E multiple of 12 times on projected 2008 earnings of $9,750. That resulted in a fair value of $121,000. For Kass, that represented a meaningful gap. Using a variation on that methodology, Kass calculated a price that melded a 1.6 times price-to-book value ratio on Berkshire's insurance and other businesses and a 1.25 times book ratio on finance and financial products. That resulted in a projected price of $125,000 a share.

Again, though only modestly below the market price, the discrepancy was sufficient to explore further.

More dramatic was Berkshire Hathaway's recent sizzling relative stock price performance. The class A shares by March 2008 had risen 12 percent over the previous six months versus an 11 percent decline in the S&P 500. Over 12 months, the stock was up 26 percent versus an 8 percent drop in the broader index. That huge performance gap was not logical given the driving forces behind the broader market selloff. Housing prices were falling, defaults on the rise, and the subprime contagion spreading to the general financial industry. Yet Berkshire derived most of its revenues from the financial sector in the form of insurance businesses, and it had a big exposure to the housing market through its Clayton Homes, Nebraska Furniture Mart, and building materials subsidiaries like Acme bricks, Shaw carpets and Benjamin Moore paints.

It only took a glance a Berkshire's annual report to see that its stock portfolio was bloated with financial companies, many of them good ones, but still at risk in the impending meltdown—Wells Fargo, American Express, Moody's Investors Services, Swiss Re, and U.S. Bancorp.

Kass was also sensitive to perennial concerns, like Buffett's advancing age of 78 at the time. "I figured with his age, you had to figure in a 15 percent discount the way you do a closed end fund on the New York Stock Exchange," says Kass. He also averred that growth prospects for Berkshire Hathaway's industrial businesses should likewise be discounted because it wasn't likely that Buffett would be able to make the kind of large transformative acquisitions that would allow it to boost future earnings.

In his methodically comprehensive fashion, Kass also noted Berkshire Hathaway's slowing earnings growth in recent years, somewhat opaque financial disclosure, and the likely headwinds in the property and casualty insurance industry. There was also the overhang of Buffett's 38 percent stake in the company, which was to be turned over to Bill & Melinda Gates Foundation and likely to weigh on the market for years.

Because Berkshire Hathaway's class A shares, at well over $130,000 each, often traded fewer than 1,000 shares a day, Kass began building a short position in the class B shares beginning in March 2008 at a split-adjusted $92 a share. Class A shares at the time were the economic equivalent of 30 class B shares, although the latter had only 1/200 of the voting rights of the pricier class. (In January 2010, Berkshire split the class B shares 50 to 1, giving them an economic value equal to 1/1,500 of a class A share).

"Of all the stocks on the New York Stock Exchange, few have a cadre of more loyal long-term investors than Berkshire. Warren Buffett has been so successful that this cadre is more than willing to endure extreme pain," says Kass. "They tend to be hostile to naysayers. Criticism is not taken well."

The reaction was incredulity. "There are certain things in life you just don't do," wrote one *Motley Fool* columnist. "You don't spit into the wind. You don't pull the mask off that ol' Lone Ranger, and you definitely don't short Warren Buffett. Apparently, that's a lesson Doug Kass is determined to learn the hard way."

The trade made for a rollercoaster ride. Berkshire class B shares stock initially ratcheted down from Kass's initial shorting position of $92 a share, adjusted retroactively, in March 2008 to the mid-70s in July. A collapsing Bear Stearns Cos. had been snapped up by JPMorgan Chase & Co. in June, and concerns were growing about the solvency of Fannie Mae and Freddie Mac. Kass was short those stocks by this point in addition to Citigroup, MBIA, and Washington Mutual. By the end of September, the two government-sponsored mortgage machines were in conservatorship and Lehman Brothers in bankruptcy. American International Group, would soon become a ward of the state, after the federal government bailed it out of a $62.1 billion portfolio of imploding CDOs it had insured in a rescue package that left U.S. taxpayers on the hook for more $182 billion.

As terror gripped the world financial markets, though, it soon looked as if Kass had badly miscalculated. Berkshire shares rallied in the last two weeks of September as panicked investors stampeded into the stock, handing Kass a paper loss as shares hit $93. In October, Buffett showed how well he could play a financial crisis by purchasing $5 billion of preferred stock in Goldman Sachs Group and General Electric. The preferred stocks each paid a 10 percent dividend and were redeemable at advantageous prices just 10 percent above where they were trading. Kass, though, didn't cover a share.

Then it got worse. As worries that the world financial cataclysm would suck down the entirety of the Western financial system increased, the Chicago Board Options Exchange VIX index, which measures the volatility of the S&P 500, pierced 80, versus little more than 20 at the beginning of the year. The S&P 500 itself lost a quarter of its value in November peak to trough, and Berkshire cratered along with it to a 2008 low of $52.40 on November 20.

Of course it wasn't over. The Treasury Department under Secretary Henry Paulson was rolling out massive rescue initiatives like the Troubled Asset Relief Program (TARP), and Bernanke's Federal Reserve flooded the system to keep markets from freezing, cutting its target rate to 1 percent. Berkshire class B shares rallied to $64 at year-end.

The first two months of 2009 were characterized by capitulation across the financial markets. The S&P 500 tumbled to 676, down 56 percent from its peak in 2007 and off 31 percent from the previous year's close. Berkshire shares bottomed at $46. Seabreeze ultimately closed out its short position below $50 in March, as it did with the remainder of its financial shorts. Kass figured the firm's gain on the Berkshire trade was 30 percent. "I was early," says Kass, who has bought and shorted Berkshire since. "But I was committed."

Warren Buffett invited a short seller to make the case publicly against Berkshire Hathaway stock at his famous annual meeting at Omaha, Nebraska's cavernous CenturyLink Center May 4, 2013. Kass, not averse to the limelight, stepped up to the challenge. As hordes of Buffett-worshipping shareholders looked on—the attendees totaled more than 30,000—Kass questioned whether the sage of Omaha was doing the kind of detailed due diligence on his investments that he had in the past, citing his 2008 investment in Bank of America Corp as an example. Buffett responded that he learns his lessons and can reapply them.

"Are you at the point where the game interests you more than the score?" Kass asked Buffett.

"I think you have to love something to do it well," Buffett responded. "The passion has not gone, I promise you."

Kass also questioned Buffett's decision to name his son Howard, who has limited operating experience, to be executive chairman after Buffett left the scene. Buffett responded that Howard's responsibility would be to make sure the CEO who was eventually chosen didn't go astray, not to run Berkshire.

Then, in his own charmingly characteristic self-promoting style, Kass asked whether Berkshire Hathaway would hire him to manage a $100 million short portfolio. Buffett turned him down flat, noting that he himself had identified frauds and inflated stocks in the past.

The normally reticent Berkshire Hathaway vice chairman Charles Munger couldn't help but chime in. "Shorting is a game that doesn't appeal to us," he said.

For the record, Berkshire's class A shares traded at $162,904 the day before the annual meeting. In late 2014, the stock was $221,925, a gain of 36.2 percent.

Kass began to suspect Apple Inc. was baked fruit in late 2012. On September 12, the Cupertino juggernaut unveiled the iPhone 5—slimmer, lighter, and with a bigger screen than its predecessors. The media enthused, even if the device itself was more an evolutionary improvement than the kind of game-changing quantum leap that had thrilled Apple enthusiasts in the past—music player iPod; Siri, the voice-activated butler; and iPad, the e-book reading laptop substitute. Kass didn't like the feel of the device, which he thought lacked heft.

Still, first-weekend sales topped five million. *Time* magazine named the iPhone 5 gadget of the year. Shares, up 65 percent through August, pierced $700—which admittedly sounded pretty cool. Kass, who in 2011 had zinged out bullish Apple comments on his blog, thought it was time to reappraise the stock and its prospects. "My experience is in looking at innovative companies that become market darlings," says Kass. "I'm wired to look for the storm clouds gathering at successful companies like Apple, Chipotle, Salesforce.com, and Google."

Valuation was problematic as a starting point. Apple shares were trading at a seemingly ridiculously low 9.9 trailing earnings in September. If you backed out the cash on Apple's balance sheet, $110 billion worth, the remaining company would be trading for just 7.9 trailing earnings. That was two-thirds the P-E multiple IBM traded for—and less than half that of Google.

The problem with that calculation was that it wasn't a particularly useful metric given Apple's history of super-splashy product launches and super-high margins, which were likely to be unsustainable as rivals caught up. Kass, like some other analysts, preferred to look at the company's share price compared to its annual sales. On this count, at 4.4 times sales, Apple was wildly expensive compared to other hardware makers like Hewlett-Packard and Dell, which traded for 0.5 times sales.

In his characteristically exhaustive style, Kass published a litany of other observations: Apple products, while still costlier than those of rivals like Samsung, Google, and Hewlett Packard, were no longer qualitatively better. The company faced product cannibalization—new, cheaper offerings like the iPad mini did the same job as pricier models. Carriers like AT&T and Verizon, pinched by tough economic terms forced on them by Apple, were pushing rival phones on customers. And most of the apps that tied users to the Apple ecosystem were now available on Android and Microsoft. "The first-mover advantage was evaporating," says Kass.

Of course, Steve Jobs's death the previous year had left a huge hole in the company: Apple's attempt to replace Google Maps with its own version was evidence of that. It was a fiasco; the app generated streets in the wrong neighborhoods, and the company was forced to reintroduce the Google application for its iPhones. "The map boner was one of the signs that a Jobs-less company was less attentive to quality," Kass says. "Pride goeth before a fall."

The reaction to Kass's e-mail post of September 26 was immediate. "The blogosphere went ballistic," says Kass. "Few addressed my 10 points. There is a tendency to spout sparkly generalities and not address issues." One example: "These guys should be caged in the zoo with all the other animals."

Kass published his research just days after Apple's all-time high of $702. When Apple released fourth quarter earnings on October 25, 2012 the $8.45 earnings per share were 10 percent shy of analysts' consensus estimates and gross margins were down. The stock, trading at $609.54, fell to $604. Shares continued to break down over the rest of the year, ending at $532.17. The fact that the company beat estimates by only 2 percent in January 8 spurred another downward leg. Kass covered his short position on February 4, 2003, at $442. He figures he gained 25 percent—and went long Apple for a couple of days that month as well.

Jerry Jordan likes to tell the tale of Kass's call on the bottom of the financial crisis in February 2009—about the time he was closing out his Berkshire Hathaway short. The two friends talked about the market.

"Doug, this market is moving into a climactic bottom," Jordan recalls telling him.

"I think it is, too,"

That Friday, Kass wrote: "This is the market bottom I've been talking about."

Kass covered most of his shorts and went long.

Then, just over one month later, he about-faced—selling all his positions and writing that he planned to go short.

Jordan asked him why.

"I don't like the way it feels," Kass responded.

As Jordan explains, at his core, Kass will never be comfortable as an optimist. "He truly is a bear," says Jordan.

Kass doesn't argue the point. "The average long-short investor sees the world as America and apple pie," he shrugs. "We are facing secular headwinds that have been accumulating for decades. I view the world as a kaleidoscope of problems."

Chapter 8

Tice: Truth Squad Leader

ongress was in for some fireworks. It was June 2001 and the House Subcommittee on Capital Markets was investigating the ties of Wall Street analysts to their investment banker colleagues. "We are going to inquire into disturbing media and academic reports about pervasive conflicts of interest," Chairman Richard Baker told the half-empty chamber, filled mostly with sundry aides and lower level staffers milling about. But if the Louisiana Republican thought the proceedings were going to be dry, he didn't know much about the first witness—David Tice, founder of his eponymous investment firm.

Tice lived and breathed research; a numbers geek, he had devoted the better part of his career to picking apart financial statements, using what he found as the cornerstone for not one but two thriving businesses—an accounting-focused market research service and a short-selling mutual fund. Tice let loose.

"This is an outrage," he proclaimed. "Wall Street's research is riddled with structural conflicts of interest."

Tice said bogus analyst recommendations were just the tip of the iceberg. The entire financial system had become irredeemably tainted. "This problem is much larger," he said. "A sound and fair marketplace is at the very foundation of capitalism."

The corruption of hundreds of stock analysts contributed to the channeling of vast sums of money into risky and money-losing ventures. "When the marketplace's reward system so favors the aggressive financier and the speculator over the prudent businessman and investor, the consequences will be self-reinforcing booms and busts, a hopeless misallocation of resources, and an unbalanced economy," Tice said.

He linked Wall Street excesses to the growing credit bubble—one that would explode years later in the credit crisis of 2008–2009. "The financial sector is creating enormous amounts of new debt that's often being poorly spent," Tice said. "Wall Street's lack of independence has fostered this misdirection and camouflaged the fact that our U.S. economy is in danger because of our capital misallocation and credit excess."

Representative Baker eventually cut him off, but Tice says he's proud of his fiery testimony that day. "We were the good guys," he says. "I liked to refer to us as 'the truth squad.'"

Tice's career was built on this blunt outspokenness. He was among the first in the 1980s to sound the alarm about a rising tide of accounting distortions. Worried that small investors were being suckered into a rigged investment game, Tice launched his first mutual fund—the Prudent Bear—dedicated to shorting stocks promoted by Wall Street. As his understanding of the bubble economy grew, Tice says he connected dots and saw that the inflated technology stock prices of the late 1990s were manifestations of a bigger issue: out-of-control credit that had for years levitated the stock market. By 2001, that bubble was collapsing—and vaporizing trillions of dollars of speculative capital as it did.

Tice was never one to lay low. He penned columns and opinion pieces at every opportunity and grabbed television time whenever he could. In 1999, he sponsored a conference at New York's Waldorf Astoria hotel entitled the "Credit Bubble and Its Aftermath—A Symposium." Keynotes were delivered by Henry Kaufman, the former Salomon Brothers chief economist dubbed "Dr. Gloom"; hedge fund manager Marc Faber, publisher of the *Gloom, Boom & Doom Report*; and former Federal Reserve Governor Lawrence Lindsey, at the time the top economic advisor to presidential candidate George W. Bush. The *Wall Street Journal* cited Lindsey's bearish outlook expressed at the symposium on the front page: "In an era of prosperity and optimism, the economist shaping Republican presidential front-runner George W. Bush's economic thinking has been one of the country's leading pessimists."

A bearish outlook is no way to make friends. He received hate mail. When his firm, David Tice & Associates, moved to larger space, Tice made sure his own office was as distant from the front entrance as possible—with a nearby stairwell through which to beat a hasty exit if necessary. He kept a loaded Smith & Wesson revolver in his top right hand drawer—part of Texas gun culture, but also a sign of his relentless wariness.

Nobody cut through smoke-and-mirrors accounting like Tice's "truth squad." At the threadbare offices in Dallas, the blond-haired CPA led a motley group of a dozen analysts and others who delved into the adjustments, special items, and footnoted ephemera of financial statements. Every five or six weeks, Tice sent out his $10,000 subscription newsletter, *Behind the Numbers*, flagging stocks with dubious accounting. The newsletter became an arsenal of potent short-selling ideas for storied investors—George Soros, Jim Chanos, and Michael Steinhardt among them.

Among the hits: a 1990 item on Procter & Gamble. The company reported sizzling earnings-per-share growth of 23 percent, but Tice showed that when adjusted for restructuring charges and other aggressive accounting, pre-tax earnings were up just 7 percent. P&G shares lagged those of rivals over the next year. In a 1998 *Behind the Numbers* issue, Tice's analysts questioned the write-offs that WorldCom took after buying MCI Communications. Analysts calculated that of the $1.97 earnings per share Wall Street forecast for 1999, $1.50 was due to aggressive accounting. WorldCom's CEO Bernie Ebbers is now serving a 25-year sentence for fraud. It was dead-on, lethal research. Tice eventually turned the newsletter over to the analysts who worked on it.

A populist of sorts, Tice fretted that it was mostly hedge fund barons benefiting from his bearish analysis. So in late 1995, Tice started Prudent Bear with the purpose of shorting the stocks that *Behind the Numbers* was warning about. "I felt I could help protect the great unwashed public who were listening to Merrill Lynch analysts," he says. "Wall Street was selling people a bill of goods. I felt that was morally wrong."

Tice's timing was astonishingly poor. The stock market had entered a historic speculative frenzy—the fund dropped 13.7 percent in 1996, 4.3 percent in 1997, 34.1 percent in 1998 and 23.4 percent in 1999—a span during which the Standard & Poor's (S&P) 500 Index delivered a 26.3 percent annualized return. Fund assets were just $160 million at the end of the decade. Tice notched an expense ratio of 2.5 percent. Critics savaged Tice and the fund, which financial publisher Morningstar named to a roster of "top wealth destroyers."

Did Tice worry that his bearish stance was a disastrous mistake?

"No," he says. "I told myself, 'This is just an asset bubble.'"

Did he consider pulling back—say, buying Treasuries to balance his negative bets?

"No. We told investors that we would be there for them," Tice says as he leans back in his 12th-floor office overlooking downtown Dallas's gleaming, skyscraper punctuated skyline. "We were a hedge."

Tice remained constant. "We told them that we would be that ship in the storm when the market goes down." Having that lodestar to refer to helped him through much of the worst of Prudent Bear's losses. "People asked 'Weren't you pulling your hair out? Didn't you think you were wrong?'" Tice recalls. "No. I was bloodied but unbowed."

When the technology bubble burst in mid-March 2000, Tice was vindicated. The S&P 500 tumbled 21 percent that year as Prudent Bear surged 30.5 percent. Tice rolled out the Prudent Bear Safe Harbor fund, which buys short-term sovereign debt of nations with strong currencies—Norway, Singapore, and Switzerland. "I felt with all the credit being created, our currency would decline," says Tice. "People needed a fund that would protect them." Safe Harbor notched a 7.1 percent return annualized from its founding in early 2000 to the end of 2008, with only a single money-losing year.

As for Prudent Bear, Tice adroitly navigated the fund through the treacherous rebound years of 2002–2004, working to keep losses manageable as the S&P 500 surged and surged—and even successfully posted profits in 2005–2007.

The surprise payoff for Tice, though, came in December 2008. As credit markets seized up across the globe, Tice struck a deal to sell his funds to Pittsburgh-based Federated Investors, a big money fund manager. Tice got $43 million up front, with a further $99.5 million over four years conditional on asset growth. That totaled 8.4 percent of assets versus the usual 4 percent or less that an asset manager fetches. "We were able to justify that because we were the only fund doing what we were in shorting individual stocks," says Tice. "We were very profitable."

On a warm November afternoon in Dallas, Tice wears a black-and-white check polo shirt and black corduroy slacks. He is five feet eight inches tall and weighs a lean 160 pounds. Tice is hyperkinetic. He stands and sits frequently over the course of an interview, is quick to laugh, and speaks with the slight drawl of his adopted state. Having divorced his wife Louise in 2006, Tice lives in a high-end 22nd-floor bachelor pad, with pricey modern furniture and a genteel feel of clutter about the place.

Away from short selling, Tice continues to work a 45-hour week, hopping into his black Mercedes-Benz sedan to speed off to meetings and oversee a half dozen projects and businesses he's since embarked upon. Tice is chairman of his family office, Tice Capital LLC and of Encryptics, a Frisco, Texas–based cyber security company he funded. He has put money into a Singapore diamond exchange, stem cell research, and social media ventures. Tice also heads his own 501(c) nonprofit, True Spark, that encourages children to watch movies that provide ethical role models—he's funding it to the tune of $3 million over five years.

Hollywood is a particular interest and a lucrative one. As executive producer, Tice bankrolled *Soul Surfer*, a 2011 movie about a evangelical Christian girl who loses her left arm to a tiger shark, and then goes on to embark upon her professional surfing career. It stars AnnaSophia Robb, Dennis Quaid, Holly Hunt, and Carrie Underwood. With a domestic gross of $43 million, it is the highest grossing live action surf film in history. He also scored when, together with legendary Hollywood executive Peter Gruber, he co-financed the script for "When the Game Stands Tall", a 2014 inspirational movie starring Jim Caviezel about famed high school football coach Bob Ladouceur, who took the De La Salle Spartans from obscurity to a 151-game winning streak. It grossed $30 million.

Closer to Tice's market roots: *The Bubble*, a documentary about the causes of the financial crisis, written as a response to the Academy Award–winning polemic *Inside Job*, by director Charles Ferguson. While *Inside Job* focuses on avaricious bankers, compromised government regulators, and co-opted academic research, *The Bubble*, directed by Jimmy

Morrison, highlights the Federal Reserve and failed Keynesian policies, as well as—and I'm not sure I get this—the Community Reinvestment Act of 1977, which encouraged banks to lend to the economically disadvantaged. It's based on the *New York Times* bestseller *Meltdown* by Thomas F. Woods Jr. (Regnery Publishing, 2009). Tice says he pulled out because it didn't meet his standards.

A middle child, David Wayne Tice grew up in Independence, Missouri, the birthplace of Harry S. Truman, a President who had no problems tilting against popular opinion. His father, a radiologist, and mother, a Presbyterian church elder, were children of the Great Depression, and drilled into him the value of a dollar earned.

Born in late September, Tice was typically the youngest in his class. He was less social, at times a loner. "I didn't date much," he says. "I don't have good friends from back then." Tice was no prodigy. "I was a decent student," he says. "But super excellence was not my goal."

A sports enthusiast, Tice's stature held him back, as did his near-sightedness, which required his wearing thick, two-toned horn-rimmed glasses as early as the third grade. Tice's father encouraged his interest in golf; ultimately, he couldn't make much progress with his stroke. Tice showed much more promise in high school math—geometry, trigonometry, and mathematical analysis. His Scholastic Aptitude Test (SAT) scores were evidence of his talents—580 verbal and 640 math.

Tice found a surrogate for athletic stardom in a fantasy baseball game—Strat-O-Matic. Tice excelled at selecting imaginary teams of star players and then rolling the dice to see how they performed. Strat-O-Matic mixed probability with research and depended on understanding numbers—skills that would later come in handy. "You could play the 1962 Minnesota Twins against the 1967 Yankees," Tice recalls. "You were putting together the line-up, you could make decisions about relieving pitchers, and you rolled the dice, so there was an element of luck."

His mother interested him in the stock market, tuning in to the television program *Wall Street Week* in its earliest days. She opened a brokerage account in his name.

After high school, Tice headed out of state—seeking to put some distance between his teenage years and the vibrant future he hoped would lie ahead. Texas, with its sun, warm climate, and booming economy, beckoned. It was 1972, the oil boom was in full swing, and Tice landed at Texas Christian University in Fort Worth, known for its tan-bricked beaux arts campus and its premed and undergraduate business programs.

There, Tice hit his stride, academically and socially. It helped that freshman year, he lived across the hall from a scion of the local Budweiser beer distributorship. "I was in with a cool group of guys, we played intramural baseball and basketball," Tice says. Neither he nor his friends rushed for TCU's popular fraternities. They preferred being outsiders.

The 1973–1982 bear market dragged on. TCU business majors were held in low esteem at TCU by some of his classmates. "If you were just a business major, people would say, 'So what, you'll run a Pizza Hut someday,'" Tice says.

Tice impressed professors—especially with his ability to tie together disparate subjects in class discussions. "He had the amazing ability to integrate economics and accounting and even history," associate professor Chuck Becker told a campus newsletter. "He was really ahead of his time."

TCU offered an elective called the Educational Investment Fund (EIF), a sponsored $100,000 pool of money run by a team of 12 students—who were required to pitch two investment proposals. Competition was tight, but Tice landed an analyst slot. "It was easy to see who had talent and who didn't," Tice says.

From his work on the fund, Tice decided that fluency in accounting differentiated superior managers from their peers. He resolved to become a CPA. Tice thought he was headed for the Big Eight accounting firms he applied to. Instead, upon graduation, Tice was turned down by each of them. He blames a green and blue tweed suit he wore. "They were looking for partnership material," he says. "I did not exude confidence."

Without prospects, Tice opted to shoot for an M.B.A. in finance and won a paid teaching internship. Gathering up his degree in 1977 he again applied to the Big Eight. Despite his graduate school grade point average, each of them again rejected him. He was wearing the same green and blue tweed ensemble. Ruminating as he looks out over the Dallas skyline, Tice says: "I should have just gotten a navy blue suit."

A despondent Tice took a job at the oil giant Atlantic Richfield (ARCO), which had an army of 500 accountants working at eight offices in cities like Bakersfield, California, and Tulsa, Oklahoma. They kept track of oil production history, revenues, and royalties. The ARCO career path was clear. "I saw my boss's job, I saw my boss's boss's job," Tice recalls. "I knew I didn't even want my boss's boss's boss's boss's job."

After four years, Tice left for ENSERCH Corporation, an exploration and production company that wanted an eye on its prospective purchases. Tice helped draft acquisition memos that went to the board of directors, laying out discounted cash flow scenarios, prospective rates of returns, and the impact of acquisitions on ENSERCH's earnings.

By 1984, it was time for a change. The bull market was in gear and Tice joined financial planning firm Concorde Financial, which catered to wealthy doctors and businessmen. His focused on real estate, energy partnerships, and tax shelters. But Tice figured Concorde could save money by corralling stocks into a fund which he launched, Concorde Value, hiring Gregg Jahnke, an alumnus of the TCU's Educational Investment Fund, to run it.

The hours were long. Tice had a young wife, a new baby. Late one night, driving down Dallas's Central Freeway, Tice looked up and saw a single light burning near the top floor of an otherwise totally dark skyscraper. "I didn't want to be that person," Tice says. "I wanted something else in life."

A change in Wall Street regulation pointed the way. More than 10 years earlier, an adjustment had been made to the Securities & Exchange Act of 1932, allowing for independent analysts to sell research to clients and be compensated by third-party brokerage firms. An independent analyst would publish a report. If a buy-side firm found it useful, it could place a trade through a designated brokerage, identifying the analyst involved. The brokerage executed the trade and split the commission with the analyst. This was the start of what became known as "soft dollar research." Now, in the late 1980s, the bull market was fueling demand for such independent analysis.

His friend, Jahnke, had already jumped ship to start JKE Research. Tice figured he too could make a living doing something he was good at doing. "I had skepticism toward Wall Street," says Tice. "I knew 95 percent of recommendations were nonobjective."

Tice launched *Behind the Numbers* in 1987, just months before the October meltdown. Working at a card table in a spare bedroom with two plastic chairs, Tice loaded a Compaq portable computer—a 45-pound behemoth equipped with a 5.25 inch floppy drive—with SuperCalc spreadsheet software and subscribed to information provider Compustat for financial data and news. Tice keyed in financial data from the 300 companies whose financial reports he received.

Macros, preprogrammed commands, would go to work churning out calculations of days sales of inventory, which show investors how long it takes to turn inventory into finished goods, or the growth rates of earnings per share, research and development, and advertising expenses. It was rudimentary stuff. But it allowed Tice to flag potential problems. Clients loved it.

Tice personally drummed up sales, keeping a brutal travel schedule. Still in his early 30s, Tice looked 10 years younger. "I grew my moustache," he recalls. "I was so young then and wanted to look mature and credible."

Clients included New York investors Leon Cooperman, George Soros, Stanley Druckenmiller, Jim Chanos, and Carl Icahn. Tice would travel there and schlep his Compaq from one client's office to the next, in summer months perspiring in the hot New York City subways. Booking nine or ten meetings a day, it was as far from the glamor of Wall Street as possible.

Initially focused on pure accounting, Tice began incorporating fundamental analysis—venturing opinions about acquisitions, capital allocation, and marketing efforts. "Sometimes I'd see fundamental issues and no quality of earnings issues," he says. "Sometimes I'd see quality of earnings issues and no fundamental issues."

If *Behind the Numbers* found an accounting concern, it would flag the stock with a warning for investors to sell. If no further problems surfaced after six months, that would lapse. In early 1989, *Behind the Numbers* showed inventories at Noxell Corp., a cosmetics company, were growing far faster than sales. Tice duly placed a warning on the stock.

Procter & Gamble, as it turned out, bought Noxell in October 1989 for $1.6 billion—a 31 percent premium. Visiting Michael Steinhardt, Tice walked him through some issues relating to another company. Steinhardt erupted.

"You're full of *s--t!*" Steinhardt yelled.

The hedge fund manager took the passel of research Tice had brought with him and dumped it into a wastepaper basket.

"Noxell was acquired!" he shouted, his veins bulging. He accused Tice of deliberately not revealing the accompanying price run up in its performance figures. He told Tice *Behind the Numbers* was cooking its own numbers.

"You're misrepresenting your track record!" Steinhardt said.

Tice walked to the trash bin and removed his research.

"No, Michael," he said calmly. "You were looking at a report on Noxell from a couple of years earlier."

He then showed the subsequent appropriate *Behind the Numbers* reference that acknowledged the Noxell buyout, showing that the recommendation was indeed unprofitable. Everything had been properly disclosed.

Tice needed analysts willing to dig, infuriate companies, and settle for pay that might be half what they could get on Wall Street. One of his first hires was a Wharton MBA with investment bank experience. He lasted two months.

Tice gathered an eclectic crew, recognizing overlooked talent. Many were neophytes whom he trained personally, molding business majors from TCU into balance sheet-devouring analytical animals. "What makes a great analyst?" says Tice. "Someone who thinks outside the box, can be skeptical, understands accounting, will dive deep, and uses his time well."

They made an interesting cast. The disheveled Jahnke was an ex-card-counter who for a couple of years made a living at Las Vegas blackjack tables. Albert Meyer, a former accounting professor at Spring Arbor College of Michigan, had in the early 1990s uncovered a Ponzi scheme run by the nonprofit Foundation for New Era Philanthropy. Will Garner was a semipro golfer whose resume included a stint at *Grant's Interest Rate Observer*. Over the years, Tice's roster of analysts included an aspiring football coach, and sundry graduates of TCU, many of whom had participated in the EIF.

Offices were spartan. There were cubicles and wood-laminated desks—barebones. "If you walked in, you'd say I don't know what this business does, but managing money would be the last thing you'd expect," says Jim Smith, a personal friend.

Forensic sleuthing could be epically frustrating. Beginning in early 1990, *Behind the Numbers* zeroed in on General Electric, captained by CEO Jack Welch. Lionized in the business press for promising predictable earnings growth of 15 percent, Welch delivered it. In a *Fortune* article, he had vigorously defended the practice of managing earnings. "What investor would want to buy a conglomerate like GE unless its earnings were predictable?" he asked.

Tice poked around General Electric's financial unit, mostly the part known as GE Capital—and what he found set off alarms.

GE Capital's loan portfolio, at $30 billion to $40 billion, made the financial unit look like a money center bank—it was about the size of J.P. Morgan & Co. at the time. Banks traded at five to eight times earnings, while GE was selling at 12 times earnings. Other analysts—daunted by GE Capital's complexity—downplayed it, preferring to view the company as a specialized manufacturing juggernaut, worthy of higher valuation.

Tice, instead, zeroed in on GE's growing exposure to commercial real estate loans, residential mortgage insurance, and—amidst a collapsing junk bond market—dicey leveraged buyout (LBO) loans. He noted that GE Capital's credit card lending and other consumer loans were vulnerable in a recession. The upshot was that Tice didn't think it likely that the GE parent company would grow at 15 percent because of GE Capital's sensitivity to credit losses.

Nobody paid attention. "Our criticism was a gnat on an elephant," Tice says.

Nevertheless, he persevered, pointing out five months later the suspicious manner in which GE Capital was reporting its nonperforming loans. The company shifted repossessed loans from its leveraged buyout category into an asset called "other investments," that was similar to "real estate owned." Tice knew most analysts were not aware that this maneuver, while legal, was hiding growing nonperforming loans. From 1988 to 1989, "nonperforming loans" dropped from 1.4 percent to 1.2 percent. Adding in "other investments," however, they grew from 3.0 percent to 3.8 percent. Investors generally hit the panic button when a

THE MOST DANGEROUS TRADE

bank's total nonperforming loans rise above 1.5 percent, and GE's figure was twice that.

Tice kept at it, and in October, with the stock down 20 percent, *Barron's* published a bylined story by Tice reiterating his concerns. The stock fell 3 percent the next Monday morning in Europe. The gnat, it seems, was a major nuisance. GE held a conference call disputing Tice's analysis.

Ultimately, though, investors preferred Welch's sleight of hand to Tice's hard-nosed analysis. "I can't say this was a great success financially," Tice says about the analysis. "GE went on to do great for another 10 years. The warts remained hidden because they were able to keep borrowing in the commercial paper market and were able to grow out of their potential problems." GE outperformed spectacularly throughout the 1990s.

Tice and Jahnke chewed over their idea for a "bear" mutual fund. Each day, they would cross the street to discuss their plans at the local outlet of a Mexican restaurant chain, Taco Bueno. Texas didn't allow mutual funds registered there to short more than 25 percent of their portfolios. Tice petitioned the Texas State Securities Board, explaining that any savvy manager could circumvent the restriction by buying put options and selling call options, essentially creating a synthetic short position. The securities board voted to lift the 25 percent limit. "The board members hated derivatives more than they hated short selling," Tice laughs. "We should have a Taco Bueno law degree." So Tice started the fund with $500,000, most of it his own money.

The dynamics of running a short mutual fund were daunting. Say Prudent Bear was usually targeting a 70 percent short exposure and had assets of $100 million. That means $70 million of its assets would be short. But if stocks rallied 10 percent in a quarter, assets would draw down to $93 million. The value of its short positions—assuming it maintained the same share exposure—would rise to $77 million, increasing Prudent Bear's net short exposure to 83 percent. Unlike hedge funds, which have lock-up periods that prevent investors from pulling their money, mutual fund investors can redeem daily. A market move of 10 percent would prompt outflows. If investors pulled just $5 million, the move would send short exposure to 88 percent. Invariably, they added money after market selloffs and redeemed after spikes.

Tice worried that as a short-selling fund, they would be deliberately singled out for punishment by bulls to squeeze. "This was dangerous for me," Tice says. "Wall Street didn't like me because I was going against Goldman Sachs. I was putting out sell recommendations on Merrill Lynch's corporate clients."

Dallas, though, provided a nurturing climate for the short-selling sentiment Tice espoused. Texas, after all, was the epicenter of the saving and loan (S&L) crisis—huge money makers for short sellers in the late 1980s and early 1990s. Around that time, the Feshbach Brothers made headlines betting against and publicizing frauds. The three brothers—Joseph, Kurt, and Matt—were all based in Palo Alto, California, but much of the firm's research was run out of Dallas by Tom Barton. In 1993, the Feshbachs closed shop after an ill-timed short against Wells Fargo & Co. The Feshbachs moved on, and so did Barton's short-selling analysts in Dallas, including such notables as Jim Carruthers of Third Point.

Among other noted Dallas short sellers were Frederick "Shad" Rowe of Greenbrier Partners, who penned a column for *Forbes* magazine in which he often ruminated on his métier. A gifted writer, he referred to short selling as the Financial Bear. "Central to the Financial Bear is the notion that somewhere out there is Financial Truth and that when people learn the Financial Truth they will be better for it," he wrote. He describes short selling as not dissimilar to two adversaries standing 30 feet apart throwing footballs at each other's crotches. "The fun of winning is nowhere equal to the pain of losing," Rowe chuckles. It was his mother's comment that prompted him to abandon the profession. Noting his moodiness after a spate of particularly upbeat economic news, she tried to comfort him. "Now don't worry, Shad," she told him. "I'm sure something terrible will happen sooner or later." Today, Rowe runs a mostly long portfolio at Greenbrier as well as an annual investor conference that benefits Parkinson's disease, from which he suffers.

There was also Rusty Rose, founder of Cardinal Investments LLC, best known for buying the Texas Rangers Baseball Club and installing George W. Bush as its general manager, raising his public profile after his departure from Harken Energy and setting him up for his successful run for Texas governor in 1995 and President in 2000, a campaign to which he contributed generously. Rose, who garnered a reputation for high profile litigation, was a frequent visitor to Camp David during the Bush administration.

And Kyle Bass, not related to the Bass brothers, was a local Bear Stearns broker who founded hedge fund Hayman Capital in 2006 and wagered massively against subprime mortgage–backed securities to post a 300 percent profit in 2007. He is profiled in Michael Lewis's book *Boomerang* (Alfred Knopf & Co. 2009). The list goes on. "I do think Texans are pretty independent, more commonsensical, more libertarian," says Tice. "They're less likely to buy into the bubble."

Tice often did best steering clear of blue chips. In May 1993, *Behind the Numbers* began coverage of Paging Network, the largest independent paging services provider in the United States. The stock was trading at $30.25, or about 15 times cash flow, defined as earnings before interest, taxes, depreciation, and amortization (EBITDA). Wall Street emphasized the price relative to EBITDA in research reports—and on the surface, it seemed like a reasonable way to value a paging company. Paging required big capital expenditures on things like transmitters, relay towers, and individual pagers. Since these all depreciate over time, analysts argued, it made sense to price the stocks based on cashflow, which ignores both depreciation and capex. Analysts often do the same with cable companies.

Tice thought differently. That's because 55 percent of the capital expenditures were on pagers that had to be replaced every year or two just to keep the business operating—Tice labeled them "maintenance capital expenditures." These were required ongoing cash expenditures which had to be made or the company wouldn't remain competitive. This was far different from some capital expenditures that were more discretionary as they supported expansion into new business.

The difference was crucial. "In the paging business, you needed a huge amount of maintenance cap-ex just to keep the business alive," Tice says.

Behind The Numbers ran its own calculations, subtracting, what it called "maintenance depreciation" from the reported EBITDA. By 1994, Paging Network was trading at a heady 16 times EBITDA, but the newsletter's adjustment for maintenance depreciation cut the EBITDA figure by more than half, and meant it was trading at a sky high 44 times adjusted EBITDA.

Meanwhile, according to the newsletter's calculations, revenue per pager at Paging Network was steadily declining from $29.30 in early 1993 to $26.09 in September 1994. Long-term debt and interest expense had more than doubled over that time. And *Behind the Numbers* showed that the average purchase price for a paging company ranged from $140 per pager to a high of $353 per pager. Paging Network, Tice pointed out, was already trading at nearly $500 per pager. "Maybe P.T. Barnum was right," Tice wrote.

Ultimately, mobile phone technology wiped out Paging Network. The company had big plans for rudimentary text messaging and voice services, but by the mid- to late-1990s, cellular phone prices were plummeting and usage surging. Paging was obsolete for most general applications.

Tice isn't sure when the Prudent Bear Fund began shorting Dallas-based Paging Network. The fund's September 1996 annual report, its first full-year version, shows it was short 10,000 Paging Network shares, worth $20 each for a total exposure of $200,000—its third-largest short position at the time. The next year, the fund's semi-annual showed no short position in Paging Network—that might have been because it was temporarily covered for any number of reasons. But in 1998 the fund was again short the stock—40,000 shares at $6.00, for a total exposure of $241,250. By then, the company was on the ropes, as were many paging services. Paging Network filed for bankruptcy in August 2000.

Over time, Tice and his analysts recognized patterns in prospective shorts. One was the tendency of one accounting distortion, once uncovered, to be followed by more. Another was for confusion thrown up by serial acquisitions, restructurings, and one-time charges to obscure a company's performance, hiding disappointing news from shareholders.

A marquee example was Sunbeam Corp., the home appliance maker run by "Chainsaw" Al Dunlap, a self-styled turnaround artist recruited by Michael Price, head of the Mutual Series Funds, which controlled 20 percent of the company's shares. Dunlap's track record included restructurings and layoffs at companies like Crown Zellerbach and American Can. His most recent success was Scott Paper, which he quickly cut down to size and sold to rival Kimberly-Clark Corp., tripling its share price in his two-year tenure.

Dunlap took the reins at Sunbeam in July 1996, as the company's profits were sandbagged by the cost of both a new factory and a steep peso devaluation in Mexico, where it did a lot of business. Dunlap publicly savaged previous management. Under his own "dream team" of new executives, his cronies, Dunlap promised to double sales to $2 billion from $1 billion over three years, boost operating margins to 20 percent, and post a return on equity of 25 percent. "A new Sunbeam is shining—and the best is yet to come," he wrote in the 1996 annual report.

Sunbeam embarked on restructurings and plant closings, laying off half its employees. Shares rose from under $30 to a high of $50 in October 1997. For the 1997 calendar year, net income swung from a loss of $228.3 million in 1996 to a profit of $109.4 million in 1997. Then, in early March, the company announced three acquisitions: Coleman Co., the camping gear company; appliance maker Mr. Coffee; and fire alarm manufacturer First Alert. Shares surged to $52.

Jeff Middleswart, the lead analyst at *Behind the Numbers*, was skeptical. Sifting through the charges the company booked, he felt the goal was to make 1996 look as bad as possible compared to 1997, when Dunlap could begin taking credit for improvements. Sunbeam booked a $92.3 million inventory charge at the end of 1996 for goods it actually sold in 1997. It was legal, but fishy. Dunlap hiked Sunbeam's advertising budget 25 percent in 1996, only to slash it the following year. Likewise, the company took a sharply higher, $23.4 million bad debt expense in 1996, as well as a steep $5 million hit as "other expenses." Both expenses declined sharply in 1997.

It fit a pattern. "CEOs realize they have the latitude to take all these charges," says Tice. "Dunlap was classic. Just take big restructuring charges."

Behind the Numbers accused Sunbeam of "channel stuffing"— shipping goods and booking sales to customers in amounts greater than they are likely to sell as a way of frontloading earnings and sales. Why was there a sudden rush to buy outdoor grills in the winter? Sunbeam's accounts receivables soared to $355 million in 1997 from $213 million in 1996.

The goods Sunbeam was sending to retailers, it turns out, were going to third-party warehouses. The tactic is legal as long as the company books the sale after the product is shipped, but it's still channel stuffing. Neither Sunbeam nor its backers ever complained to Tice about *Behind the Numbers'* accusations. "We never heard from Dunlap or his backers," says Tice. That may have been because even worse news was percolating.

Just weeks after its March acquisitions announcement, Sunbeam announced it might miss consensus earnings estimates for the quarter ending March 1998. It was clear the company was not going to grow 25 percent. Shares plummeted 26 percent to $38. In the second quarter of 2008, Sunbeam lost $60 million, as stores refused shipments of additional grills, toasters, and hand irons. It was as *Behind the Numbers* had forewarned. In August 1998, Sunbeam directors fired Dunlap.

Prudent Bear had 105,500 shares short on Sunbeam on September 30, 1998, equal to $745,500 or $7.07 a share. That was after the vast majority of damage had been done. The next year, filings show no short position on Sunbeam. Federated Investors declined to provide access to Prudent Bear trading records. Nevertheless, it took until February 2001 for Sunbeam to file for chapter 11 bankruptcy. In September 2002, Dunlap paid $500,000 to settle SEC charges that he had defrauded investors by inflating sales figures. Dunlap did not admit or deny guilt, but agreed not to work for a public company again.

Management at Prudent Bear was evolving. Doug Noland joined Prudent Bear as market strategist in 1999, bringing with him a macro-orientation hitherto lacking: A talented, experienced, and highly strung short seller who had worked with Bill Fleckenstein. Noland was a fan of the writings of Kurt Richebacher—an economist whose writings helped Tice understand asset bubbles. Richebacher was a newsletter publisher and acolyte of the Austrian School of economics, which includes such laissez faire stalwarts as Ludwig von Mises and Friedrich Hayek.

While John Maynard Keynes wrote that central banks should act to spur demand during recessions by lowering rates, printing money, and using other stimuli, Richebacher and his ilk argued such moves reinflate bubbles, postponing and worsening the day of reckoning. To Tice and other "credit bubble bears," economics boils down to a series of truisms. "What goes up, must come down," Tice says. "You can't borrow against the future. I don't think you print your way to prosperity."

Noland began writing the *Credit Bubble Bulletin*, offering trenchant analysis of trends—trade imbalances, credit, cheap money—from an Austrian School perspective. Noland's track record as a prognosticator is not well known. In the bulletin and elsewhere, he forecast the market's future calamities with breathtaking acuity—ballooning derivatives exposure, the housing bubble, the collapse of Fannie Mae and Freddie Mac, the risks to money market funds. Going as far back as the 1990s, Noland nailed them all.

In 2013, Noland—who declined to talk with this author—forecast a cataclysmic deflationary cycle. Since the sale, he has served as portfolio manager for Prudent Bear, which has lost money in every year since Tice's departure as the stock market has rallied.

What in the 1990s the sharp-eyed Tice had seen as myriad instances of accounting legerdemain began to fit into a larger pattern of economic dislocations. By the turn of the 21st century, total credit market debt outstanding had nearly doubled to $26 trillion since 1991, and the money supply was ballooning to close to $7 trillion. With access to such easy money, investors and corporations had become dangerously speculative. The stock market was in the midst of a swelling asset bubble and the house croupier—Alan Greenspan—was dispensing chips at the casino, in critics eyes, as he strove to keep things humming.

As the new decade progressed, Tice began turning responsibilities for *Behind the Numbers* over to Middleswart, now research director at the firm. That gave Tice and Noland time to overhaul and refine the management of Prudent Bear. The goal of the fund remained to serve as a hedge to the overall stock market. That did not mean that the fund shouldn't try to mediate losses when the stock market was rising, however. "Our feeling was that we are going to try and lose as little money as possible," Tice says.

Tice employed defensive tactics—he would avoid the stocks of companies with high short interest, for example, viewing them as subject to likely squeezes. Noland would keep watch on the portfolio, suggesting Tice cover a position if it began to rise higher than the market overall—again, a sign it might be targeted for a squeeze. Noland was on the lookout for stocks as they began to "break down," or tumble. The tactic risked leaving him empty-handed as he tried to locate stock to borrow, but it reduced the possibility of being caught flat-footed in a short squeeze or being pummeled if a company were acquired.

"I called him the 'secretary of defense,'" says Tice. "We were a great team. People said I was too aggressive. People said he was too defensive." The bottom line was that the partnership worked.

Tice saw that gold prices had been moving inversely to stocks—not unusual. The London spot price for the metal had ratcheted down to $252 per ounce by the end of 2000 from a high of $415 in early 1996. The Philadelphia Stock Exchange Gold & Silver Index lost 60 percent of its value peak to trough between 1997 and 2000. And big gold-miners like Barrick Gold and Newmont Mining were unloading mines around the world.

A Vancouver broker named Cal Everett of Pacific International Securities cold-called Tice in early 2000 pitching small gold miners that were early stage exploration companies often selling for nickels and dimes. Many such stocks were frauds, little more than a phone and a desk looking for money. But Everett was seasoned and a geologist and who knew firsthand which mines had reasonable merit. He scoured Africa, North and South America, and Asia.

Prudent Bear piled into the "junior miners" in industry argot. Capstone Mining Corp. surged from 50 cents to $3.50, East Asia Minerals Corp. from 15 cents to $5.00, Western Silver Corp. from $1.35 to $15, and Fortuna Silver Mines from 50 cents to $7.50. All told, Tice estimates the mining stocks contributed $100 million in profits to the Prudent Bear Fund.

The change in Prudent Bear's management style and move into gold stocks was crucial. In the bear market year of 2002, when the S&P 500 dropped 22 percent, Prudent Bear shot up 62.9 percent. More impressively, Tice managed to keep losses manageable as the stock market roared back in 2003 and 2004, when the broad S&P benchmark soared 28.7 percent and 10.9 percent, respectively. The fund lost 10.4 and 14.1 percent those years—nothing to cheer about, but acceptable. Tice could take losses—the fund prospectus said so. "I never said we're so damn smart we'll make money every year. That made it easier."

Then, as the index rose 4.9 percent, 15.8 percent, and 5.5 percent in the bull market years of 2005, 2006, and 2007, Prudent Bear managed gains of 2 percent, 9.1 percent, and 13.4 percent.

Unlike other short sellers who built bearish positions before pushing their analysis on journalists, Tice wouldn't initiate a short before he issued a research note in *Behind the Numbers*, and waited 10 days after publication before doing so. On occasion that meant missing an opportunity.

Tice and Noland would huddle. They'd look at the macro picture, but also ask where the stock was breaking down. Is the likelihood of a short squeeze growing? What is the cost of the borrow? Should they cover ahead of an earnings pre-announcement? Is it rallying back?

These were not the kinds of questions *Behind the Numbers* was meant to answer. The contribution of the newsletter's recommendations to Prudent Bear's short portfolio steadily declined. In 1996, they comprised an estimated 80 percent of Prudent Bear's short exposure but only a quarter by 2000 and five percent by 2005. "What David learned was that short selling was 90 percent tactical. When you're getting crushed, you have to get out," says Jahnke. "There's a big difference between publishing research and running a publicly traded short portfolio."

Instead of concentrating on individual stocks, the increasingly macro-focused fund was shorting exchange-traded funds (ETFs) and similar index-like products such as HOLDRS. By March 2000, more than a third of the fund's short positions were on ETFs and their ilk—NASDAQ-100 Shares, DIAMONDS Trust Series I, S&P 500 Depositary Receipts, the B2B Internet HOLDRs Trust, the Internet Architect HOLDRs Trust, and the Internet HOLDRs Trust. Later, as the technology bubble collapsed and the universe of ETFs expanded, Tice would use them to wager against the specific sectors of the economy most likely to suffer: the Industrial Select Sector SPDR Fund or the Financial Select Sector SPDR Fund.

Prudent Bear was in the process of evolving from a bottom-up fundamental portfolio to using more of a macro model. In fact, the fund didn't make a nickel off of what turned out to be *Behind the Numbers'* most famous call—Tice's 10-day rule prevented it. In early 1999 he hired Albert Meyer, a South African-born accountant. The new hire's previous big hit: In 1995, Meyer had uncovered a Ponzi scheme at the Foundation for New Era Philanthropy that cost universities millions.

In July 1999, Meyer wrote a report on Tyco International Ltd., the fast-growing Hamilton, Bermuda–based multinational conglomerate led by Dennis Kozlowski. Tyco, with $60 billion in revenue in 1999, was a classic roll-up whose shares had risen an astonishing 54 percent annualized over the previous five years as it bought companies, shuttered factories, and found ways to goose productivity. It made everything from medical devices and home alarms to heat-shrink tubing to electronics parts, and it did so in scores of countries.

Meyer began investigating Tyco because so many sell-side analysts were recommending it. To this day, Meyer isn't quite sure why the report garnered the reaction it did—he made no accusations of financial improprieties, and only a passing criticism of Kozlowski's colossal pay package.

The crux of the report was simply an analysis of the company's operating profits and associated margins from 1996 through 1999. Tyco reported total operating profits of $6.3 billion over that span, reflecting margins of 15 percent. That, however, excluded nonrecurring restructuring and merger-related charges that totaled $4 billion. Including those numbers would have reduced profits to just $2.3 billion, and operating margins would have been just 6.4 percent. Meyer questioned whether the "nonrecurring" charges, which seemed to be booked with clocklike regularity, should be considered "nonrecurring" at all—a fairly standard complaint among skeptical accountants.

Meyer also pointed out that the various merger-related accruals Tyco booked for plant closings, lease terminations, and severance seemed consistently higher than necessary, leaving the company with hundreds of millions of dollars of reserves—reserves that theoretically could be used to boost earnings in the future. He warned that a "cookie jar" of accruals was developing—but made no accusations that anything was being done with them. "Surely, this is not what accounting rules based on accrual accounting have in mind," he wrote. This is not the prose of a gasoline-soaked anarchist.

The report was issued October 6, but—perhaps because of its tame language—didn't have a major impact until the following week. Then shares plummeted from $41.03 to $31.57 over seven days, a drop of 23 percent. (They eventually bottomed in early December at $21.77.)

The New York Stock Exchange stopped trading in Tyco shares due to an order imbalance in the options market. Kozlowski went on the offensive on CNBC, *Bloomberg News*, and in press releases sent around the world. Kozlowski continued. "We don't know this David Tice," he said in a statement. "He has never spoken to anyone at Tyco, and we don't know who he is or what he does."

It continued. "I heard the reports being circulated about our company. And I can state unequivocally that they are false and baseless." He then proffered a not-so-veiled threat to Tice. "Because we take our commitment to our shareholders and our reputation very seriously, we will pursue this matter until we are satisfied that both have been adequately protected."

Wall Street analysts lined up behind Tyco—lacerating the *Behind the Numbers* report even if there were no major contentions that were even debatable. "It's a bad report, and the more I look at it the worse it gets," huffed Jack Blackstock, an analyst with Donaldson Lufkin Jenrette Securities. "I hope they covered their short position because I think the stock is going up tomorrow." Of course, Tice held no short position—and by the time 10 days had lapsed, the cost of borrowing Tyco shares had spiked, and short interest made it unattractive.

"There was a battle of words," says Tice. "Twenty-six Wall Street firms came to the defense of Tyco. The company was, after all, a fee-generation machine for Wall Street."

Tyco shares rebounded in December—until the SEC disclosed an inquiry into Tyco's accounting practices, which may or may not have been linked to Meyer's report. Ultimately, on unrelated matters, the SEC demanded Tyco restate earnings going back five years. Tyco shares rebounded, hitting a high of $48.40 in January 2001.

Meyer's *Behind the Numbers* warnings were effectively brushed aside. But in 2002, Kozlowski was charged, along with chief financial officer Mark Schwartz, by New York District Attorney Robert Morgenthau with grand larceny, conspiracy, securities fraud, and nine counts of falsifying business records. Most of the charges stuck: Kozlowski was systematically looting the company, to the tabloid papers' delight. Among other things, he had helped himself to a $25 million Manhattan apartment on the shareholder's dime, complete with a $14,000 umbrella stand and $6,000 shower curtain. Then there was the matter of Kozlowski's wife's 40th birthday party on the Italian island of Sardinia, which cost $2.1 million and featured an ice statue of Michelangelo's David urinating vodka, all paid for by Tyco.

More than 200 of Tyco's top 250 managers were fired for either accommodating Kozlowski's pilfering—or knowing about it and doing nothing. He served eight years after convictions on tax evasion, theft, and other charges. Tyco the company, it should be pointed out, not only survived Kozlowski, but thrived. The company, whose shares traded $40 in early 2015, has gone through multiple spinoffs and sales of business lines.

The stock has generated annualized returns of more than 13 percent since their nadir in July 25, 2002, when they hit $6.36.

By the mid-2000s, Tice was arguably at the top of his defensive game. Despite a surging S&P 500, which in 2005, 2006, and 2007 notched gains of 4.9 percent, 15.8 percent, and 5.5 percent, Prudent Bear was not only *not* losing money—thanks largely to its gold mining stocks, it was making money for fund shareholders: 2 percent in 2005, 9.1 percent in 2006, and 13.4 percent in 2007.

Things were changing in the world of research. In the mid-2000s, institutions—especially mutual funds—were becoming less willing to use soft-dollar brokerage arrangements to pay for research. The feeling was management firms should use their own money, and not the brokerage commissions that came out of their shareholders' pockets. Business at *Behind the Numbers* suffered. At the same time, Tice was shorting more indices and ETFs, and using more futures than ever before. By 2005, just 5 percent of the short positions in the portfolio were generated by *Behind the Numbers'* research. Tice decided to turn the research service over to employees, led by Middleswart, in 2007. It became a stand-alone company.

As the housing bubble inflated in the mid-2000s, Tice built and maintained big short positions in financials like Lehman Brothers Holdings, Bank of America, Citigroup, Wachovia, and Washington Mutual, as well as collateralized debt obligation (CDO) insurers MBIA and Ambac Financial Group, and homebuilders KB Home, Lennar, and Toll Brothers. Yet the game had changed. Tice says he had no edge on the accounting problems that enveloped Lehman, MBIA, or others. He was in many cases betting on industries, not stocks. "We fear the risk of a run on 'Wall Street finance' and resulting systemic credit crisis is high and rising," Tice told investors in his 2007 annual report. The stock selection was more likely to be driven by such issues as the short interest in a stock or other essentially technical factors.

By 2007, Prudent Bear, now with $900 million in assets, had just 10 short positions of more than $7 million on individual stocks. Prudent Bear had a quarter of its short exposure in ETFs—Industrial Select Sector SPDR Fund and the iShares Russell 2000 Growth Index Fund, for example. The individual stock shorts were weighted to liquid, heavily traded names—Starbucks, Wal-Mart Stores, Xerox. That theoretically minimized the likelihood of short squeezes. Tice avoided trades in stocks that were crowded, as quant-driven funds and classic long-short hedge funds all found themselves piling into the same short positions.

Tice was already shifting gears in early 2008, switching out of the increasingly heavily shorted financials—staying a step or two ahead of the crowd. But other positions turned against Prudent Bear—retailers, homebuilders, and restaurants. Even the fund's gold positions began falling. The world was turning to Tice's viewpoint, turning the market into a gigantic crowded trade. As it fell, the short-term rebounds were steep, sometimes 10 percent in a couple of days. Individual stocks like Freddie Mac and Fannie Mae, on their way to zero, or close to it, would reverse course back up 10 to 20 percent. It was time to cover—at least the most obvious shorts. Prudent Bear was out of financial stocks by the time the SEC issued its short-selling ban on them in September 2008.

Instead, Prudent Bear targeted a swath of big cap technology companies—EMC, Lam Research, KLA-Tencor Corp., and Juniper Networks. This was a reflection of Tice and Noland's belief that the economic trauma shaking the markets would extend far beyond the housing and banking sectors. He also targeted consumer stocks like Coca-Cola, Amazon.com, ConAgra Foods, and Sara Lee. The thinking was that in a general collapse, some of the stocks that held up best would have more downside pain ahead of them.

The sale of the Prudent Bear funds to Federated went though as planned—closing on December 8. The flagship, Prudent Bear, under Tice and his colleagues, had fulfilled its promise to the funds investors, finishing out 2008 with a 26.9 percent gain in the midst of the greatest financial calamity since the crash of 1928.

It's not unlike a line by AnnaSophia Robb, who plays Bethany Hamilton in the movie *Soul Surfer*. "I don't know why terrible things happen to us sometimes," she says. "But I have to believe that something good will come out of this." Whether it does or not is still very much open to debate.

Chapter 9

Pellegrini: Behind the Great Subprime Bet

P aolo Pellegrini has a nose for trouble. He smelled it in the rising housing prices of early 2006, when he cranked through decades of home price data and concluded the bubble was poised to burst. Pellegrini then engineered a series of massive wagers against subprime mortgages that catapulted Paulson & Co. hedge funds to 2007 gains of as much as 590 percent—and firm-wide profits of more than $15 billion. The negative bets boosted Paulson, his firm, and Pellegrini himself to superstar status in the world of short sellers and beyond. (Parts of this chapter are based on an article written by the author for a *Bloomberg Markets* magazine article published in the November 2009 issue, as well as other stories he wrote.)

Pellegrini, a former computer programmer with an engineering degree, pocketed $175 million as a bonus for 2007, allowing him to buy a couple of what he laughingly calls "entry-level supercars": a silver Ferrari F430 with a base price of $168,000 at the time and a black

Audi R8. He decamped from a one-bedroom apartment in suburban Westchester, New York into a sprawling yet spare full floor apartment overlooking the pastoral dells and bridle paths of Central Park. Today, he sails the Mediterranean in a 48-foot sailing yacht.

The trade did more than make Pellegrini and his colleagues rich. It triggered a U.S. Securities & Exchange Commission (SEC) suit alleging that Goldman Sachs, the investment bank with which Pellegrini worked most closely, committed fraud by withholding critical information from clients on a key and lucrative deal that Pellegrini worked on.

So Paulson & Co., its founder, and Pellegrini himself were soon lumped together, perhaps unfairly, with Goldman Sachs Group in the public's eye as avatars of the greed, conflicts and deceit that fueled the crisis. The SEC, however, ultimately only accused Goldman Sachs of wrongdoing, charges that the investment bank settled for a record $550 million, along with a hapless low-level salesman whose case became tabloid fodder.

The collapsing housing market that Pellegrini wagered on played to his hidden aptitude. "I'm more drawn to doing analysis of scenarios of what can break down and go wrong instead of go right," he says. "It's an engineering thing. For shorting to work, certain things have to take place and then it happens quickly. Escalator up, elevator down."

By April 2008, the Rome native was smelling danger again. Nearly six months before the collapse of Lehman Brothers Holdings and the bailout of American International Group, he and his colleagues at Paulson & Co. foresaw that the unfolding crisis would trigger U.S. government intervention: costly bank rescues, a massive stimulus plan, and yawning deficits. Those moves would eventually undercut the dollar and U.S. stocks, unleashing market havoc, Pellegrini reasoned.

"The losses would be massive," he says. "I knew the policy response would be commensurate."

So, after wowing the investment world with Paulson & Co.'s subprime bet, Pellegrini went on to show he was no one-hit wonder. While still working for Paulson, Pellegrini plowed a chunk of his personal winnings from the subprime bet into PSQR LLC, a private fund he created to protect his newfound riches. He began shorting bank-heavy exchange-traded funds (ETFs) and later, as the stock market collapsed, those that track the broader Standard & Poor's (S&P) 500 Index.

Then, at the end of 2008, as panicked investors stampeded into Treasuries, sending the yield on the 30-year bond down 184 basis points, or 1.84 percentage points, to 2.52 percent, Pellegrini began betting against U.S. Treasury futures with underlying maturities of 15 to 30 years.

PSQR's returns initially set Wall Street abuzz. From its launch on April 15, 2008, through December of that year, the fund gained 52.4 percent, according to a fund document.

That's when Pellegrini quit Paulson & Co. to start his own firm, PSQR Management LLC. He seeded his firm with $100 million of his own money.

Pellegrini continued his aggressively contrarian short-selling strategy. As the markets collapsed, he was in his element, like a Yankee slugger on a hitting streak. In January 2009, Treasury prices plunged, with 30-year yields rising 92 basis points. PSQR's short position generated a return of more than 65 percent that month, contributing to an 80 percent gain for 2009, according to fund documents. It was as if he could do no wrong.

Pellegrini, a former member of Italy's Radical Party with a Harvard Business School M.B.A., continues his against-the-grain strategy, wagering on fundamental world economic trends. Like such storied short-selling macro investors as George Soros and Julian Robertson before him, he buys and sells futures on government bonds, stock indexes, currencies and commodities like oil. It was Soros who famously structured one of history's most profitable shorts—wagering in 1992 that the Bank of England would be forced to devalue the British pound, which it ultimately did, netting the Hungarian-born investor a profit of $1 billion.

PSQR returned outside investors' money after losing 11 percent in the first eight months of 2010. Yet Pellegrini continues to manage his own substantial fortune.

Friends and former colleagues say Pellegrini has a rare ability to apply rigorous analysis to complex financial markets, as he did with the subprime trade. "Paolo is a deep thinker," says William Michaelcheck, founder of Mariner Investment Group, a New York hedge fund firm where Pellegrini worked. "He was able to synthesize the situation into a hedge fund position. It's the iconoclast's ability to see things other people can't see."

Pellegrini described his contrarian operating style in a 2010 letter to PSQR investors: "We look to develop insights from readily available but complex data—same information, different conclusions—and position ourselves for the market to catch up."

Pellegrini is especially critical of the bouts of quantitative easing, engineered by former Federal Reserve Chairman Ben Bernanke and his successor, Janet Yellen. So-called QE, in macro-speak, refers to the Federal Reserve's purchasing of long-term Treasuries and mortgage bonds to keep interest rates artificially low. The easing is hammering responsible investors by making it impossible to preserve the inflation-adjusted value of one's assets without taking uncontrollable risk.

"The [social] implications of QE are horrendous because it punished responsible savers while rewarding a financial-services industry that should be vigorously curbed as it extracts an exorbitant rent from society," Pelligrini wrote in response to a *Bloomberg View* editorial on the Federal Reserve in September 2012. "There's no way to achieve positive real returns in an extreme QE environment without being leveraged long, and there is no way to protect oneself from crippling losses if one is caught leveraged long at the wrong time. The trick is to be leveraged long only at times of market-moving policy decisions."

That was one reason Pellegrini returned money to investors in his hedge fund in 2010 and decided to manage only his own money.

Pellegrini, who is six feet two inches tall and weighs 183 pounds, is a former jazz disc jockey whose views on how to fix global finance are downright radical—at least for a career-long Wall Streeter. In its response to the financial crisis, the U.S. government shamelessly placed bank interests ahead of the common good by bailing them out, he says. He sees no reason why Americans should deposit their savings in private banks at all, since the government already guarantees those deposits.

Indeed, there is no need for banks at all. The public's cash, he says, can be held with the Federal Reserve in individual accounts. Loans can be made by nonbank lending institutions—entrepreneurial pools of capital that could include hedge funds or similar entities that would never become too big to fail.

At a minimum, Pellegrini says, there should be limits on bank profits—perhaps a 10 percent return on equity—to keep them from taking the kinds of risks that led to the housing bubble. "You need a system where people won't be incentivized to take risks," Pellegrini says. "We don't need bankers to take risks with our money."

Pellegrini, who lives on the Upper West Side of Manhattan with his third wife, Henrietta, and her daughter, seems incapable of sugar-coating his insights for expediency's sake. He has a predilection for long, free-wheeling conversations in which he tosses out incendiary snippets.

How has the Federal Reserve handled the crisis? "It's going to be viewed on a par with the torture at Guantanamo Bay," he says, sipping from a bottle of mineral water.

What does he think about the U.S. central bank otherwise? "The Fed steals from everyone," Pellegrini snorts. "It is printing money, as instructed by the financial services industry, so that they can stick all of us with the bill."

And ex-Federal Reserve Chairman Ben Bernanke? "I think he is a buffoon—I have zero confidence in what the Fed is doing."

Pellegrini has offered his subversive solutions for the financial system in opinion pieces on financial Web sites and blogs and in correspondence to legislators and senior officials in the Obama administration. One proposal was to use the Term Asset-Backed Securities Loan Facility (TALF) program, enacted as part of the 2008 bailout to help struggling homeowners, as a mechanism to reset inflated real estate prices. Hedge funds and private equity firms would get cheap funds from TALF to help homeowners refinance their underwater mortgages at realistic, lower levels. To do so, they would bid for their own homes in competition with other prospective buyers. The existing mortgage holders would get paid the reduced amount the auction fetched and be forced to eat the difference—punishment for their profligate lending practices. The homeowner's credit rating would be damaged—the price for erasing the debt.

"Nobody escapes reality and the pain is apportioned fairly," he wrote on the *New York Times* DealBook website in May 2009. "Credit starts flowing again and the market decides what houses are actually worth."

Economists have taken note of Pellegrini's maverick ideas to drastically reduce the footprint of behemoth banks, known as "narrow banking" in academic argot. "They are very crisp and different and provocative," says Kenneth Rogoff, an economics and public policy professor at Harvard University. "As an academic, I find that refreshing."

With his professorial air and penchant for theorizing, Pellegrini muses that he might have made a better contribution as a policy planner or macroeconomist than an investor. "I've been completely in the wrong place as an actor," he chuckles. "I could have helped design different mechanisms for running the financial system, and guiding the economy."

He argues that the Federal Reserve's policies are based on analyses that are unreliable—an example of the so-called Lucas critique, which states that predicting the impact of changes in economic policy based solely on historical information is dangerously simplistic.

In this case, the notion that historically low long-term rates will generate gross domestic product (GDP) and job growth has proven unfounded. "Whenever the central bank decides to use a particular indicator to measure an economic outcome, it ceases to be a relevant indicator," Pellegrini says.

The Federal Reserve has succeeded in pumping up asset prices—pushing investors into riskier asset classes, Pellegrini says. People in general are frightened of missing a run-up in equities, and the system is awash in excess liquidity. "We are basically through the looking glass," he says. "Now all the old relationships have become irrelevant."

This is all bad news for those who champion a free-market economy. "If you think ours is a market-based system, what Bernanke is doing is making this less of a market economy," Pellegrini says. "The system is not in balance."

Pellegrini says his fund's name, PSQR, is a play on his own initials: P.P. or P Squared. And it's also an anagram for SPQR, the initials of the ancient Roman Republic that stand for Senatus Populusque Romanus, or the Senate and the People of Rome. The four letters are still emblazoned on monuments, buses, and signs around Rome, where Pellegrini was born and spent his first five years amid the cobblestoned alleys of the bohemian neighborhood called Trastevere—that is, on "the other side of the river Tiber."

Pellegrini's quantitative disposition traces back to those early years. The oldest of three children, Paolo Marco Pellegrini was born in 1957 to a household steeped in the sciences. His father, Umberto, was a physics professor, and his mother, Anna, worked as a biology researcher.

Paolo was different. As a four-year-old, he used LEGO blocks to build a replica of a bank—perhaps a portent of his future interests.

The Pellegrinis moved north from Rome in 1962 when Umberto was appointed a professor at the University of Milan. There, Paolo took up classical piano and attended a "liceo classico," studying Latin and ancient Greek. Dinner table conversations were often political. While a teenager, Paolo joined the Partito Radicale, a pacifist, antiestablishment party that advocated the legalization of divorce and abortion.

His antiestablishment stance found ample expression at school too. "I was what you called a very uncooperative student," he laughs. "I was daydreaming in class, not doing my homework." One requirement was to read a Greek tragedy, whose title eludes him today. "I didn't buy the book," he says. "It wasn't that I didn't read it carefully. I didn't buy it at all."

Nevertheless, in 1975, he was admitted to Politecnico di Milano, where he pursued a degree in electrical engineering. Many nights, he volunteered as a disc jockey at Milan's Radio Radicale, spinning vinyl by bebop greats Dizzy Gillespie, Bud Powell, and Charlie Parker.

While a student, Pellegrini circulated Radical Party petitions, including one calling for the strengthening of civil liberties. He stayed clear of demonstrations and student groups advocating violence. The 1970s and early 1980s were Italy's Years of Lead, during which hundreds were killed or wounded in bombings and assassinations by both left- and right-wing extremists. In 1978, Red Brigade terrorists kidnapped and murdered the former Christian Democratic Prime Minister Aldo Moro.

Pellegrini focused on school, especially computer programming classes, at which he excelled. In the summers, he found work at big multinationals, including a stint in France with Hewlett-Packard and another with Honeywell International in Boston. He graduated cum laude in 1980.

Amid the strikes and demonstrations, the Italian economy was a shambles. "There were few opportunities in terms of a real career track," Pellegrini says. He looked abroad and landed a low-level job in the Netherlands at Praxis Instruments, a computer company. He found the work boring. "Business school seemed like a good investment," he says.

Pellegrini headed to Harvard Business School in Boston, where professors stoked his interest in finance, economics, and especially the markets. Pellegrini's field study adviser was Professor Andre Perold. "He was into data and patterns," Perold says. "He was intrigued by the potential of math-based systems to trade stocks."

At Harvard Business School, Pellegrini also met his first wife—Claire Goodman, daughter of the prominent New York State Senator, Roy Goodman, a progressive Republican. The two, who married in 1984, would go on to have two boys.

Michaelcheck, a partner in the fixed-income division of Bear, Stearns & Co., recalls recruiting the Italian student as a summer associate that year. Pellegrini wrote pitch books on possible mergers and acquisitions for the firm's clients.

There, Pellegrini shared an office with a mergers and acquisitions (M&A) vice president and a fellow Harvard Business School graduate who also had something of an independent streak—John Alfred Paulson. He and Pellegrini soon became friends.

With his Harvard M.B.A. in hand, Pellegrini landed an associate's position in corporate finance at Dillon, Read & Co., a small investment bank with a prestigious pedigree. The bull market was in full swing. It was 1985, and swashbuckling raiders—Carl Icahn, Ronald Perleman, T. Boone Pickens—had corporate America on the run. "I must have worked on a dozen major deals over a few months," Pellegrini says.

Dillon Read itself was bought by Travelers Corp. in 1986, and Pellegrini moved to Lazard Frères & Co., the Franco-Anglo-American investment bank run by Michel David-Weil. Pellegrini specialized in insurance, an industry that appealed to him for its complexity and quantitative orientation. Among other deals, he advised Munich-based Allianz AG on its 1990 acquisition of Fireman's Fund Insurance Co., a unit of Fund American Cos.

At Lazard, the pace was famously brutal. Pellegrini often worked 14-hour days, turning off the overhead lights in the office at night and blasting Mozart and Beethoven on his stereo. He trolled through reams of insurance data generated by his clients and their potential targets or acquirers.

Yet Pellegrini was not a natural investment banker. "It involved a lot of salesmanship," he says. "That's not my forté."

Pellegrini's blunt honesty was likely a hindrance, as was his Italian accent. Did he really understand the fine print? And his often biting sense of humor sometimes did not go over well with some American clients. Nor did it help that his marriage had run into trouble, too—he separated from Claire that year.

In 1994, the fees he was generating dropped as he failed to rope in new clients. The next year, Pellegrini says, Lazard's head of investment banking at the time, Kendrick Wilson, fired him.

In 1996, Mariner's Michaelcheck teamed up with Pellegrini to start a Bermuda-based firm called Select Reinsurance Ltd. He also remarried, this time to another prominent socialite—Beth DeWoody Rudin, daughter of powerful New York real estate developer Lewis Rudin. After two years, he and Michaelcheck, together with the firm's board, decided an executive with more sales experience should replace him.

"I was fired from that too, I suppose," he says.

In 1999, he started a consulting firm named Global Risk Advisors LLC to counsel companies on reinsurance and other risk-related matters. The venture didn't gain traction, and Pellegrini closed it in 2002. "Trying to reinvent myself was tricky," he shrugs.

Pellegrini compares these wilderness years to his treks as a youth in the Italian Alps. "There are times when you are hiking that you are really exhausted; you just put one foot in front of the other," he says. The important thing is to keep walking. "When you sit down, that's when things just fall apart," he says.

Pellegrini found his way back to Mariner, where Michaelcheck hired him as an analyst in early 2003. At the time, a Mariner hedge fund was trading CDOs, or collateralized debt obligations—bundles of housing loans and other debt—and Pellegrini developed a fascination with these complicated pools of bonds and other loans, as well as a relatively new kind of insurance-like derivative called a credit-default swap.

Eventually, Michaelcheck assigned him to the fund. Innately curious and fascinated by complex systems, the former computer programmer and engineer delved into the details of the esoteric instruments—how they were structured, how they traded. "Mariner was at the frontier of what was being done at the time," says Pellegrini.

In fact, CDOs and their predecessors were hardly new, having been around for more than a generation; they were the latest iteration of the mortgage-backed security, originally pioneered in the 1980s by Lewis Ranieri, the flamboyant Salomon Brothers trader profiled in Michael Lewis's best-selling book *Liars' Poker* (Viking, 1989).

CDOs were the high-octane fuel behind the growth of the skyrocketing housing market. By allowing banks and other lenders to package loans into securities and unload them onto investors around the world, they freed up bank capital, permitting them to make still more loans in a seemingly unending virtuous cycle. Because the loans were packaged and sold off so quickly, little attention was paid to their quality, and lending standards dropped precipitously. Originators like Ownit Mortgage Solutions, People's Choice, and Ameriquest Financial led the way, flogging interest-only, low-document and even no-document mortgages along with option arms and payment option arms. These were simply mortgages that were destined to fail, but they could be fed into a kind of financial instrument that could seemingly transform them into conservative bonds—the CDO.

At its simplest, a CDO is a pool of residential or commercial mortgage-backed securities and other debt instruments whose projected payment streams are mixed and sliced into tranches, based on the likelihood of their continuing to be paid out over time. The most secure of these, the super senior slices, paid out the lowest rates, (e.g., 5.5 or so percent in 2005), since the probability that they will stop paying was perceived to be quite low.

As rating agencies like S&P got into the business of measuring the riskiness of CDOs, these senior tranches would usually get labeled as triple A, equivalent to the top-notch grade of the U.S. Treasuries at the time. Further down the pecking order, successive CDO tranches were built to absorb the hits when problems arose. These slices would stop paying investors when mortgage holders defaulted. They might be rated A or lower and so sport higher yields, 6 or 8 percent.

The so-called "equity" tranche of the CDO was called that because it was assumed to be the riskiest—designed to be the first slice to stop making payments at the first hint of trouble. However, until it imploded, this risky slice paid double-digit rates of return.

The ratings from S&P, Moody's, and Fitch were based on a fallacy: that the geographic diversity, mix of different kinds of mortgages and sophisticated modeling of projected payments would allow the agencies to anoint tranches with a high-grade rating, even if the underlying mortgages were shaky. That proved disastrously wrong when housing prices reversed gears.

The credit default swaps (CDSs) Mariner was trading, by contrast, were of more recent vintage, having come into fashion only in the early 2000s. The CDSs were originally designed to provide insurance for investors holding corporate bonds. Credited to a red-haired JPMorgan derivatives whiz, Blythe Masters, the concept is straightforward: A bank or insurance firm, say, JPMorgan Chase or MBIA Inc., writes an insurance contract on a particular corporate bond, offering to pay the interest and the full principal amount if the issuer defaults. That's why it is routinely referred to as protection.

Originally, swaps were bought by holders of a particular bond, who paid, say, 10 basis points, or $100,000 annually for insurance on $100 million of bonds. Beginning in 2000, swaps were increasingly traded independently of whether the purchaser owned the underlying bonds. The value of the swap would rise as the creditworthiness of the bond's issuer declined or fall as its outlook improved. That could be helpful if, say, Bear Stearns was financing your business and you wondered whether the investment bank would go belly-up.

So swaps became an efficient way to wager against a particular company or its bonds. They had fewer hurdles than shorting a company's bonds—the difficulty of finding bonds to borrow and the unpredictable cost of buying them back if somebody engineered a short squeeze on those particular bonds.

It was the combination of CDOs and CDSs that was to prove critical to Pellegrini when he found his way to Paulson & Co.

At Mariner, Pellegrini worked on a project to build a triple A-rated derivatives product company to sell CDS protection on highly rated bonds, including CDOs. Because the bonds were of high quality, the company could have obtained a triple-A rating from credit agencies even if it insured a very large portfolio of bonds. As a result, the company could generate a high return on equity. Given its rating, the company did not need to "collateralize" the swaps it wrote and, therefore, had a better chance of surviving a market downturn. (The need to provide collateral on credit default swaps was what brought down American International Group Inc. and its AIG Financial Products subsidiary.) Soon, though, he began casting about for other work.

A Harvard Business School alumni service mentioned that Paulson & Co. was looking for a chief operating officer. Pellegrini, then 47, called John Paulson in the summer of 2004, even though he suspected he was underqualified. Paulson seemed happy to hear from him. The COO job had been filled, and the only thing available was an analyst's position that had opened up.

Pellegrini said immediately he was interested.

Paulson was hesitant. "My analysts are more junior than you," he said.

"I don't care," Pellegrini responded.

Today, Paulson's ascendancy into the pantheon of short-selling greats is Wall Street legend—and the subject of a best-selling book, *The Greatest Trade Ever*, by Gregory Zuckerman (Crown Business, 2010). Paulson's tale, like Pellegrini's, is that of an outsider catapulted into the uppermost echelons of the investing world.

Paulson long kept a low profile, even by hedge fund standards. Raised in the waterside neighborhood of Beechhurst, Queens, he was the third of four children of Alfred and Jacqueline Paulson.

Paulson's father, Alfred, was an accountant who became chief financial officer of public relations firm Ruder-Finn. His mother, Jacqueline, was a child psychologist. Paulson gives credit to an unlikely institution for giving him an early lift—the New York City public school system, with its programs for gifted children and accelerated curriculums, which are often under fire because they tend to exclude blacks and Hispanics disproportionately.

"I always had reading and math skills four or five years ahead of my grade," Paulson says.

Yet, Paulson had an entrepreneurial side even in elementary school. He would buy packages of six Charms lollipops for eight cents, breaking them up so he could sell the individual pops for five cents each—quite a mark-up.

By eighth grade, in New York City's accelerated program, he was studying Shakespeare and calculus. And after graduating from Bayside High School in Queens, he headed to New York University, where he earned a bachelor's degree in finance, summa cum laude, in 1978. As valedictorian, Paulson gave a graduation speech on corporate responsibility.

He went on to earn an M.B.A. at Harvard Business School in 1980, finishing in the top 5 percent of his class—a Baker's Scholar. Paulson decided on a career in finance. At the time, banking jobs were scarce, and he settled for a spot at Boston Consulting Group, a relatively obscure proving ground whose alumni include former U.S. presidential candidate Mitt Romney and Israeli prime minister Benjamin Netanyahu.

Two years later, he landed an associate position at New York-based Odyssey Partners, an investment firm run by the legendary Leon Levy and Jack Nash. An Odyssey specialty was risk arbitrage, in which traders often buy the stock of takeover targets and short that of the acquirer.

Paulson says Levy and Nash, both now deceased, taught him the ins and outs of risk arbitrage, real estate investing, and how to profit from bankruptcies. "Leon was brilliant," Paulson says. "A lot of what I know about deals today, I learned from them."

Paulson left Odyssey to join Bear Stearns' M&A department in 1984, rising in just four years to managing director. The firm had an outsider status on Wall Street under chairman Alan "Ace" Greenberg, eschewing standard Ivy League M.B.A.s in favor of what he called "PhDs"—candidates who were poor, hungry and with a deep desire to become rich.

Paulson wasn't thrilled when Bear sold shares to the public in 1985, and he eventually decided he didn't want to work for a big, publicly traded company, where the impact of his work was diffused. In 1988 he joined privately held Gruss Partners, another risk arbitrage firm. Founder Joseph Gruss taught Paulson an important lesson.

"Joseph Gruss used to say, 'Risk arbitrage is not about making money; it's about not losing money,'" Paulson says. That lesson seared in his psyche a career-long aversion to risk that, despite reversals in 2011 and 2012, continues to this day.

Paulson set out on his own in 1994, initially taking a desk at the office of his old colleague, Manuel Asensio. Paulson & Co. started as an arbitrage firm. Over the years, Paulson launched new funds to exploit market trends and on occasion closed them. Still, by the time Pellegrini approached Paulson, the firm was known primarily for two strategies. First was the aforementioned merger arbitrage—playing takeover candidates. The other was event arbitrage—a fancy way of wagering on corporate developments such as earnings surprises and stock buybacks.

The distinguishing feature at Paulson & Co. was risk control. "We always operated with a lot of hedges," Paulson says. "We try to minimize market correlations. If you don't, you're going to be exposed when a market event happens."

Paulson explains his philosophy thus: "Investors will forgive you if your returns are below average for a period. They won't forgive you if you lose money."

By the time Pellegrini joined in 2004, the merger arbitrage business was getting tough. There was plenty of volume—Pellegrini worked on the three-way merger that created Mitsubishi UFJ Financial Corp—but too much competition. "There was so much capital chasing any return," says Pellegrini. "Merger arbitrage spreads were being compressed more and more."

The flagship Paulson Advantage Fund, with $300 million in assets returned just 5 percent net in 2005, versus 9 percent for the average hedge fund. "That gave John the incentive to look for other opportunities," Pellegrini says. "What we tried to do was identify situations where betting against the consensus was inexpensive in both relative and absolute terms."

The signs of a growing real estate bubble were evident for anybody who cared to take note. Manhattan cocktail parties buzzed with news of the latest $25 million celebrity coop sale. The S&P/Case-Shiller 20-City Home Price Index had more than doubled from 2000 to mid-2006. Paulson had witnessed roller-coaster rises and drops in the volatile Manhattan coop market. "I did not subscribe to the theory that real estate prices only go up," Paulson told the Financial Crisis Inquiry Commission. Meanwhile, investment banks were printing massive amounts of CDOs—$157.8 billion in 2004, $251.3 billion in 2005, and $520.6 billion in 2006.

"John was worried about a credit bubble, particularly a consumer credit bubble," says Pellegrini. Although he shared Paulson's concerns at the time, Pellegrini insists that Paulson deserves the lion's share of the credit for initiating the trade. Paulson did and still does make all investing decisions at his firm; in Wall Street argot, he "pulls the trigger." Besides, as Pellegrini puts it: "I'm always pessimistic about everything, so John's view was more significant."

In his hedge fund's offices in the black granite IBM Building on Manahattan's Madison Avenue, Paulson and Pellegrini began discussing ways to profit from a collapse in the housing bubble he suspected was developing in early 2005. One obvious way was shorting the shares of banks with outsize exposure to the subprime mortgage market. In February 2005, Paulson & Co. initiated short positions on Countrywide Financial Corp., the Calabasas, California, mortgage lender co-founded by CEO Angelo Mozilo (the well-tanned poster child of the housing boom), and Washington Mutual, a Seattle bank that had expanded at breakneck pace across the country to comprise a nationwide network of more than 2,200 bank branches.

The danger of shorting financial stocks in a housing bubble was soon apparent. In little more than a two-week period from mid-April to early-May in 2005 the shares of both companies surged more than 12 percent, partly based on takeover rumors. Pellegrini calls the shorts modestly profitable. Both Countrywide and Washington Mutual were in fact eventually purchased by Bank of America Corp. and JPMorgan Chase & Co., respectively, but long after Paulson & Co. covered its positions. Paulson also bought credit protection on MBIA, a municipal bond insurer that had expanded into the faster-growing business of writing CDSs on CDOs. At the time the Armonk, New York, firm was the target of a short campaign by Bill Ackman, founder of Pershing Square Capital Management LP, who had spent years criticizing the rationale behind the triple-A ratings it was accorded by S&P and Moody's. The trades were only modestly profitable.

The lesson to Pellegrini was clear. "I told John the better way to express a negative view of consumer credit was to short subprime mortgage debt through credit derivatives," he says.

The lure of doing so was simple—by using a swap to bet against a bond, the only capital at risk was the premium paid. That was often as little as .50 basis points—or $50,000 for protection on $10 million worth of bonds. That was chump change if the bonds performed. But if they defaulted, swapholders would win a 2000 percent return on the investment. By contrast, shorting a stock in the traditional fashion leaves an investor virtually unlimited downside if, for example, an acquirer offers to pay significant premium to the market price.

Paulson began buying protection on tranches of Residential Mortgage-Backed Securitizations (RMBS)—specifically those rated BBB, or one step above junk. This, to his mind, was the sweet spot: The swaps cost just 100 basis points, or $1 million to cover $100 million of bonds. If he had dipped down just a single rating point, to the BBB- tranches, the price would have tripled.

The problem for Paulson & Co., with $3 billion in assets under management at year-end 2005, was supply—it was fiendishly difficult to find enough BBB tranches to buy protection on, since that particular slice represented less than 2-3 percent of the RMBS capital structure. Wall Street, innovative as always, was working on the problem with a new instrument—the synthetic CDO, a product of which Pellegrini was well aware.

By now, Pellegrini was devoting most of his efforts to analyzing the housing bubble. "We began to peel the onion," he says. He was worried that his work so far on mergers hadn't been particularly impressive—and wanted to show his old office mate and friend that the decision to hire him had been right.

The first year the trade was in effect was a nervous time, even though the Paulson Advantage Fund's notional exposure was relatively small. "From early 2005 to early 2006, it wasn't clear the trade was going to work," Pellegrini says. He would wake up in the night pondering the trade. "People thought we were throwing money down the drain. We asked, 'Are we missing something?'" It turns out they were.

Initially, he and Paulson believed that housing prices were a function of the current low "teaser" rates on many residential mortgages—just 4.25 percent on an adjustable-rate subprime mortgage in late 2005. Once mortgage rates "reset" to the higher contractual rate at the end of the typical two-year teaser-rate period, homeowners would begin to default on their adjustable-rate mortgages—and the bubble would burst.

At a November 2005 conference at New York's Grand Hyatt Hotel, New Century Financial Corp. CEO Robert Cole gave an upbeat presentation to analysts. Afterwards, Pellegrini approached Cole at the lectern, asking him whether the "rate reset" rates would trigger defaults.

Cole blithely responded that defaults would be minimal because New Century would simply refinance existing mortgages coming up for rate resets with new, larger mortgages starting out again at the low teaser rate. The upfront refinancing fees New Century charged the homeowners would compensate for the lower initial rates.

Paulson and Pellegrini suddenly had a problem. They had staked their housing bet on the premise that rising mortgage rates would trigger a wave of defaults. Now the head of one of the biggest subprime mortgage originators had told them the company was happy to refinance mortgages to avoid such defaults.

What Paulson & Co. needed now was some sort of proof that housing prices were unsustainably high and due for a major correction, regardless of the direction of mortgage rates. In such a scenario, homeowners would not be able to refinance their mortgages because the value of their homes would have declined below the existing mortgage balance, rendering a refinancing impossible. As it was, housing bulls were arguing loudly that home prices had never declined in value in the United States—and they were proffering plenty of evidence that there was good reason for housing prices to be as high as they were.

Paulson desperately needed evidence that prices were out of whack and Pellegrini volunteered to look for it. "The mortgage market lends itself to deep quantitative analysis and modeling," Paulson says. "Paolo excelled in this area."

Pellegrini and his colleagues zeroed in on numbers from the Office of Federal Housing Enterprise Oversight's home price index from 1975 to 2000. Previously, research had shown that, indeed, home prices had never fallen on a national basis—a key argument for housing bulls. However, the argument overlooked the fact that inflation had declined substantially since 2000.

Pellegrini decided to inflation-adjust all the numbers. Sure enough, inflation-adjusted prices showed peaks and troughs—when he drew a regression line through the data points, it showed prices would have to fall 30 percent to 35 percent in inflation-adjusted terms just to get back to the historical trend. With almost zero inflation, this meant that nominal prices would have to fall by a similar percentage. And since falling prices tend to overshoot in a sell-off, the United States and much of the world were facing a meltdown of cataclysmic proportions. "After hearing a lot of arguments for and against the presence of the bubble, we had a simple and clear insight of our own to go by," Pellegrini says.

He recalls that Paulson broke into a smile when he showed him the proof that houses were overpriced. "John doesn't smile," Pellegrini says. "It felt great."

The next step was to determine the relationship between home prices and defaults. Pellegrini hired a New York firm called 1010Data Inc. to help him integrate two databases: One, compiled by Santa Ana, California–based First American Corp. and called LoanPerformance, tracked 6 million securitized subprime mortgages. The other was based on a Case-Shiller home price index, sorted by postal code. The combined database showed that even if home prices merely flattened, defaults would surge. "There was a very strong relationship between mortgage losses and home prices," Pellegrini says.

Even before the exchange with New Century's Cole, Pellegrini and Paulson were ramping up the housing bet. One way of doing that was what acronym-happy Deutsche Bank Securities called the Static Residential Trust, or START, series of CDOs, which Pellegrini called cash-synthetic CDOs. Paulson & Co. would be involved from the beginning, buying protection on various tranches—typically those rated BBB by S&P. Work started in the summer of 2005. "I decided it was better to buy wholesale than retail," says Pellegrini.

Better yet, it meant Paulson & Co. wouldn't have to buy in the open market, upsetting prices and tipping its hand. Paulson purchased the risky equity tranches, too. These were the hardest to sell, but necessary in this structure to get the entire deal done. Though the equity tranches were the first to be wiped out as defaults rose, until they did, they generously paid 10 percentage points above the London Interbank Offer Rate or LIBOR, reducing the impact of the eventual loss.

START and most synthetic CDOs worked like this: Bullish investors put their money into the CDO, which "referenced" to a portfolio of existing mortgage-backed securities selected by Deutsche Bank or other firms. The synthetic portfolio was tracked and sliced into tranches, just as if there were real residential mortgage-backed securities in it, as they would in a normal CDO. Those looking to bet against the housing market bought credit protection on the specific tranches they wanted. The bearish investors' premium payments then flowed to the bullish investors, mimicking cash flow payments of the referenced mortage-backed securities.

The CDO tranches absorb losses on all the residential mortgage-backed securities referenced by the CDO in reverse order of seniority. If an RMBS is written down, the equity tranche absorbs the loss. If the equity tranche is wiped out, the next tranche absorbs the loss and so on. In that situation, the cash paid in by the long investors is used to pay the buyers of the credit protection on the CDOs.

Because START didn't hold actual mortgage-backed securities, Deutsche wasn't limited by the supply. It could simply "reference" existing ones and crank out cash-synthetic CDOs to meet demand.

Paulson & Co. bought almost all the credit protection on two START CDOs—the $900 billion START 2005-C and the $1.2 billion START 2006-B, launched in December 2005 and February 2006, respectively. Loreley Financing, an investment firm, later sued Deutsche Bank, accusing it of using synthetic CDOs, including START, to defraud it by designing them to fail. The suit was settled for undisclosed terms in March 2012.

But now, Paulson & Co. had hit another wall. The funds he was making his investments through, Paulson Advantage and Advantage Plus, were ostensibly event arbitrage funds. He rationalized to investors that his growing bets against the housing market were a kind of market hedge. Now, with the notional value of the trades teetering at more than a $2 billion dollars, that artifice rang hollow.

Paulson resolved in early 2006 to launch a fund dedicated to the subprime bet—Paulson Credit Opportunities I, and later, a less leveraged version called Credit Opportunities II. Pellegrini was charged with finding a portfolio manager for the two funds—a tall order, since he would be hiring somebody to take over the trade that he had played so large a role in developing. Paulson eventually surprised him by naming him co-portfolio manager of the funds.

Paulson and Pellegrini launched a full-court press to market their investors on Credit Opportunities. It was a tough sell. "There was skepticism and hostility from people within the industry," says Pellegrini. "They told us we were early, that we didn't understand the game."

With the housing market still galloping upward, investors wanted details of both Paulson & Co.'s research and how the trade would work.

"I remember Paolo stopping by the office at 5 p.m. and staying to 9 p.m. explaining his research," says Jack O'Connor, chief investment officer of AI International Corp., a family investment office. "We were impressed." So were others. Over nine months, the firm raised $1.1 billion.

As home prices continued to rise, Paulson & Co. took advantage, paying as little as one cent for every dollar of credit protection. Former investors still marvel at the payoff. "It was technically a beautiful trade," one money manager says. "The asymmetry was incredible."

The housing market peaked in mid-2006. "Once the year-over-year change in home price appreciation went negative in June 2006, we thought the collapse of the market was almost inevitable," Paulson says.

Not everybody agreed. Indeed, Paulson and Pellegrini were furious at the refusal of bank counterparties to their swaps to mark their CDS positions down to realistic prices. All the data showed rising defaults, but the counterparty banks simply pretended that had no impact on the sometimes thinly traded credit protection.

Fortuitously, the Markit Group had just launched an index tied to the value of subprime mortgages—the ABX Index. The benefit of the new benchmark, as for most indices, is that it provides a tool for enhanced liquidity and soon Paulson was buying protection on the index in force—another tactic to extract profit from the housing collapse he was predicting.

Even better, the index was calculated to show the returns of specific tranches—BBB, Single A, and so on. Accordingly, Paulson had a pretty good idea of the firm's real winnings, even if its counterparties were fudging their marks on the swaps the firm had bought. For the last half of 2006, Credit Opportunities gained 19.4 percent, according to investors.

Although extremely liquid, and useful in expanding the Paulson & Co. subprime wager, betting against the ABX Index was far more expensive than buying CDO protection. Finding counterparties to wager with was also tough.

With the new funds up and running, Paulson kept looking for ways to expand, enhance, and press his subprime bet. The firm was in constant discussions with Wall Street firms, asking about their willingness to structure synthetic CDOs that Paulson & Co. could bet against. Originally targeting the tranches rated BBB, as home prices declined and defaults began rising Paulson & Co. started buying protection on those rated A as well.

In early 2007, Josh Birnbaum, head of Goldman Sachs' CDO trading desk, stopped by Paulson & Co.'s office with some colleagues to meet with Paulson, Pellegrini and the firm's head trader, Bradley Rosenberg. They wanted to meet the hedge fund that was beginning to have a major impact on their profit and loss statement (P&L) and to deliver a message: Paulson & Co. was overreaching. "Basically, he said, there's no way the single A tranches were going to have write-downs," says Pellegrini. "They had been accumulating single A credits."

Birnbaum offered to buy back some of the protection Goldman Sachs had sold Paulson & Co. Paulson said he'd think about it.

Birnbaum then began probing for an idea about how big a bet Paulson & Co. was planning on CDOs. He pitched the notion that Goldman Sachs was there to help. Goldman, after all, was the hedge fund's main prime broker. It had helped Paulson & Co. raise capital.

"We're partners," Birnbaum said. "You should tell us how much you intend to buy so we can make a market."

Paulson didn't commit to anything. Still, with two new hedge funds ramping up, Paulson & Co. needed to buy more CDO protection quickly.

Morgan Stanley was one prospect. Pellegrini approached Trust Company of the West (TCW) about acting as portfolio selection agent on a structure like START. TCW replied that Morgan Stanley would have a problem with Paulson shorting tranches of a CDO it was sponsoring. "Morgan may have a tough time with [Paulson] shorting the whole portfolio," one TCW executive wrote.

Pellegrini turned to Paulson & Co.'s own prime broker, Goldman Sachs, a growing force in CDOs, with the idea of buying protection on $1 billion of residential mortgage-backed securities through a new synthetic CDO, the latest in a series of synthetic CDOs under the ABACUS moniker—rolled out by Goldman some years earlier. His day-to-day contact was an affable and wise-cracking young Frenchman named Fabrice Tourre, a vice president in the group called Structured Product Correlation and Trading.

Dubbed ABACUS 2007-AC-1, the CDO would be what Pellegrini likes to call "synthetic-synthetic." No cash would be paid into the CDO, although the long "buyers," as in the case with the START CDO, would still receive the protection payment streams from the swapholders and pay them when downgrades and defaults occurred.

Getting a deal done quickly was crucial. By eschewing real securities and real cash and relying on credit default swaps to mimic cash flows of real securities with underlying collateral, a synthetic CDO could be done quickly—a critical consideration because the market, as Pellegrini and Paulson figured, was beginning to crumble. This type of CDO also didn't require every tranche of the synthetic CDO to be spoken for.

Goldman Sachs's Tourre suggested hiring a "portfolio selection agent" who would determine which mortgage-backed securities to include in the referenced portfolio.

Again, there was pushback. Tourre and Pellegrini met with GSC Partners LLC, a Florham Park, New Jersey, asset manager run by a group of former Goldman Sachs distressed debt traders to see if they would serve as portfolio selection agent, working with Paulson, who they acknowledged intended to short the CDO. No dice.

Later, when GSC was approached by Goldman to participate as an investor, it had a withering response. "I do not have to say how bad it is that you guys are pushing this thing," the e-mail read.

At least one other asset manager was also approached, and ultimately did not sign on.

By contrast, ACA Financial, a once-staid underwriter of municipal bond insurance, was hungry. Bear Stearns' merchant banking division had bought a 28 percent stake in the company in 2004, pushed aside existing management and refocused ACA on managing and insuring CDOs. By year-end 2006 it had $15.7 billion in assets under management, a combination of credit default swaps, asset-backed securities like CDOs, and leveraged loans.

Heading the ACA CDO business: senior managing director Laura Schwartz, a former Merrill Lynch asset-backed finance executive who took charge of the portfolio selection process. Whatever mortgage-backed securities Pellegrini wanted in the reference portfolio would have to meet with her approval.

What ensued was a months-long game of complicated, billion-dollar gin rummy, played out in e-mails, face-to-face midtown meetings, and one dimly lit bar in Jackson Hole, Wyoming. Pellegrini would pitch to Schwartz a portfolio of risky securities to be included in the reference portfolio. Schwartz would volley back, nixing some and approving others and suggesting replacements. It was an arduous process.

Troves of e-mails were disclosed in the SEC's suit against Goldman Sachs and Tourre, and in another suit filed by ACA itself against the investment bank and Paulson & Co. as well as in hearings by the U.S. Senate and House of Representatives concerning Goldman Sachs' role in the financial crisis. They shed light on how the CDO factories worked—as well as the characters involved.

Throughout, the personable Tourre hustled to keep both parties at the table, encouraging them to come to terms. Along the way, he e-mailed his girlfriend in London, Marine Serres, another Goldman Sachs yearling, opining on the housing bubble's impending collapse—segueing seamlessly between English and French as he did.

"More and more leverage in the system the entire building at risk of collapse at any moment ... the only potential survivor, the fabulous Fab," one whimsical missive reads. "Standing in the middle of these complex, highly levered, exotic trades he created without necessarily understanding all the implications of those monstruosities!!!"

From the start there was confusion on ACA's part about Paulson & Co.'s role in putting together the deal. In a January 8, 2007 e-mail, Schwartz questions a colleague of Tourre's about it, after an early meeting. "I think it didn't help that we didn't know exactly how they [Paulson & Co.] want to participate in the space. Can you get us some feedback?"

Whether Schwartz ever got feedback is unclear—the issue was the crux of ACA's suit against Goldman and Paulson & Co. The insurer claimed that Goldman and Paulson conspired to hide the fact that the hedge fund planned to short the ABACUS portfolio and not, as is implied in subsequent Goldman e-mails, buy the equity tranches.

In fact, like a lot of bearish investors at that time, Paulson often did both. Cash flows from equity tranches, which threw off double-digit payments, were often sufficient to pay for the credit protection the company was buying on the rest of the portfolio—so the trade could be self-financing. In the second half of 2006, more than half of the equity tranches of CDOs were bought by hedge funds that also shorted other portions, according to the Financial Crisis Inquiry Commission.

In the kind of housing meltdown Paulson and others predicted, defaults would be triggered across the CDO's capital structure—not just the unrated equity tranche.

Schwartz was aware of the strategy, since in a January 28 e-mail she described Paulson as a "Magnetar-like equity investor," referring to the Chicago-based hedge fund whose bets against subprime mortgages were accompanied by long investments in the equity tranches. ACA had served as selection agent on at least one of those CDOs.

On January 9, Goldman forwarded to ACA a roster of 123 mortgage securities that Pellegrini was suggesting for the reference portfolio. ACA had previously purchased more than half of the securities—and was thus reasonably comfortable with them. A Goldman colleague of Tourre's emailed Schwartz that he was "very excited about the initial portfolio feedback."

Still, negotiations were tortuous. In general, Pellegrini sought out pools of mortgages from California, Nevada, and Arizona, the so-called "sand states" with the sharpest run-ups in home prices. He also wanted a high percentage of adjustable rate mortgages sold to homeowners with low FICO credit scores.

In a January 14 e-mail to a Tourre colleague, Schwartz fretted she might have been too tough with him, and once again referred to her understanding that Paulson was an equity investor in ABACUS. "I certainly hope I didn't come across too antagonistic on the call with Fabrice last week but the structure looks difficult from a debt investor perspective. I can understand Paulson's equity perspective but for us to put our name on something, we have to be sure it enhances our reputation."

About a week later, on January 22, Schwartz e-mailed Tourre and colleagues a list of 86 subprime mortgage securities that ACA would consider for the reference portfolio. Just 55 of Pellegrini's original 123 names were included. She wrote:

> We do not recommend including the other 68 names because either: 1) we did not like them at the recommended attachment point; 2) there are lower rated tranches that are already on negative watch; and 3) some names (i.e. Long Beach and Fremont) are very susceptible to investor push back.

Schwartz added that the names she was suggesting were mostly new issues, which she believed to be of higher quality.

Despite the back and forth, four days later, on January 26, Tourre felt confident enough to start asking about lawyers for the deal, engagement letters, and fees.

Pellegrini took a couple of days off to go skiing with his elder son in Jackson Hole, Wyoming, booking a room at the Snake River Lodge. By coincidence, he bumped into Schwartz, who was attending a structured product conference sponsored by UBS at the nearby Four Seasons Hotel.

The two agreed to meet up at the bar at Snake River Lodge to work on the all-important portfolio composition. Schwartz ordered a soft drink and Pellegrini a beer. They then opened up their respective laptops and began working through changes to the roster of reference securities. Pellegrini says the negotiations reflected their different outlooks. "This is one the few examples where a difference in intellectual paradigm determined the outcome," he says. "They missed completely the notion—what happens if home prices go south?"

Pellegrini recalls having a spreadsheet with 100 or so lines of data on it. By contrast, he says, Schwartz had a 20-page report on each securitization.

For an hour, the two swapped the securities in and out of the hypothetical ABACUS portfolio. "We changed the portfolios four or five times before we were done," Pellegrini says.

Certainly, the one-on-one smoothed the path for ABACUS. "He may be as much of a nerd as me since he brought a laptop to the bar and he also seemed to have a worksheet from DB and another manager," Schwartz joked in an e-mail to Tourre the next day, January 28. "I certainly got the impression he wanted to move forward on this with us."

Goldman, Paulson, and ACA continued to cull and add names to the portfolios: At Goldman's suggestion, out went SAIL 2006 BNC1 M7 and SAIL 2006 BNC2 M7, which Moody's had placed on negative credit watch; in came GSAMP 06-HE-4 M8 and GSAMP 06-HE5 MB.

At least one long investor, Jorg Zimmerman of IKB Deutsche Industriebank, a huge buyer of CDOs, asked for his own changes to the portfolio, specifically to remove bonds serviced by Fremont General and New Century. The securities in question remained in the portfolio.

On February 5, Schwartz e-mailed two lower level colleagues, Keith Gorman and Lucas Westerich. "Attached is the revised portfolio that

Paulson would like us to commit to—all names are at the Baa2 level. The final portfolio will have between 80 and these 92 names. Are 'we' okay to say yes on this portfolio?"

Gorman responded. "Looks good to me. Did they give a reason why they kicked out all of the Wells deals?"

Though there is no record of Schwartz's response, Wells Fargo was, in fact, known for its relatively strict underwriting standards.

Two days later, lightning struck. While New Century's share price had held up amid mounting worries in the housing market, Paulson had begun shorting the stock in January. He neither believed the firm's cultivated reputation at the time as a conservative lender nor respected the fact that Greenlight Capital founder David Einhorn, a successful hedge fund manager, sat on its board.

New Century reported that it would restate earnings for most of the previous year's results because banks were returning troubled loans it had sold them. The next day, New Century shares plunged 36 percent. More importantly, the news triggered a rout in the ABX Index, which tumbled five points that day. Holding $25 billion in subprime insurance, Paulson & Co. earned $1.25 billion in a single day.

ABACUS 2007-AC1, though, moved forward. On April 10, Schwartz e-mailed ACA CEO Alan Roseman. She stated Paulson & Co. was a buyer of the equity tranches. "We did price $192 million in total Class A1 and A2 today to settle April 26," she wrote. "Paulson took down a proportionate amount of equity (0–10% tranche)."

In 2010, Laura Schwartz told the FCIC she was blind to Paulson & Co.'s intentions to the end. "To be honest, [at that time,] until the SEC testimony I did not even know that Paulson was only short," she said. Whether she believed the firm was net long or short would be a good question.

The fateful CDO closed on April 26, as the subprime mortgage markets accelerated into a vortex of home wealth destruction. Credit was drying up and bids for subprime loans fell below the cost to originate them. Firms like Fremont General and New Century stopped making the loans altogether. Two prominent Bear Stearns hedge funds that invested heavily in subprime mortgage bonds racked up double-digit losses for the month, triggering headlines and stirring panic among investors.

The mortgage markets just kept getting worse—which is to say, much better for Pellegrini and his funds. For March, Credit Opportunities posted a 66 percent return—one investor called to complain that there was there was a typo in the e-mail announcing the fund's gain. It must have been 6.6 percent, no?

The ABX Index, however, soon rallied from its February plunge as bargain hunters entered the market. After tumbling from 100 to 60, in March the index began a climb to 70 and then nearly 80 by mid-May. Paulson Credit Opportunities gave back half of its year-to-date gains.

The rally had no legs. By mid-May, the ABX was collapsing once again. And now the bad news seemed relentless, mounting into the summer. In late June, Bear Stearns paid $3.2 billion to shore its hedge funds; those were shuttered the next month when rating agencies S&P and Moody's downgraded billions of dollars worth of subprime mortgage bonds. IKB, the German bank that had been the biggest long investor in ABACUS 2007-AC1, had to be bailed out by German bank regulators because of soured U.S. mortgage bets.

The Goldman Sachs CDS trading desk, by going short the subprime mortgage market in late 2006, was well positioned to observe the carnage and profit from it.

Birnbaum, for one, was in awe. "Many accounts throwing in the towel," he wrote to a colleague in July as the bad news mounted. "Anybody who tried to call the bottom left in bodybags." His colleague was effusive. "We hit a billsky in PNL today," he wrote, using trading desk argot for $1 billion for a single-day profit. "I'm no John Paulson though."

At Paulson & Co.'s midtown offices, with their muted blond wood built-ins and bold Alexander Calder gouaches, Paulson and Pellegrini kept a measured calm, even as their profits began to accelerate. Twice a day, the firm's head trader, Brad Rosenberg, would walk into Paulson's office and tell him the marks, or prices, of the firm's credit default swaps. Employees, many of whom kept real-time quotes of the ABX Index on their computer screens, would strain to read Paulson's expression as he did so—but the former investment banker usually succeeded in maintaining a perfect poker face—revealing nothing.

By August, the ABX had tumbled to 35. Pellegrini, his net worth tied up in the fund, begged Paulson to be allowed to cover at least part his funds' short positions. Paulson agreed to Pellegrini's pleas to take some profits—but initially covered only its subprime short positions in its merger and event arbitrage funds. He, Pellegrini, and research director Andrew Hoine by now realized a logical corollary to their mounting riches—if they and other hedge funds were racking up outrageous gains, who was ultimately going to book the losses to pay them? The answer to one degree or another had to be the thinly capitalized banks.

Paulson assigned the project to Hoine, a former investment banker at JPMorgan Chase. Paulson's funds began buying credit protection on a range of financial institutions—Bear Stearns, Lehman Brothers, UBS, and Credit Suisse Group—at prices as low as 20 basis points, or $200,000 for protection on $100 million worth of bonds. At prices that low, Paulson & Co. could spread his bets around.

Assets had been pouring into the funds—especially Credit Opportunities and Credit Opportunities II, the two swelling to a combined $8.9 billion. They stopped taking new money in late- and mid-2006, respectively. New money was going to the Advantage funds. By October, though, Paulson & Co. had covered 60 percent of its subprime bets. By that point, every security in the ABACUS 2007-AC1 reference portfolio had either been downgraded or placed on negative credit watch. Investors lost $1 billion, including $15 million lost by Goldman Sachs itself, when it failed to unload or hedge a portion of Paulson's credit protection. Paulson made about $1 billion on the CDO's collapse.

Who bears the onus for ABACUS 2007-AC1? In an interview with the Financial Crisis Inquiry Commission, Schwartz for one did not deflect responsibility. "ACA … selected that portfolio," she said. "[E]very name in that portfolio has been reviewed by ACA."

Perhaps the whole issue is a bit of a straw man. Paulson, in his FCIC interview points out that synthetic CDOs are by their nature zero sum bets between two parties with losers and winners. In this case, arguably, the scales were tipped in his favor with the help of Goldman Sachs.

Schwartz herself points out that ABACUS 2007-AC1 did not perform particularly poorly, in light of the thorough collapse of the mortgage markets. "Unfortunately, almost every deal went bad," she says. "ACA's structured credit business lost a significant amount of money on almost all the super-senior protection it wrote."

For his part, Pellegrini says the evidence backs his claim that the portfolio of residential mortgage-backed securities included in ABACUS was meant to create a reflection of the subprime market, not engineer a train wreck. "We wanted a CDO that wasn't better than the market, wasn't worse than the market," he says. If that's not the case, he was less than expert. Those securities he initially recommended for the doomed CDO, and that Schwartz rejected, ultimately performed better than those Schwartz selected to replace them.

Pellegrini, when questioned twice by the SEC, in December 2008 and again in March 2011, said he told them that he doesn't recall specifically telling Schwartz about his Paulson & Co. plans to short ABACUS.

The SEC suit, filed in April 2010, alleged that Goldman Sachs defrauded investors by not telling them that Paulson & Co. had helped select the ABACUS reference portfolio. Goldman settled that suit in October 2011 for $550 million, a record. "The marketing materials for the ABACUS 2007-AC1 transaction contained incomplete information," the firm said in a statement:

> In particular, it was a mistake for the Goldman marketing materials to state that the reference portfolio was "selected by" ACA Management LLC without disclosing the role of Paulson & Co. Inc. in the portfolio selection process and that Paulson's economic interests were adverse to CDO investors.

Tourre, not surprisingly for a junior-level investment bank employee, was left holding the bag. In August 2013, he was found liable for six of seven of SEC fraud charges in connection with the case. His lawyers, paid by Goldman Sachs, brought no witnesses in his defense. He was ordered to pay $650,000 in civil fines for defrauding investors. And Tourre was also required to give up his $175,463 bonus that derived in part from the ABACUS deal. Tourre entered the University of Chicago to pursue a doctorate degree in economics.

By contrast, in 2007, Paulson Credit Opportunities posted a 590 percent return. In 2008, a year when the average hedge fund lost 19 percent, Credit Opportunities posted an 18.3 percent return. Firm assets rose to $36.1 billion at the end of 2008 from $7 billion two years earlier. Over two years, the firm's total gains amounted to a stunning $19 billion.

Pellegrini's lucrative Paulson & Co. trade was based on numbers.

"People were pretending they were earning a living, and they were not," he says. "Banks lent them the money so they could live beyond their means, and I don't mean lavishly." That's a lesson and a warning going forward.

Chapter 10

Cohodes: Force of Nature, Market Casualty

"**G**aston! Gaston!" It was November in Las Vegas, and Marc Cohodes, general partner of Rocker Partners LP, was calling across the convention floor of Comdex 1999, the giant consumer electronics show. He had just caught sight of Gaston Bastiaens, CEO of Lernout & Hauspie Speech Products, a Belgian maker of voice recognition software, switchboards, and other gear. Bastiaens was not happy to see Cohodes—and began making his way to the exits, with a posse of underlings in tow. Rocker Partners had been shorting the company's shares since July 1998, soon after Cohodes discovered its speech-to-text software didn't work—just 15 percent of the words a person spoke would be accurately transcribed. The salespeople at big box retailers agreed the stuff was junk and told him so. L&H, as people called it, would claim revenues of $344.2 million that year, but already

Cohodes was having a hard time figuring out who was buying the software. Neither L&H rivals nor Wall Street analysts could figure it out either.

Bastiaens had a checkered past. He had helped preside over Apple Computer's disastrous Newton personal writing tablet, a pen-based device that that bombed spectacularly in 1993. Bastiaens went on to head Quarterdeck Office Systems, a software company that flamed out in the late 1990s. Other than his nationality—Bastiaens too was Belgian—Cohodes could see no credentials that qualified him for the top spot at L&H.

"Gaston! Gaston!" Cohodes called out again as he hurried through the crowded exhibition floor filled with booths of software and electronic gadgetry. "I want to ask you some questions."

Bastiaens quickened his pace ahead of Cohodes, who at six feet two inches and 260 pounds made for a formidable, bearlike pursuer. The CEO's retinue of handlers tried to keep up as best they could.

Bastiaens certainly knew about Cohodes—a regular visitor to L&H chat rooms, where he posted critical questions under his own name. Cohodes was open about his short position on L&H, and grilled Bastiaens' investor relations staff on any number of issues. He even bashed L&H on an Internet radio program he hosted.

"Gaston, don't run away like a girl," implored Cohodes. "I want to ask you about the sales."

Bastiaens didn't respond. The head of L&H public relations, Ellen Spooren, a tall blonde Dutch woman, positioned herself between Cohodes and her boss.

"Go away," she scolded. "You're a bad, bad man!"

Cohodes continued peppering Bastiens with questions.

"Keep away," Spooren warned. "I'll call security."

Soon, guards arrived to unceremoniously escort Cohodes from the building. The next day he was back, undaunted, but Bastiaens was nowhere to be seen. Cohodes picked up some L&H T-shirts from the corporate booth for his son and Rocker Partners analysts.

Cohodes relishes the limelight as much as some fellow short sellers disdain it. In the end, combined with persistence and spot-on investigative work, this has proven lethal for a roster of companies.

In the case of L&H, the short seller's dogged research, and that of his colleagues, triggered a fusillade of damning media coverage, including Herb Greenberg, who wrote for Marketwatch.com at the time, and most notably, the *Wall Street Journal's* Jesse Eisinger and Mark Maremont. The company was forced to open an internal audit, the U.S. Securities & Exchange Commission began an investigation, and L&H filed for bankruptcy before year-end 2000.

The enduringly bitter dynamics of the short-selling business insured that Rocker Partners' investors suffered. Initially shorting L&H at prices as low as $10 a share, Cohodes agonized as the stock rose in 1999 to $23. The company was billing itself as the premiere play in the white-hot translation software market, and using its rising stock to buy out rivals—including Dragon Systems of Newton, Massachusetts, and Dictaphone, a Stratford, Connecticut-based company. The leaders of the U.S. technology industry bought into the hype, and Microsoft Corp at one point became the largest holder of L&H stock, with a 10 percent position. Intel was in, too.

As reported L&H sales accelerated, the stock went into hyperdrive, hitting $72.50 at the peak of the technology bubble in March 2000.

Rocker Partners was losing tens of millions of dollars. By mid-2000, even as tech stocks in general were tanking, L&H shares were up 70 percent for the year. "This thing had tripled on us," Cohodes recalls. "We're getting killed. We were losing clients." Following the immutable laws of short-selling, the Rocker Partners' exposure was growing as it was forced to post more collateral to maintain its position. Because the share price was rising, L&H was accounting for more and more of the Rocker Partners' portfolio—7 to 8 percent instead of the normal 4 to 5 percent.

Cohodes, normally self-assured, began to doubt his own research. "You start losing your ability to realize you're right," he says. "The stock is going against you so you can't see right."

Then came a serendipitous phone call. On his radio show, Cohodes had been speculating on the identities of L&H customers. Who would purchase the software that he and others found so flawed? At his office in Larkspur, California, Cohodes picked up the receiver one morning to hear what he'd been hoping for—an ex-L&H executive, Michael

Faherty, who'd headed sales in the northeast region of the United States. "You're dead right," Faherty told him. "I used to work there in sales. We make the stuff, we ship them out, we write up false invoices."

The call proved a game changer. "It was like finding the proverbial needle in a haystack," says Cohodes, who put Faherty in touch with the SEC's enforcement division, with whom he had been sharing information about L&H. Faherty's revelation was the first clear evidence the company was fundamentally a fraud. Certain now that he was on the right track, Cohodes redoubled his efforts—and resolved to maintain his short position with invigorated confidence.

More damning evidence was en route. L&H's purchases of Dragon Systems and Dictaphone meant the majority of its assets were now domiciled in the United States. L&H was now required to file 10-Qs, the extensive quarterly financial information required of U.S. companies with the SEC, rather than the less specific, semiannual reports that foreign-based corporations can get away with.

The new disclosures cast light on L&H's business. Specifically, the company's 1999 10-K broke out sales by geographic region, showing that revenues in Europe and North America were falling. The 70 percent rise in 1999 sales to $342.2 million, which had helped to fuel the rise in L&H shares, was almost entirely attributable to a spike in South Korea and Singapore. In those two countries, sales had risen from just $300,000 in 1998 to $143.2 million in 1999. Now, Cohodes thought he knew where most of the suspicious revenues were being generated. "Korea is one-tenth the size of the United States, but it's generating the same volume of business," Cohodes recalls thinking. "How can that be?"

Cohodes hired an Asia-based analyst to track down the purported customers that L&H listed in its SEC filings. Many, it turned out, had never heard of L&H. Others had bought some software, but in amounts far lower than L&H was claiming.

There was also the matter of special purpose entities that were set up by "independent" investors to develop speech translation software applications for more than a dozen languages—Urdu, Czech, Arabic, Polish and Farsi, for example. These entities paid L&H between $3 to $4 million for software franchise rights tied to specific languages. It was a byzantine financing scheme that, multiplied many times over, drastically boosted revenues. L&H declined to provide anything like a complete roster of the investors. One, however, was FLV Fund—an entity set up by L&H founders Jo Lernout and Pol Hauspie, who had stepped back from management but remained co-chairmen. Though the pair were no longer connected to the FLV fund, Cohodes viewed it as a sign of rife conflict—a bright red flag.

As the importance of these vehicles sank in, L&H shares dropped, tumbling 19 percent on August 8 alone. On August 15 the company's somnambulant board stirred, ordering an audit of its South Korean operations—and ten days later CEO Bastiaens resigned. The *Wall Street Journal* reported on September 21 that the SEC was investigating the company. In October, Bastiens's replacement, John Duerden, flew to South Korea to confront the local business head—Joo Chul Seo. During a meeting, three toughs barged into the office and hauled Seo out of the office, and he was never heard from by L&H again. The company announced on November 9 it would restate financial statements for two and one half years because of "errors and irregularities." By the end of the year L&H was bankrupt, with its shares trading in the pennies.

Despite L&H's ignominious collapse, Rocker Partners' profit was slim on the trade—about $10 million over two and one half years. In the interim, the $700 million hedge fund had been forced to endure paper losses of as much as $100 million, exacerbated by customer redemptions.

Rocker Partners sued L&H's investment banker, SG Cowen & Co. and auditor KPMG Peat Marwick. Without their assistance or negligence, the suit argued, L&H would not have been able to continue its fraud and run the company's share price up to the nosebleed levels it reached in early 2000, costing Rocker Partners so much money. "We weren't able to maintain a position because of what they had been doing with their accounting," says Cohodes. The suits were settled for undisclosed terms, but Rocker Partners made some money—not a lot. "Lawyers got most of it," he shrugs. Still, the case was vitally important in establishing the legal rights of short sellers to sue for damages.

Such conviction stands as a Cohodes hallmark. "Marc's tolerance for being wrong until being proven right is amazing," says Carter Dunlap, of Dunlap Equity Partners, a San Francisco investment firm. "That confidence, or capacity to stand the pain, is what sets him apart." So does his humor and utter lack of pretense—Cohodes would most typically show up at investor conferences in his trademark polo shirt, khaki shorts, and Crocs, the brightly colored rubber clogs beloved by chefs and gardeners. Cohodes has a way of connecting—persuading people by force of his personality. "When he says something, you believe it," says Paul Landini, an analyst colleague of Cohodes at Northern Trust Company in Chicago in the 1980s. He has a way of connecting with people—even adversaries—winning them by both logic and charisma. Says Landini: "He means it. Marc Cohodes is an amazing human being."

L&H certainly validated Cohodes's pit-bull tenacity and investigative techniques—including stake-outs and endless cold-calling combined with hours of forensic accounting. "Marc understands how to research a company," says Landini. "He turns over stones, he grovels, he is relentless."

Like many dedicated short sellers, Cohodes is juiced by a passion for calling out bad actors. His hit list over the years includes a roster of companies whose products, at least in some people's eyes, could arguably be called as dubious as their share prices. In 2003, Cohodes began shorting the stock of Kansas City, Missouri–based NovaStar Financial, a subprime mortgage lender that targeted the poorest, most vulnerable population seeking to buy a home, saddling them with untenably expensive mortgages. In 2005, he wagered against Taser International, a Scottsdale, Arizona, maker of high-voltage stun guns that were found to induce cardiac arrest in people with common heart conditions. The company calls the studies detailing the phenomenon flawed. Cohodes's bet against the shares of high-flying Monster Beverage Corp., the Corona, California, maker of caffeinated energy drinks, included having one of his analysts stake out emergency room admissions of teenagers who mixed the brew with vodka or other alcohol. Monster says its energy drink has less caffeine than many Starbucks beverages. "As difficult as it is, winning becomes that much sweeter," says Cohodes.

Ultimately, Cohodes's tale would end disastrously—a case study in how a short seller can be upended by the forces arrayed against them: government agencies, a dysfunctional legal system, and, perhaps, the machinations of Wall Street banks. The successor fund to Rocker Partners, Copper River Partners, was forced to liquidate in late 2008, even as other short sellers were minting fortunes in the meltdown of the financial crisis.

Navigating the winding back roads of California's Sonoma County, Cohodes ruefully shakes his head as he talks about his former line of work. In the distance are the Mayacama Mountains, from which you can see the Pacific Ocean and, to the south, San Francisco. At Hunt & Behrens, a cavernous farm supply store, he swaps banter with the owner and staff, who load $450 worth of feed onto the flatbed of his Dodge "Viper" pickup—it has the V10 engine of a Viper sports car—on a sunny December afternoon. "There's a lot of wear and tear in the business," Cohodes says in a booming voice as he careens along. Since Copper River's liquidation, he is focused on Alder Lane Farms, a 20-acre equestrian center, where he also raises free-range organic chickens whose eggs fetch $12 a dozen in San Francisco markets.

"I'll never be in the business again," he says. "Underline 'never.'"

Back at Alder Lane Farms, Cohodes sits at the kitchen table in a sparsely furnished, immaculate, sun-dappled dining area. On the table are fresh-baked bread, butter, and jam made from pluots—a mouth-puckering hybrid of plum and apricot. There are no artworks on the white walls, no computer terminals, and no mementos to remind him of his colorful career. It's as if Cohodes has wiped away his short-selling past. Regardless of his height, he fills up the room even more with his persona than his physical presence. With a tendency for irreverent banter, Cohodes has been a delight for quote-hungry journalists over the years.

Markets? "I think they are rigged," he says.

Short selling? "The smart guys are extinct. The good minds are out of the business."

Goldman Sachs? "For them, everything is just a cost of doing business."

And on the meaning of his own short-selling career? Cohodes pauses. "The question is whether you want to make a difference or not," he finally responds, and knocks back a shot of espresso. He leans forward and reveals a truth that informs his life and work "What you see is not what it really is," he says.

For all his talk about outing bad guys and protecting Joe Six-Pack, Cohodes describes himself as a bounty hunter—surprisingly not too far from what his adversaries call him. He credits his successful years as a short seller to an innate sense of pattern recognition that goes a long way in helping him sniff out dubious businesses programs. Bad companies sport some similar characteristics that turn up again and again. Their headquarters tend to cluster geographically, for example. "There are no legitimate companies in the state of Utah," Cohodes declares flatly. Other prime breeding grounds for problem companies are Florida, Arizona, and New York's Long Island.

Cohodes looks for serial acquirers—so-called "roll-ups" who use their inflated stock to buy legitimate companies on the cheap. Accounting for mergers and acquisitions allows for all kinds of obfuscation, and continual restatements and charges are a way to cover up a fundamental lack of growth. He trawls in the mid-cap and small-cap stock arena, figuring that more often than not, larger companies have proven business models. "I stay away from the [Standard & Poor's] S&P 500," he says. "Those companies are big for a reason."

Cohodes combs through senior management resumes—and his ears prick up in cases where a CEO has a track record of poor performance, as was the case with L&H's Bastiaens. When an executive can't answer seemingly simple financial questions about his business—say, about rising inventories—warning lights go off. "You shouldn't walk away from the building, you should run away from the building," he chuckles. "Then you should short the f--k out of the building."

This skill set in pattern recognition rises to ethnic profiling on occasion: He pays special attention to South Asian Indians and Sri Lankans. "For nine years I told the SEC that Raj Rajaratnam was dirty," Cohodes fumes. "I've never met an honest Indian CFO or CEO." Rajaratnam, founder of hedge fund Galleon Group, was found guilty of conspiracy and securities fraud in May 2011, sentenced to 11 years in prison, and fined more than $150 million.

Cohodes's rough-hewn disposition bespeaks a troubled and unhappy youth—one that likely would have held a less determined person back, but which no doubt contributed to his outsider's perspective on the world. Marc Cohodes was born on June 18, 1960, the oldest child of Donald and Meryl Lyn Cohodes, who divorced when he was three. Along with his younger sister, Nancy, he grew up on Chicago's Near North Side, an affluent neighborhood adjacent to Chicago's famed central business district, the Loop.

Cohodes doesn't wax sentimental about his past. "My father sold water coolers," he says, flatly. "He was a drunk. He's dead." Cohodes stares straight ahead as he says this, and then later mentions that he doesn't speak with his estranged mother, either—following his divorce from his first wife, Leslie. "It is what it is," he says, and shrugs.

As a child, Cohodes didn't seek to impress grown-ups—and was quite successful at that. A second grade report card he keeps is stark about his prospects. "It said that I'd end up in jail or a mental institution," he says. His mind wandered in class and he was derelict in homework assignments. "In this era, I think you'd say I have attention deficit disorder," he says. "I still have issues sitting still."

Nature abhors a vacuum. Lacking a father figure, Cohodes found one at sleepaway camp, in the form of a counselor—Bob Mercier. "He taught me more about life than anybody before or since," says Cohodes. Foremost amongst Mercier's admonitions: Don't act on impulse. Analyze a situation, research any predicament before acting. "When things get squirrely or out of control, don't just do something, stand there," he says. "Take the time. Think it out. Then act. People do something on a dime and 95 percent of the time it's the wrong thing."

In high school, Cohodes's situation improved. He attended the private Latin School of Chicago, an elite preparatory school with a curriculum heavily influenced by the classics. Cohodes's 10th grade economics class piqued his interest in financial markets—especially after he embarked on a portfolio management project, picking and monitoring stocks. It was not enough to inspire him to academic greatness.

With mediocre grades, Cohodes attended Babson College in Wellesley, Massachusetts, a business-focused school known for turning out financial industry functionaries, as well as a fair number of entrepreneurs. There, Cohodes noticed that the easier the work, the worse his grades. He aced "Policy Formulation," studying real-world business case histories, while pulling Ds on gut introduction classes. Cohodes worked part-time for a Merrill Lynch broker, the kind more concerned with churning accounts than enriching clients. It gave him a front-row seat to the markets. In 1976, Bache Group got swept up in the Hunt Brothers' failed attempt to corner the silver market—and Cohodes watched in awe as the brokerage firm's stock tumbled to $6 from $32. "I remember thinking, if you could see this coming that would have been really sweet," says Cohodes.

The early 1980s provided Cohodes with his first direct experience with a stock collapse. He sank $50,000 of his own and clients' money into Blackwood, New Jersey–based Data Access Systems, a computer terminal distribution company. The stock fell from $8 to $2 before he got out. "The feeling was so awful," Cohodes recalls. "I thought I better bone up on my skills so this never happens again." The company eventually went bankrupt.

After graduation in 1982, Cohodes headed back to Chicago to Northern Trust Company as an investment officer, and was soon taken under the wing of Paul Landini, a leisure and food stock analyst. It was long before Regulation FD, and lucrative information could be gleaned legally from conversations with corporate executives—if you knew who to call and what to ask. Most days, around the close of business, the two would huddle and call up CEOs or treasurers of the companies Landini covered and, like lawyers at a trial, entice them into revealing clues about sales, profits, or the competition. "We wanted information," says Landini. Often they got it.

Interest rates were at 20 percent and the Dow Jones Industrial Average at 776, down 40 percent from its high three years earlier. Chrysler was in bankruptcy, and word was that Ford could join it.

Cohodes was innately contrarian. "I was so bullish I was dizzy," he recalls. Cohodes's tendency was to see opportunity where others saw danger, and vice versa. Example A was Coca-Cola Co., then trading at a split-adjusted 70 cents a share. Cohodes figured people always drank Coke and would continue to do so, regardless of economic vagaries. It was yielding a fat 8 percent. "I bought a s--t-pot full of Coke," he recalls. It would go down as one of the best-performing large capitalization stocks of the decade, returning some 1,000 percent.

Sugar prices were on the rise, and Archer Daniels Midland Co., the Chicago-based grain processor, was making money on the low-priced alternative, fructose. A conversation with Landini and an ADM executive persuaded him that Coke would increase its use of fructose as a way to expand margins. The upside was formidable. "We bought a s--t-pot full of ADM," Cohodes said. Shares more than tripled by the end of the decade.

Cohodes learned the art of the short sale, too. One of the hottest leisure stocks was Bally Manufacturing Co., maker of arcade games like Pac-Man and Space Invaders. Cohodes walked to the local venue, Rubus Games, and pestered the manager about which games were doing well. "I'd ask, 'What's your coin drop today?" Cohodes recalls. "We shorted the hell of Bally and shifted the money into Warner Communications, whose video games were doing better."

He was developing an alternate view of how things worked—a priceless skill for a short seller. "I think most people are full of crap," says Cohodes. "I like to verify. I like to know. I view myself as a conviction player."

Still, most of Cohodes's work at Northern Trust was handholding accounts. "Marc wanted to succeed," Landini says. "He didn't want to type up letters to little old ladies telling them their accounts were up 3 percent."

Cohodes soon hooked up with a gruff, New York-based hedge fund veteran who was looking to hire an analyst as he got a new business off the ground. It was 1985, the bull market in full swing, and finding a smart analyst difficult. The two had breakfast at the Waldorf Astoria hotel. The manager was David Rocker.

By this point in his career, Rocker, had paid his dues—with long stretches at Mitchell, Hutchins & Co., Steinhardt, Fine, Berkowitz & Co., and Century Capital Associates, where he was a partner. Rocker today, following an acrimonious break up with Cohodes, won't meet in person, and doesn't seem at all happy being quoted talking about his former partner. But interviews with acquaintances and former colleagues at his former hedge fund, as well as rivals in the short-selling business, paint a picture of Rocker as someone who thrived in the short-selling industry.

David A. Rocker was born in 1943 in Elizabeth, New Jersey, just south of Newark. His father Robert, an accountant, and housekeeping mother Beatrice, were affected by their experiences during the Great Depression. Ever thrifty, they reflexively switched off light-switches to save a penny or two on electricity and never risked much career-wise. As Jews, the family inculcated David Rocker in the credo of Tikkun Alom, that a just person's life mission is to repair a damaged world. And Rocker embraced that notion. "Do the right thing," he would say in difficult times.

Rocker says he learned that from his father. "My father was a very honest man," says Rocker. "He imbued me with that." Rocker's noble intention in life, it should be noted, never prevented him from launching a high-decibel take down of whoever was upsetting him.

Class president at West Orange High School, a sprawling working class institution, Rocker excelled in the classroom and athletics. He won admission to Harvard. "It was a big deal for me to get in there," he says. "West Orange was not a feeder school."

In 1961, Rocker joined Harvard's Naval Reserve Officers Training Corps, partly because he was a naval history buff but also on principle. The Jewish kid from New Jersey was impressed by professor Otto Eckstein, who helped develop the notion of core inflation—which excludes volatile food and energy costs. Rocker majored in economics.

Commissioned as a Navy ensign, Rocker spent two years on the USS *Little Rock*, including six months in the Mediterranean where the light cruiser served as the flagship for the U.S. Sixth Fleet. He was officer of the deck when the *Little Rock* helped pick up the injured from the USS *Liberty*, an American spy ship attacked in error by the Israeli Air Force and Navy during the Six-Day War. He says he is ashamed of how Vietnam War veterans were treated upon their return.

Having returned to Harvard Business School for his M.B.A., he recalls learning a life lesson. His preoccupation with a new stereo prevented him from properly preparing for a class one day. The professor called on Rocker. He tried to wing it—and failed disastrously. "I got torn apart," he chuckles. "Justifiably."

Nevertheless he graduated with distinction and joined research firm Mitchell Hutchins as a real estate and finance analyst under the stewardship of Donald Marron, who later rose to head PaineWebber. He covered the homebuilding industry and hung sell recommendations on land developers whose accounting he thought misleading. Soon after, their stocks collapsed. Rocker's gutsy calls caught the attention of buy-side managers.

From there it was on to what would become a famous hedge fund—Steinhardt, Fine, Berkowitz, & Co. Rocker initiated his first professional short sale in 1977 on Tampax, the maker of tampons. Such products were heavily restricted in their ability to advertise on television or radio.

New rules were about to change that, and Rocker felt that Tampax was due for a wallop. The first weeks of the sale went awry as word leaked about his short position. "Some schmuck at a bank who was long Tampax heard about the short position and marked it up," Rocker says. The stock, briefly rose to $125 from $115. Rocker ultimately covered the position when Tampax shares dropped to $25.

Rocker remained until 1982 when he joined Century Capital Associates. That firm was sold, and Rocker founded his eponymous firm in 1985.

Rocker and Cohodes both recall their breakfast at the Waldorf Astoria. "He was cheap and I was cheap," says Cohodes. For his part, Rocker says he was impressed by Cohodes's enthusiasm. "He was fresh-faced, honest, aggressive, a tireless worker," says Rocker. "The person who recommended him prophetically said, 'He's very smart and aggressive, but you're going to have to put fences around him.'"

Rocker says that advice was spot on. "Marc had intense passion," he says. "Why be short 100,000 shares when you can be short 300,000 shares? We're going to win so why not win bigger?" Cohodes was taking a risk, too, because Rocker Partners was a startup. And it was backed initially only by the Zimmerman family, owners of the Pic 'N' Save stores, which they had just sold. The pair developed a father-son relationship over the years.

Rocker Partners started as classic long-short fund. David Rocker eventually saw more opportunity in the short-selling side as the bull market in stocks surged in the 1980s, raising hundred, even thousands of companies to what he viewed as dubious valuations, and suspect accounting flourished. The fund went net short in 1990. Besides, he was a better short seller than long investor.

Rocker Partners was a distinctive outfit in many ways. "It was like a family," says Rocker. "We adopted a cooperative rather than an eat what you kill culture to foster cooperation." Six of the twelve working there were partners, sharing profits. Over 21 years, only two principles left the firm. Rocker Partners responded to employee's preferences to work where they wanted. The chief financial officer, Phil Renna, was in Millburn, New Jersey, with David Rocker and trader Carol Ju. There was an office in Manhattan's Rockefeller Center, where Cohodes worked for a while. Analyst Terry Warzecha out of Boston.

Cohodes says he can't remember what his first short sale at Rocker Partners was, but among his earliest was a toy company—Coleco Industries, Hasbro Inc., or Tonka Toys. In 1986, all three had monster fad products tearing up the market—and goosing their share prices. Coleco hawked Cabbage Patch Kids, wildly popular cloth and foam dolls; Hasbro had Pound Puppies, a droopy-eyed toyline of canines; and Tonka flogged its Transformers, diminutive robots based on an animated television show with movable parts that, as their name implied, could change their shape and functions.

The stocks were true high-fliers, trading for 27 trailing earnings or more. In the case of Coleco, sales had more than doubled the previous year. Cohodes did simple channel-checking to see how sales were going at big retailers like Toys 'R' Us, Child World, and Toys Plus.

To be sure, at the time this was no dark art. Executives were generally happy to talk about their businesses. "If you pester people enough and are persistent, they'll talk to you," says Cohodes.

A typical phone call to, say, a Toys 'R' Us executive would follow a template:

Cohodes:	So how are Cabbage Patch Kids selling this season?
Executive:	Here's what we're seeing. Sales are still growing fast but not anywhere near last year.
Cohodes:	So are we talking 10 to 20 percent growth?
Executive:	More than that.
Cohodes:	30 to 40 percent?
Executive:	That's about right.
Cohodes:	What are you budgeting for the upcoming season?
Executive:	We're figuring high single digits.

Meanwhile, Wall Street analysts were forecasting growth of 40 percent—for the current and future years—as if such growth was sustainable.

Naturally, as Cohodes points out, people are far more willing to talk about the business of their suppliers or customers than they are about their own. He isn't sure how much money Rocker Partners made shorting the toy companies. The shares of all three companies collapsed spectacularly beginning in 1987, with Coleco filing for bankruptcy in 1989 and Hasbro eventually buying Tonka in 1991.

A life-changing event for Cohodes hit in 1987. His son, Max, was born prematurely and diagnosed with cerebral palsy, the congenital disorder that impairs motor reflex skills and sometimes intellectual development. Max, who displays extraordinary aptitude in such areas as math, name recognition, and memory, would be mostly wheelchair-bound for his life.

Max's diagnosis fundamentally changed Cohodes—in ways even today he has trouble putting into words. "I really turned it up," he says. "I became edgier. Wherever I was before, I became more motivated. I will out-hustle anybody."

Cohodes's research convinced him that the best treatment for Max's specialized issues was Feldenkrais therapy—a holistic approach to alleviating pain, and fostering physical and intellectual development. One leading Feldenkrais therapist was based in the San Francisco Bay area. Cohodes told Rocker that he and his family were moving to San Francisco. "Then Rocker Partners is opening a San Francisco office," Rocker replied.

Separated by a continent, the two split some of the funds responsibilities—Rocker dealing with outside investors and Cohodes focused on portfolio issues and devoting time to personnel matters. "He was Mr. Outside and I was Mr. Inside," Cohodes says.

The fund's 40 to 50 short positions were typically allocated between the two. Generally, if Rocker initiated a position, he would be in charge of maintaining it; ditto for Cohodes. "It was a high functioning yin-yang," says Russell Lynde, who worked at Rocker Partners from 2000 to 2007. "Marc was more of a risk taker and David was more conservative. They balanced each other well." Still, it was certainly a different way to run a hedge fund.

The results were undeniably impressive—though volatile. Between its founding and December 2007, it generated returns of about 11 percent. That included years like 1999, when Rocker Partners gained 31.7 percent, and others like 2003, when it lost 35.6 percent. Rocker says the firm's alpha, excess returns provided by stock selection above the S&P 500, was 17 percent annualized from its start until when he stepped down in mid-2006, offering investors the opportunity to redeem if they chose to.

The volatility was the killer. As the L&H experience showed, being right was by no means a guarantee of making money for investors. Beginning in 1996, for example, Rocker initiated a short position on America Online, the Internet access firm now known as AOL. Rocker could see plainly that the company's accounting stank. Though there were several issues that came to light after its merger with Time Warner in 1999, Rocker was initially concerned with the capitalization of marketing expenses.

America Online did mass mailings of CD-ROMs that would allow people to set up their AOL accounts and then dial into AOL to be connected to the World Wide Web. To Rocker, and most anybody else with an inkling of accounting savvy, these were clearly marketing expenses and should be accounted for as such. AOL, however, insisted on accounting for them as capital expenditures, like plant and equipment—costs that could be amortized over 10 years. This had the effect of artificially inflating earnings.

Rocker, a regular contributor to *Barron's* "Other Voices" section, penned a letter on the subject to the financial newsweekly's editors. "America Online would have huge losses today if it handled its accounting as other Internet companies like PSI and UUNET do," he wrote. "America Online capitalizes subscriber acquisition costs, whereas they expense them. To put this in perspective, America Online reported pretax earnings of less than $12 million in its September [1995] quarter, while capital acquisition costs increased $56 million." The stock didn't budge. Even worse, after the SEC began an inquiry into the matter, America Online about-faced and wrote off the $365 million of capitalized costs in the fourth quarter of 1996. Rather than fall because the company had lied to investors, AOL shares soared 15 percent, because they were relieved the company needn't amortize those costs. The short-selling business is never short on irony.

For his part, Cohodes routinely disagreed with some of Rocker's positions, including AOL, which to this day he calls "another David Rocker Special." But he thrived on the independence Rocker gave him, especially after being named general partner in 1987. Cohodes ran the West Coast office his own eccentric way. Tucked into a Larkspur office park in Marin County for most of Rocker Partners' time there, he held court over a tight-knit cadre of analysts who, at his urging, expended copious shoe leather tracking down accounting chicanery of various stripes.

Cohodes had a talent for attracting talent from curious corners. There was Richard Sauer, a lawyer and former investigator with the SEC who, after working on the L&H case, decided to hang his hat at Rocker Partners working for Cohodes, his favorite tipster. There was Mark "Monty" Montgomery, who had worked with short seller Jim Chanos. Russell Lynde, a newly minted M.B.A. from Wharton, stumbled into Rocker Partners after his wife got a fellowship at Stanford University and an acquaintance recommended he call Cohodes. Jerome Souza was a batboy for the Oakland A's who developed a fondness for Cohodes' son Max, tossing him foul balls.

Much of Cohodes's strategizing took place on long coffee walks, 20 minutes each way, under the Highway 101 overpass that brought them to the local Peet's Coffee in the adjoining town of Corte Madera. Like a lot of West Coasters, Cohodes would go in at 5:30 a.m. and wrap up by 2:30 p.m. He generally didn't eat during market hours, preferring to drink water out of a large cup. If his positions were paying off, Cohodes would wear the same the clothes—often a Yale sweatshirt.

Cohodes prized creativity. Accordingly, he seldom did more than suggest that he suspected something was amiss at, say, Joseph A. Bank Clothiers, the Hampstead, Maryland, chain of discount business attire outlets. Souza, now a Drug Enforcement Agency officer, began by cold calling stores.

"Are you busy?" he asked.

"No."

"Do you have any sales coming up?"

"Sure."

"I'm looking for a cashmere top coat, size 38 regular."

"We have that."

"Do you have enough?"

"We have three."

With great patience, Souza created a reasonable facsimile of a Joseph A. Bank store's inventory. He learned what was selling or not. He counted customers parked outside of Bank's stores. And Souza even sent dress jackets to a lab to verify whether they were 70 percent wool as advertised. (They were).

"I'd tell [Cohodes] what I found out and he'd hug and kiss me," Souza recalls.

For the record, Rocker Partners began shorting Joseph A. Bank in early 2007, when it became apparent that the company was goosing sales with frequent clearance events. The fund held that position until September 2008.

Cohodes developed an encyclopedic understanding of the various instances of corporate malfeasance. Friends, family, and anonymous sources would routinely tip Cohodes off to questionable companies. That was the case with AAIPharma, a Wilmington, North Carolina, generic drug maker that Paul Landini, by then working at Morgan Stanley, suggested he look into. The tell-tale signs were certainly there. One red flag was the company's changing business model. Up until 2002, AAIPharma had generated reasonable profits as a contract research firm—performing the mountainous amounts of analysis and number crunching necessary for big pharmaceutical companies to shepherd their drugs through the exhaustive Food and Drug Administration approval process. Shortly thereafter, it switched gears under CEO Philip Tabbiner, moving in a new direction—buying rights to existing, often problematic drugs such as painkillers Darvocet, Darvon, and Roxicodone. Often AAIPharma could tweak formulations or dosages slightly, notching up sales before rival generic manufacturers could tool up to imitate the changes.

Cohodes was suspicious right off the bat. "The cash flow was negative," he recalls. "The receivables were out of control." Cohodes launched into his analysis of AAIPharma's numbers and didn't let up.

It worked like this: AAIPharma would signal to drug distributors such as McKesson, AmerisourceBergen, and Cardinal Health that it was going to increase prices ahead of time. Sometime it was a 10 or 20 percent increase from $1.00 a dose, say, $1.10 or $1.20. Other times, it was a bigger hike, as when the company jacked up the price of the injectable asthma drug Brethine to $25 a vial from $2. The distributors would order huge amounts of inventory to lock in the lower price. That allowed distributors, who operate on relatively thin margins, to double or triple them. AAIPharma sales would surge; though the price hikes invited generic rivals to move in, that would take from several months to a year. Distributors could return what they couldn't sell of the inflated merchandise.

AAIPharma was in effect channel stuffing—pushing through sales that were likely to be returned as a way of boosting current earnings.

One brokerage firm with a relationship to AAIPharma was Raymond James Financial, of St. Petersburg, Florida. Its pharmaceutical analyst was Michael Krensavage, who had a buy recommendation on the stock when he received a call at his Manhattan office. It was Cohodes, who immediately began talking about some of the discrepancies he was finding as he researched AAIPharma. "I saw the West Coast telephone prefix on my phone and figured it was some whacko," says Krensavage. "It didn't take long for me to realize he knew his stuff."

At the time, Cohodes was struggling to stir interest in AAIPharma with journalists and other analysts. When Krensavage showed interest, he began calling him more frequently, daily, and even on nights and weekends. Cohodes figured if he could turn one respected analyst, others would become more receptive, not unlike a chink in a dam. He kept after Krensavage. "After an earnings call, he would call and question charges and accounting treatments," Krensavage recalls.

Cohodes's analysis made sense. The smoking gun: Data from research firm IMS Health showed that AAIPharma claimed to be selling more than twice of some drugs than the research firm showed was being bought by institutions.

Ultimately, Krensavage downgraded the stock in March 2003 to "underperform," citing, among other things, skyrocketing inventories. It was a move the company would not take lying down. AAIPharma management swung into action, dispatching an investor relations executive to talk Krensavage out of the downgrade. When he refused to budge, senior AAIPharma executives berated Raymond James executives, who along with Krensavage and Cohodes were watching in horror as shares rose from $11.90 to $30 by January 2004. That contributed to Rocker Partner's 2003 loss of 35.6 percent.

Things were hardly better at Raymond James. AAIPharma canceled a loan facility with the firm. But a smattering of mostly local news media began to pay attention—exactly what Cohodes was hoping for. In March 2004, the company announced that outside board members would conduct an investigation into "unusual sales" in Brethine and Darvocet. In March, the SEC and the U.S. Attorney for the Western District of North Carolina told the company they might issue subpoenas. The company defaulted on $175 million in senior subordinated debt. It filed for bankruptcy in May 2005. Rocker Partners covered at a profit. "We did quite well on that," Cohodes says.

It was 1998 when Cohodes first took note of NovaStar Financial—a Kansas City, Missouri-based mortgage originator. He could hardly avoid doing so: His brother-in-law at the time had taken a job there and regaled him with tales of outrageous behavior. "All he would tell me was what a complete and utter zoo the place was," Cohodes says. "These people would lend money to dead animals; they put in hidden fees that their borrowers knew nothing about; they lied about documentation." The company was founded in 1996 by Scott Hartman and Lance Anderson, who had worked together at a mortgage lender called Resource Mortgage Capital, and was initially financed by GE Capital. Shares of NovaStar traded in penny stock territory at the time, just $2 a share, and Cohodes had other fish to fry. His brother-in-law soon left and Cohodes more or less forgot about NovaStar.

In 2004, his brother-in-law told him to take a look at the company again. NovaStar's shares had bolted to $30 amidst the booming housing market—and the company was minting money. NovaStar had fashioned a business making mortgage loans to subprime borrowers either directly, through an expanding network of its own branch offices, or through independent brokers. It would then securitize most of the loans, eventually pooling them into various collateralized debt obligations (CDOs) whose highest rated slices, or tranches, would be sold off to bond investors. Novastar kept the lower-rated ones. The company also serviced the loans, taking in 0.50 percent of the balances. *New York Times* columnist Gretchen Morgenson and analyst Joshua Rosner do a great job detailing the story in *Reckless Endangerment* (St. Martin's Griffin, 2011).

The lure for investors was NovaStar's payout of 18.6 percent. The company, like a lot of property-focused businesses, was structured as a real estate investment trust (REIT). That meant 90 percent of earnings had to be paid out as a dividend. Not surprisingly, NovaStar caught the fancy of gullible and yield-hungry investors. "There was a whole crowd of clowns that were attracted to NovaStar," says Cohodes. There seemed to be an organized effort to goose the shares. On the *Motley Fool* message board, for example, investors would enthuse over the NovaStar's prospects. A nominally independent site called NFI-info.net also flogged the stock, notably via the missives of a character who called himself Bob O'Brien, who sang NovaStar's praises and smeared critics and skeptics. O'Brien, who creepily sometimes called himself "the Easter Bunny," blogged on his own site, SanityCheck.com, painting short sellers or most any other critic of NovaStar as part of vast conspiracy to drive down the share prices of fast-growing companies.

His talk veered to the scary-weird side, with O'Brien suggesting investors use their credit cards to buy the stock. The spread between 12 percent card debt and the 18.6 percent yield on Novastar meant a lock of 6 percent points. If investors loaned out their shares at 6, 8, or 10 percent, they would be sitting on a yield of 12, 14, or 16 percent. The Easter Bunny was going to play a role in Cohodes's fortunes beyond NovaStar as well.

Sifting through NovaStar's financial statements, Cohodes zeroed in on the crux of its gamey accounting. In calculating profits, the company used "gain-on-sale accounting," a dicey but thoroughly legal practice that lets a company book today the profits it expects to realize on loans it holds over extended period of time. If the interest rate environment or credit quality changes, the company accordingly needs to book charges or gains to account for that. In doing so, NovaStar had enormous latitude in determining how much the portfolio was worth and its income, based on such assumptions as the rate of prepayments, loan losses, or the discount rate. It made full use of this. In the face of declining interest rates which should speed up prepayments, Cohodes realized that management decreased the discount rate on some of its mortgages, along with loss assumptions on others. That conveniently netted out the hit from the expected rise in prepayments.

NovaStar's dividend, of course, had to be paid in cash—not assumptions. Even a back of the envelope calculation proved to Cohodes that the company was selling stock in order to finance the extravagant payouts it was shoveling to shareholders. The math was simple enough. NovaStar sold shares worth $94 million in 2003, $194 million in 2004,

$142 million in 2005, and $143 million in 2006—Cohodes calculated these approximated the total dividend payment for those years.

None of this even touched on the appalling underwriting practices Cohodes's brother-in-law had told him about years earlier. There was plenty of evidence to suggest matters since then had gotten worse, not better. NovaStar virtually boasted about it. In a 2002 interview with American Banker, NovaStar CEO Hartman had crowed: "In 30 seconds, brokers can complete an application and get multiple approvals back. In a call center environment, it's nice to give them approval on the phone." Cohodes found memos to brokers. One read: "Did You Know NovaStar Offers to Completely Ignore Consumer Credit!"

He checked in with companies doing business with NovaStar. Mortgage insurance brokerage PMI had simply stopped selling insurance to NovaStar after it discovered blatant tampering with loan documents—specifically in areas dealing with borrowers' income levels.

All the while NovaStar's branch system was seemingly ballooning, from 246 offices in the first quarter of 2003 to 432 by the end of the year. Yet general and administrative expenses grew just 19 percent over that time. NovaStar was either hiring deadly efficient office managers or something was remiss. Cohodes decided to check out some of these new offices. He drove out to Las Vegas, taking a tour of NovaStar's branches in Nevada, one of its fastest-growing markets. The branch offices were often fictitious. One turned out to be a private residence, another a massage parlor.

The State of Nevada noticed, too. In late 2003, it issued a cease and desist order, shutting down the branch offices there because NovaStar had never obtained appropriate business licenses. The move followed a similar one by Massachusetts. And the Department of Housing and Urban Development, which had been investigating NovaStar, issued a critical report in the summer of 2004. It recommended penalties based on the company's violation of myriad HUD regulations.

More was to come. ABN AMRO, a big buyer of NovaStar mortgages, sued the company alleging fraud. All these cases had something in common. NovaStar never bothered to tell its investors about the regulatory actions or the suit, despite their seriousness—and despite SEC requirements that it disclose such material information.

Cohodes initiated his short position against NovaStar in January 2003, when shares were trading at $45 each. Soon, he began turning over reams of data and research to the SEC. What investigators there did with it remains unclear. Cohodes said there were frequent and lengthy conversations, conference calls, and bucket loads of documents that he e-mailed to Washington. Cohodes says he never got the impression that the SEC knew the first thing about how the subprime business worked.

Meanwhile NovaStar shares were climbing as the housing mania expanded; Cohodes had counted on fraud, not a real estate bubble. He began sharing his research with journalists—swapping tips and insights. Cohodes was also active on message boards and blogging, discussing his short position—and disparaging NovaStar's business model and accounting. Even as Cohodes's losses mounted, he was aware that the number of ways he could win by betting against NovaStar were multiplying—there was the sham accounting, a flawed business model, an unsustainable dividend. Nevertheless, rising shares of NovaStar, together with the bet against AAIPharma, contributed to Rocker Partner's 35.6 percent loss in 2003, which would take years to recover from.

Cohodes wasn't the only short seller beating the drums on NovaStar. By the first quarter of 2004, short interest comprised 16 percent of the company's shares. On April 12, the *Wall Street Journal*'s Jonathan Weil wrote a column flagging NovaStar's problems with Nevada and Massachusetts regulators. The article included this damning observation: The Nevada Department of Business and Industry's mortgage lending division found that of the 15 state branch offices listed on NovaStar's website, only 6 existed. NovaStar said it had shut some of its offices down recently. "What happens in Vegas stays in Vegas," Weil clucked. NovaStar paid an $80,000 fine. Its shares, trading at $54, fell 31 percent in a single day.

Bob O'Brien, or Easter Bunny, was keeping busy in the message boards. The revelation of NovaStar's fraud infuriated him. He targeted Cohodes for reprisal and posted a photograph of his special needs son, Max, the one with cerebral palsy, along with his address. "Still feel like playing?" O'Brien taunted. "This is coming up on game over time. Figure it out. Your playbook is known." Obviously, the Easter Bunny, adept at threatening handicapped children from the anonymity of the Internet, had no concept of Cohodes's mettle.

Eventually, Cohodes asked the Federal Bureau of Investigations (FBI) to look into the harassment and threats. Nothing came of it.

Though O'Brien continued to promote NovaStar, the bloom was definitely off the rose. An SEC investigation was launched in 2004, which NovaStar duly noted in its public filings. The news of the investigation pushed NovaStar shares down to under $25 by year end 2005. The stock was ultimately delisted by the New York Stock Exchange in 2007, a victory, says Cohodes, only insofar as it highlighted how the exchange's standards had sunk. "They'll list a goat," says Cohodes.

Rocker Partners began covering its position in 2005. Cohodes figured the fund earned $20 million—over a span of two and one half years. With the stock at $1.50, NovaStar co-founder Scott Hartman was fired by the board. Notably, Lance Anderson toils on. The company survived the subprime meltdown, partly by helping itself to financing from the Troubled Asset Relief Program (TARP). A company that did so much to feed the crisis was able to survive with the aid of a plan to pick up the pieces. NovaStar changed its name to the Novation Companies. *Novation*, it should be noted, is the act of swapping one party's obligations with another's. Shares in June 2015 traded at 31 cents, and Anderson continues to be well compensated, paid $750,000 a year. You simply can't make this stuff up.

Even while the bulletin board range wars were raging over NovaStar, though, Cohodes was zeroing in on his next target—Overstock.com, an online retailer that specialized in closeout merchandise. It would not be a pleasant experience.

The case unfolded over nearly half a decade and gained publicity in the *New York Times* and elsewhere, and not just because it involved lawsuits, wild accusations against prominent journalists, and a series of rambling incoherent rants by Overstock.com CEO Patrick Byrne on the company's conference calls. Among other things, Byrne accused a *Fortune* journalist of performing fellatio on Goldman Sachs traders, attempted to board a commercial jet with a loaded Glock 23 pistol, and accused a network of journalists and brokerage firms of engaging in a vast conspiracy to undermine honest small cap companies all at the behest of an unnamed Sith Lord—a reference to a dark character in the Star Wars movie series.

The story takes up a hefty portion of one of the unsung books on the credit bubble and its run up: *Selling America Short: The SEC and Market Contrarians in the Age of Absurdity*, by Richard Sauer (John Wiley & Sons,

2010). It bears repeating for the light it shines on the depth of corporate malfeasance in America, the complicity of the country's legal system in covering up corruption, and regulators' bumbling inefficiency.

At the center of it all was Byrne—a more unlikely, certainly multitalented corporate actor would be difficult to imagine. Strikingly handsome, he burnished impressive pedigrees. His father was Jack Byrne, a storied insurance executive who had once turned around GEICO, Berkshire Hathaway's best-in-class car insurance company, before going on to lead White Mountains Insurance Group, a respected New Hampshire–based underwriter. The elder Byrne served as Overstock.com's chairman until 2006, and then rejoined the board in 2008. He died in March 2013.

As for Patrick Byrne, he had some serious cred himself, having served as CEO of another Berkshire Hathaway subsidiary, uniform maker Fechheimer Brothers. Byrne has a B.A. in Chinese studies from Dartmouth College, a master's degree from Cambridge University, and a Ph.D. in philosophy from Stanford University. He speaks fluent Mandarin and, following a bout with testicular cancer, bicycled across the United States on several occasions to raise awareness of the disease.

Byrne began his journey into the world of stock market promotion soon after he, along with extended members of the Byrne family, bought control of Overstock.com's predecessor in 1999. It was the height of the Internet bubble and the stock market was rife with dot-com hype, crazy valuations, and fraud. Byrne, who called himself a dyed-in-the-wool value investor, joined in the fanfare—touting Overstock.com and its results with the energy of a carnival barker.

The company had two revenue sources. It bought closed out inventory at a deep discount and sold it on its website. And it hawked the products of independent fulfillment partners, earning a piece of each transaction as a commission. Competition was fierce, not just with brick-and-mortar retailers, but with fast-growing online juggernauts like Amazon.com and eBay.

Before the company's initial public offering in May 2002, Byrne trumpeted Overstock.com's profitability. As it was a private company, there was no way to verify his claims. In interviews, Byrne would brag about how quickly the company had moved from startup to profitability. "That's real GAAP profit," he boasted to *Business 2.0* magazine. "Not Amazon bullshit profit."

After Overstock.com filed its IPO prospectus, Cohodes could see that Overstock had never turned a profit—at least not one recognized under GAAP standards. It wouldn't do so on an annual basis for nearly a decade.

There was no need for Cohodes to dig deep. In a June 2001 interview with the *Wall Street Transcript*, a stock research publication, Byrne estimated sales of at least $120 million for 2001, $400 million for 2002, and close to $1 billion the year after. Instead, revenues came in at $40 million in 2001, $91.8 million in 2002, and about $150 million in 2003, even after adjusting for a change in accounting that dramatically revved up sales. Forecast misses are one matter, but Byrne also emphasized Overstock.com's low marketing expenses, just $250,000 a month. The prospectus showed they were nearly triple that. And Byrne had claimed that Overstock.com required little if any new capital—yet just months later, the company announced its initial public offering. Serial stock and debt offerings followed.

There was also that classic red flag for short sellers—senior management turnover. In 2003 alone, the chief financial officer, chief operating officer, and chief technology officer were all replaced. Gradient Analytics, then operating under the name Camelback Research Alliance, issued a negative research report on the company in June 2003, based on its poor "earnings quality," or how accurately the company appeared to be reporting financial information.

Overstock.com inflated revenue. The most obvious example occurred when it changed the way it accounted for the sales of its fulfillment partners, who typically received 85 percent of each sale, with the 15 percent balance being paid to Overstock.com as a commission. Beginning July 1, 2003, however, Overstock.com began reporting its revenues from these sales on a gross basis, including not only the 15 percent commission but also the 85 percent that went to the fulfillment partner.

On December 1, 2003, Overstock.com released figures claiming that total revenue over Thanksgiving weekend had risen to $6.0 million from $1.5 million, a gain of 300 percent. It did not disclose the change in accounting, and media outlets dutifully reported the outrageous percentage gain. Overstock.com shares spiked 24 percent from $16.27 to $20.20 in a single day. It seemed like a plan to engineer a short squeeze. When asked about the possibility that it was manipulating the stock on CNN.com in 2003, Byrne said: "Opportunities come along where we can knee the shorts in the groin; that's always good for fun and amusement."

More negative reports from Gradient followed, including one in December 2003 reducing its "earnings quality" grade to an F, the lowest possible. Overstock.com press releases continued to trumpet the hyperbolic sales growth: "GAAP year-over-year Q4 revenue grew 197 percent from $41.5 million in 2002 to $123.2 million in 2003," it trumpeted in a January 2004 release. The company was not disclosing that its new methodology was grossly inflating the sales growth figures.

If nothing else, the tone of Byrne's communications should have given investors pause. "Sales were super-de-duper," he wrote. "They truly were."

Cohodes had initiated a relatively modest short position in February 2004 at $28. Yet, he was worried about Byrne's erratic pronouncements. One of Cohodes's credos is to never cross a crazy man: The results are dangerously unpredictable, though identifying such actors can be difficult at the time.

Rocker, however, looked at the Overstock.com balance sheet and thought it was a lousy business. Over Cohodes's objections, he took over the management of the position, an unusual move at the firm. "We must have told David Rocker 300 times not to get involved with Byrne," Cohodes recalls saying. (Rocker says Cohodes was aware of Byrne's questionable behavior when he began the short). In New York, Rocker attended a June 2004 road show for an Overstock.com equity offering. During the Q&A, he asked Byrne to explain why Overstock.com had failed to meet his profit and sales targets by a long shot and why he needed more capital when he had previously said he didn't need any. Byrne declined to answer.

In a July 2004 earnings call a Gradient Analytics analyst asked what kind of profits would be generated when Overstock.com hit $2 billion in revenues. Byrne pointedly did not reply. Short interest in Overstock.com began to climb, and hit 15 percent in September 2004.

Rocker, sometimes witheringly condescending and always outspoken, didn't hold back, writing an article on *TheStreet.com* entitled "Overstock Overhypes." He questioned an increase in Overstock.com's

prepaid expenses and other assets—two warning signs of possible manipulation. Rocker also noted questionable increases in Overstock.com's
cash flow and changes in general and administrative expenses.

Byrne, for his part, became increasingly strident. In an October 2004
letter to shareholders, he railed against critics. "The elephant in the room
during our conference calls and other meetings is the fact that out there
are a bunch of short sellers and their sycophants who bad-mouth everything I do or say," he complained. In the follow-up call the next day,
he lashed out at research firm BWS Financial for questioning a specific
transaction the analyst believed had been inappropriately accounted for.
And he tore into the "shoddy research" by Camelback, disparaging both
its accounting acumen and business model. "I understand how Camelback works is that hedge funds hire them, you pay them 30 grand a year,
and in return for which if you are a hedge fund you get a call up once
or twice a year and please do a hatchet job on company X," he said.

Why Rocker Partners would want Gradient, as Camelback was now
called, to write a negative research report before the fund started shorting
the stock, however, was never explained. Gradient's skeptical research
had begun over a year earlier.

The same conference call also included a toe-to-toe between Byrne
and Rocker. CNBC star and fund manager Jim Cramer had criticized
Overstock.com on *TheStreet.com* and on TV, citing a blog post from
Rocker. Byrne declared that Cramer was invested in Rocker Partners.
(Cramer wasn't, then or ever).

Rocker was furious. "The Overstock guy wants to get into a fight,"
he e-mailed Cohodes. "Well, he has. I am in kill mode."

Journalists were getting vicious e-mail from Byrne. Bethany
McLean, a senior writer at *Fortune* magazine who had once worked as
a junior-level analyst Goldman Sachs, wrote a somewhat dutiful article
optimistically entitled "Is Overstock the New Amazon?" in October
2004. Byrne e-mailed her, calling the article "crap." He added: "Why
exactly did you become a reporter? Giving Goldman traders blow-jobs
didn't work out?"

Around the same time, Gradient published a report questioning the
competence of an Overstock.com director, Gordon Macklin, a former

head of NASDAQ who had served as a WorldCom director as it engaged in its earth-shaking accounting fraud. Byrne e-mailed Gradient research director Donn Vickrey: "You deserve to be whipped, f----d, and driven from the land."

Strange things began happening to Overstock.com stock. In September 2004, its shares began to rise—and quickly too, from $30.25 to $77.25 in December. Rocker Partners was losing millions on paper in its short position. Curiously, Scion Capital LLC, a small hedge fund managed by Michael Burry that would soon make a fortune in the credit crisis, would later report that it bought 1.3 million shares of Overstock.com in the third quarter of 2005, according to government filings. White Mountains Insurance was a part owner of the fund.

Then things got more curious. In Overstock.com's January 28, 2005, conference call, O'Brien, the so-called Easter Bunny from NovaStar Financial, surfaced again. He now introduced himself to Byrne and conference call participants as a private investor, and he and Byrne both feigned that they were strangers, though it soon turned out they had known each other for months.

O'Brien laid out a conspiracy theory. "What I am going to describe is what I call a systematic serial killing for small cap companies. And I think you guys are a victim of it. I am talking more along the lines of criminal manipulation, allusions, fraud libel, n---d short selling." O'Brien linked journalists including Cramer, Herb Greenberg of *Dow Jones Marketwatch*, Liz MacDonald of *Forbes*, and the *Wall Street Journal* and *Barron's* to the plot. Federal regulators, who he did not identify, were set to go after Overstock.com. Normally callers of this ilk are disconnected from calls. Not O'Brien. "Go ahead," Byrne encouraged him. "If you have a question that would be great, but if you have something you want to tell you may go ahead."

With Byrne's encouragement, O'Brien prattled on, drawing in the Depository Trust & Clearing Corporation (DTCC) and German stock exchanges into his malign fiesta. The idea was that shares listed overseas could be borrowed, as a sort of runaround to rules restricting n---d short selling. The trades would not have to settle in the three days as domestic shares would. It made little sense.

Investors scratched their heads—and shares began falling. It's unclear whether the share price decline was a result of the conference calls or because they had previously been artificially boosted in what seemed like a classic short squeeze.

Then came August 12, 2005, when on a special conference call, Byrne let loose an epic rant announcing a civil suit he had filed the previous day against Rocker Partners, Gradient, and their key employees. The suit alleged the defendants conspired to denigrate Overstock.com's business in order to reap personal profit. The negative Gradient research reports on Overstock.com were disseminated, it said, without disclosing that Rocker Partners had had a hand in preparing them.

The suit was laughable. It didn't allege anything at all in the Gradient research reports was inaccurate. Moreover, Rocker Partners had not contacted Gradient before it initiated its short position—and hadn't done so for months afterward. Many of the assertions, namely about phone conversations and meetings between Rocker Partners and Gradient, simply hadn't occurred—and the accusations that they had came from a disgruntled former employee, Demetrios Anifantis, who had been fired by Gradient "for cause" (misappropriating company property and other misdeeds).

What Cohodes, Rocker, and Gradient couldn't laugh off was the consortium of six law firms the Byrne had brought on to handle it—these included class action lawyers John O'Quinn, Adam Voyles, and Wes Christian of Houston, Texas, a group that had famously won a $17 billion settlement from tobacco companies in 1994. "It is time someone stops these offshore hedge funds from taking advantage of average working Americans and American public companies," O'Quinn said in a statement. "That someone is us."

Still, it was Byrne's bizarre accompanying diatribe that set Wall Street abuzz. In it, he alluded to a vast short-selling conspiracy controlled by a dark "Sith Lord," whose name he would not divulge but who was in fact a "criminal mastermind" from the 1980s. He connected nefarious players, including journalists Jesse Eisinger of the *Wall Street Journal*, Carol Redmond of *Dow Jones*, Cheryl Strauss Einhorn of *Barron's*, and Herb Greenberg of *Marketwatch.com*, with a network of short selling plotters including Rocker and Gradient. The network included plaintiff's law firm Milberg Weiss, several German stock exchanges mentioned by O'Brien in the earlier call, and the DTCC. Byrne dubbed the web the "Miscreant's Ball," drawing on the title of the book by Connie Bruck, *The Predator's Ball* (Penguin, 1989), which portrayed the Drexel Burnham Lambert–financed takeovers of that era.

In a series of charts, Byrne drew arrows between the names without any elaboration—leaving it up to the viewer to figure out, say, the relationship that existed between Camelback and Greenberg, or the Department of Justice and the Feshbach Brothers. The name of Leon Black, CEO and founder of private equity firm Apollo Global Management LP, pops up unconnected to anybody. "Leon Black I've put in there just because he's a well-known financier hedge fund guy," Byrne said. "I've got nothing more to say about him." Eliot Spitzer, New York State Attorney General at the time, is included too. "Eliot wants to be governor," Byrne declared.

David Einhorn, at the time engaged in a public short campaign against Allied Capital Corp, makes an appearance—Byrne connects him to corporate sleuths Kroll Associates, which he claimed was investigating him. Einhorn was and remains married to former *Barron's* editor Cheryl Strauss Einhorn. "Anybody on the street understands *Barron's* more or less as just being a group of quislings for the hedge funds." Byrne says.

Byrne, it turns out, didn't much like the *Wall Street Journal*, either. "I've dealt with the *Journal* before and they're just a bunch of dishonest reporters," he says. He went on to disparage Eisinger's reporting in particular, accusing him of harassment.

There were also references to among other things: money laundering, Stinger anti-aircraft missile sales to Pakistani agents, as well as gay bathhouses and cocaine use, which, he confided, he had only mentioned as a way of figuring out which of his acquaintances was leaking information to the short-selling conspiracy.

Byrne snarled at his short-selling nemeses: "So I say to Rocker, to Cohodes, and all the other miscreants. 'Did I stutter? Did I stutter or did I say I was going to take this fight to you? Well now you know what I meant.'"

He ended his monologue by returning to the Sith Lord, the supernatural demigod in the Star Wars movie series who is dedicated to the

Dark Side of the Force: "And lastly, to the man I've identified here as the Sith Lord of this stuff, I just say, 'You know who you are and I hope that this is worth it, because if the feds catch you again, this time they're going to bury you under the prison. And I'm going to enjoy helping.'" Later, some speculated the Sith Lord was identified as the former Drexel Burnham Lambert junk bond kingpin Michael Milken.

When the conference call was over, investors were shocked. Those with no previous skin in the game piled on. Short interest on Overstock.com rose from 10 percent to 15 percent the following Friday. Wall Street wags promptly nicknamed Byrne "Wacky Patty."

As an aside, after SAC Capital Advisors, founded by Steven Cohen, was indicted for systematic insider trading violations in July 2013, Byrne published a full-page advertisement in the *New York Times* with his own photograph. It read: "Congratulations on the indictment, Stevie, and remember: roll early, roll often. Your friend, Patrick M. Byrnes, CEO, Overstock.com."

The Overstock.com suit, in any normal U.S. court would have been summarily dismissed. But the case wasn't going to be heard in such a venue. Instead it was filed in the Superior Court of the State of California for the County of Marin, better suited for the adjudication of tenant–landlord tiffs and noise complaints than securities litigation. There, conspiracy-sympathetic judges repeatedly ruled in favor of the plaintiff. Rocker Partners and Gradient tried to have the suit dismissed under California's anti-SLAPP laws, designed to prevent suits intended to squelch public criticism. The court rejected that motion. Rocker and Gradient appealed. The State Supreme Court ruled against them. In November 2007, Rocker and Gradient filed a cross-complaint, a point-by-point rebuttal of Overstock.com's suit. A nightmare.

The SEC decided to weigh in—naturally on the side of Overstock .com. The agency in early 2006 issued subpoenas to the journalists covering Overstock.com, including Herb Greenberg, Carol Remond, and Jim Cramer—who stomped on the request on live television. First Amendment advocates erupted in unison. SEC chairman Christopher Cox quickly rescinded the subpoenas.

Meanwhile, another target of Rocker Partners was about to turn its lawyers loose. In June 2006, Fairfax Financial Holdings, a Toronto-based insurer, whose byzantine structure and opaque disclosures had invited heavy short-selling interest from a range of hedge funds, filed suit in superior court in New Jersey against Rocker and a half dozen high-profile rivals, including SAC Capital Management, Lone Pine Capital, Third Point, and Exis Capital. The allegations were familiar: that Rocker and other hedge funds were disseminating false and misleading statements designed to drive down Fairfax's share price.

There were connections. Fairfax's CEO, Prem Watsa, was a one-time protégé of Jack Byrne from White Mountains. And on December 20, 2006, Overstock.com disclosed it had sold 2.7 million shares to institutional investors for $14.63 a share, a 12 percent discount to where they were trading. Whether that discount was extended to Fairfax Financial is unclear, but the insurer did report its first public position in Overstock.com, 3.4 million shares, in the second quarter of 2007, equal to more than 14 percent of the company.

The New Jersey court where Fairfax Financial had filed the suit dismissed Rocker Partners from it in October 2008. The charges against the rest of the hedge funds were eventually dropped too.

In May 2006, the SEC subpoenaed Overstock.com for documents related to its accounting as well as projections, estimates, forecasts—the very things that Rocker had been focusing on. The commission also asked for documents related to the Gradient suit. "I may be the first CEO in history to celebrate receiving an SEC subpoena," Byrne said. "Some of the requests suggest the whispering of the blackguards but I remain unconcerned about their hokum."

After a two-year investigation, the SEC forced Overstock.com in October 2008 to restate five years worth of results, from 2003 through 2007, shaving millions of dollars of earnings and revenues. "Other than that, Ms. Lincoln, how did you like the play?" Byrne deadpanned.

With the lawsuit taking its time, Byrne kept busy. He refashioned himself as a "new media" journalist and helped found and finance websites and blogs, including one called Deep Capture, that detailed his various and highly developed conspiracy theories—and served as a platform for often personal attacks on business journalists who were covering Overstock.com. Among those targeted on Deep Capture and various Byrne-linked websites: *Bloomberg News*'s Susan Antilla, former

Business Week reporter Gary Weiss, Dan Colarusso and Roddy Boyd of the *New York Post*, *Fortune*'s McLean, *New York Times* columnist Joe Nocera, and Bill Alpert from *Barron's*, as well as Eisinger from the *Wall Street Journal* and Redmond from *Dow Jones*.

With the suit against Rocker winding its tortuous way through the California legal system, Overstock continued to ritually notch millions in losses each year—$13.8 million in 2001, $4.6 million in 2002, $11.9 million in 2003, $5.0 million in 2004, $24.9 million in 2005, $101.8 million in 2006, $48 million in 2007, and $11.0 million in 2008. "Financial results were poor," Byrne wrote one quarter. "My bad," he admitted in another. "Terribly sorry," he said still later.

As refreshing as it might have been to hear Byrne take responsibility for the formidable capital destruction he was engaged in, it did nothing to dampen his enthusiasm for blaming shorts and other "miscreants" for the company's losses—or for clogging the system with still more lawsuits. In February 2007, Overstock filed a $3.48 billion humdinger against Morgan Stanley, Goldman Sachs, Bear Stearns, Banc of America Securities, Bank of New York, Citigroup, Credit Suisse, Deutsche Bank, Merrill Lynch, and UBS, alleging that they had executed short sales of Overstock.com shares with no intention of delivering shares to settle the trade—in other words, intentionally engaging in "n---d shorting."

Getting to the crux of the suit requires a serious drilldown into the workings of the stock market's securities lending business. A hedge fund that wants to short a stock begins by first contacting a prime brokerage and asking it to locate shares to borrow, usually from an institution eager to earn 5 to 7 percent by lending the stock out. It's only after the brokerage affirms the "locate" that the hedge fund can legally issue a sell order for the number of shares it has agreed to borrow. The prime brokerage is supposed to deliver the shares in three days to the hedge fund's account, typically at another brokerage. If it doesn't, the company that serves as a central counterparty to all broker to broker transactions—the DTCC—marks the appropriate accounts, both the lender's and the ultimate purchaser's, with a "failed to deliver"—a place holder of sorts. These FTDs, or "Fails" as they are called, can pile up to such an extent that they represent a big chunk of a company's float.

However, the truth is that a prime brokerage can affirm a locate and never borrow the stock without the short-selling hedge fund being any the wiser for it. Indeed, the brokerage firm has every incentive to do so, since it can both spare itself the effort of locating often-hard-to-borrow shares and save the interest it would otherwise pay on them to the lender. Doing so would goose it own profits enormously.

The Overstock.com suit alleged that that was exactly what had been going on in the securities lending business—ironically, something that many short sellers had quietly suspected. The amounts involved were not pocket change: In 2008, securities lending generated more than $10 billion in profits for Wall Street. Tellingly, in 2010 Goldman Sachs settled SEC charges that it had failed to borrow shares for its short-selling clients for $450,000 without admitting or denying guilt.

The suit against the investment banks would eventually be dismissed on procedural grounds; none of the allegedly crooked transactions took place in California. Still, a screw-up by Goldman Sachs' counsel was about to prove very embarrassing and offer proof that—and here's the huge irony—the Overstock.com allegations were true.

By mid-2006, David Rocker retired—years after he had said he planned to, because he felt it was wrong to leave while the fund was below its high watermark—a result of its 34 percent loss in 2003. He was barely on speaking terms with Cohodes, who blamed him for the Overstock.com mess and who changed the firm's name to Copper River Partners. Rocker says: "The relationship between Marc and myself deteriorated after the difficulties of 2003 because of changes in Marc's behavior. As for Cohodes, he says simply: "Rocker stayed too long in the game." The two have not talked to each other since then.

Amidst the accelerating credit crisis and stock market collapse, Gradient threw in the towel on October 2008, settling with Overstock.com for undisclosed terms. It issued a statement saying that to the best of its knowledge, Overstock.com's stated accounting policies conformed to GAAP, although it is not clear Gradient ever said otherwise and the company had, indeed, restated its earnings. Gradient also apologized to the family of Gordon Macklin, who had died the previous year, for doubting his suitability or independence.

Things were far more desperate at Copper River Partners in Lark-spur. The firm had entered the second week of September up 30 percent. Yet a disastrous situation was unfolding for the dedicated short fund in the midst of the calamitous selloff.

On the surface, it seemed a combination of poor planning and plain bad luck: Lehman Brothers Holdings, a custodian of Copper River's cash and some collateral, filed for bankruptcy on September 15, 2008. This had effectively frozen Copper River's cash holdings. Then, on September 19, Wall Street successfully lobbied the SEC into banning the short selling of a roster of hundreds of financial-related stocks. Washington needed fall guys for the financial collapse many of the short sellers had predicted, so they were first in line.

According to a November 2011 deposition by Cohodes in con-nection with Overstock.com's suit against the prime brokerage firms, Copper River had just a handful of financial shorts in its portfolio. The stock market continued to fall in the last week of September, but its big short positions began to mysteriously jackknife upwards, peaking on September 22 and 23. Goldman Sachs, Copper River's prime brokerage, made house margin calls, more than tripling the haircuts, or margin requirements, on its positions. Worse, Goldman began demanding that Cohodes immediately begin liquidating the funds' short positions. Prime brokerages are allowed to do so under the contracts they strike with hedge funds, but there was no obvious reason why Goldman should do so.

The point man on Goldman Sachs's side: Ravi Singh, senior vice president in the prime brokerage division's New York headquarters. He declined to take Cohodes's phone calls that desperate September, despite Copper River's 24-year history with Goldman Sachs. While the rest of the market was plummeting, Cohodes' big short positions were, astonishingly, rising, as if someone was trying to squeeze him. One big holding was American Capital Strategies, a Bethesda, Maryland, middle market leveraged buyout firm which surged to $21.08 from $13.96 five days earlier, a 51 percent gain. By year-end, it had collapsed to $2.43.

The stakeouts and other hard work by analyst Souza at Joseph A. Bank Clothiers also came to naught, with its stock surging from $17.32 on August 28 to $26.47, a 53 percent gain.

In a week's time, OpenText, a Waterloo, Ontario, enterprise management software firm, spiked 32 percent from $28.84 to $38.21.

And Tempur-Pedic International of Lexington, Kentucky, another big Copper River short position, rose to $14.04 on September 22 from $9.32 on September 17, a gain of 51 percent. The mattress maker finished the year at $7.09.

Cohodes believed that Goldman Sachs or somebody else was front-running Copper River's trading, putting in orders ahead of the fund's to reap a profit. "Someone was running in front of these trades, someone was," Cohodes said.

As his hedge fund was collapsing, Cohodes furiously tried to negotiate a transfer of his positions to another bank, Paris-based BNP Paribas. Goldman Sachs categorically refused to release them. Cohodes then started negotiations with Farallon Capital Management, a prominent San Francisco hedge fund firm. Cohodes talked to Bill Duhamel and Lee Hicks, who considered the idea of financing Copper River's positions or having them taken over by Farallon itself.

Then the two balked, telling Cohodes, according to his deposition, that Goldman Sachs's proprietary trading desk had called to tell them not to do so: Copper River would be out of business in a few days anyway. "The fact that the Goldman prop desk knew about this is not a surprise to me because I think the guys at Goldman are common criminals, just common criminals," Cohodes said in his 2011 deposition. Farallon founder Thomas Steyer worked early in his career on Goldman Sachs's risk arbitrage desk under fixed income chief Robert Rubin, later Treasury Secretary in the Clinton administration.

Cohodes estimates that Copper River, which had nearly $2 billion in assets at the time, would have earned $1 billion, or 50 percent, if it had held on to its positions. Indeed, the fund was up 20.4 percent at the end of August 2008. Instead, it was eventually shut down and suffered a loss of 53.8 percent for the year. By early 2009, Cohedes was spending most of his time trying to find jobs for his Copper River colleagues.

In December 2009, Copper River agreed to pay Overstock.com $5 million to settle its suit—avoiding a trial which, Cohodes says, would have involved putting David Rocker on the stand. "We decided that the litigation costs did not justify passing up a practical way to end four and a half years of meritless litigation by Overstock," Cohodes said in a statement at the time.

Predictably, Byrne gloated. "The good guys won," he declared in a press release and went on to excoriate the SEC, short sellers, and the financial journalists who had covered the saga. The SEC investigations into Overstock.com continued, although following the restatements, no actions to date were brought.

Overstock.com's suit against the brokerage firms was eventually narrowed to Goldman Sachs and Merrill Lynch. Though thrown out in March 2012 on a procedural matter, it had an ironic denouement.

Overstock.com had filed a motion in early 2012 to unseal certain documents that had been entered into evidence. In opposing the move to unseal the documents, Goldman Sachs' lawyers mistakenly entered an unredacted version of Overstock.com's motion, which—you guessed it—included the very same material they were trying to keep under seal. Yes, Patrick Byrne, there is a Santa Claus.

And, yes, the documents indicated that Goldman Sachs and Merrill Lynch were, as Overstock.com's suit alleged, engaged in a n---d short selling scheme—though there is no evidence to suggest it was ever intended to drive down the share price of any particular public company. Among the evidence that the investment banks attempted to have sealed was a series of e-mails, phone transcripts, and memos that explicitly showed that Goldman Sachs and Merrill Lynch were not borrowing the shares their clients would need to execute a legitimate short sale. Sometimes, it seems, this was with customers' knowledge, and other times it seems not.

The documents make for interesting reading. One e-mail was to a large Goldman Sachs client, Wolverine Trading LLC, which was concerned that Goldman Sachs might be making an effort to clear up some of its FTDs, or Fails, in trading desk argot. That's when a stock that is supposed to have been located for borrowing is not delivered to the appropriate account. "We will let you fail," a Goldman Sachs assured Wolverine. In other words, the message suggests that it would continue to let Wolverine short stocks without locating borrowed shares for the firm.

Some hedge fund clients were clearly in the dark regarding Goldman Sachs's failure to locate stocks. In one e-mail, a Goldman Sachs hedge fund client whose name is not disclosed remarks on how it would ask "to short an impossible name and expecting full well not to receive it and [be] shocked to learn that [Goldman's representative] can get it to us."

Among other things, the e-mails and phone transcripts show that Goldman Sachs provided details of its clients' short positions in heavily borrowed stocks to preferred customers. It cited John Masterson, a Goldman Sachs executive, who "sends nonpublic data concerning customer short positions in Overstock and four other hard-to-borrow stocks to Maverick Capital, a large hedge fund." Maverick is run by Lee Ainslee III, a protégé of legendary investor Julian Robertson of Tiger Management LLC.

Quotes from Merrill executives' e-mails occasionally show an attempt to stay on the right side of regulations. "We must be within the rules and we must pass these negs [the negative rebates or borrowing costs] on to the clients," one employee writes. Still, the tenor of both firms was reflected best in the response of Peter Melz, the former president of Merrill Lynch's prime brokerage division, in May 2005 to a colleague worried about the company promoting n---d short-selling against regulations. "F--k the compliance area," Peter Meltz writes. "Procedures schmecedures."

It's hardly surprising that Cohodes, in his November 2011 deposition, said he suspected that Goldman Sachs was shutting down Copper River because of its own n---d short exposures. "Basically the theory was by Goldman putting us out of business," Cohodes explained in his deposition, "and forcing us to cover would have solved their issue, their n---d issue because they had no economic reason to do what they did."

Cohodes said he tried to discuss the matter with his account manager at Goldman Sachs, Richard Sussman, a Goldman managing director and risk manager whom he considered a friend. Sussman said his hands were tied. "Sometimes when there's a house fire, you end up burning down the whole block," Sussman told him.

David Rocker is less circumspect. "Could Goldman Sachs have been caught short without having borrowed stock, legitimate stock?" he asks. "You bet!"

Cohodes believes that the prime brokerage industry—which underpins all short sellers—is corrupted. "I think the securities lending market is just like the mob," Cohodes said. "I think it's completely rigged. It's a completely manipulated black-hole, nontransparent market."

According to Cohodes, the failure of Copper River is largely to be laid at the feet of Goldman Sachs. "I think Goldman Sachs is like the mob," Cohodes said in his testimony. "I think Goldman Sachs is a racketeering entity that does whatever they can to make a dime without conscience, thought, foresight or care about ramifications."

In response, Goldman Sachs states: "Mr. Cohodes stated in his November 2011 testimony that, prior to the losses his fund experienced in the fall of 2008, he had been a satisfied customer who had received excellent service from Goldman Sachs for over 20 years. His opinion only changed when market conditions turned against the funds' short bias and the funds suffered dramatic losses."

Cohodes stands by his characterization. "I think they are cold-blooded and could care less about the law," he testified.

And he is always glad to discuss the matter. "That's my opinion," he says. "I think I can back it up."

About the Author

Richard Teitelbaum is a contributing editor to *Institutional Investor* magazine. Among other jobs, he has worked as a senior writer for *Bloomberg News*, where he shared an award from the Society of Professional Journalists for investigative reporting; as investing editor for *The New York Times*; as a writer for *Fortune* magazine; and as a traffic reporter in San Francisco. A graduate of Connecticut College, he lives in New York City with his wife, Nanette. They have three children—Nicole, Nina, and Jack.

Index